Rehabilitating Sexual Offenders

Rehabilitating Sexual Offenders

A Strength-Based Approach

William L. Marshall, Liam E. Marshall,
Geris A. Serran, and Matt D. O'Brien

American Psychological Association • Washington, DC

Second Printing, October 2015

Published by
APA Books
750 First Street, NE
Washington, DC 20002
www.apa.org

To order
APA Order Department
P.O. Box 92984
Washington, DC 20090-2984
Tel: (800) 374-2721; Direct: (202) 336-5510
Fax: (202) 336-5502; TDD/TTY: (202) 336-6123
Online: www.apa.org/books/
E-mail: order@apa.org

In the U.K., Europe, Africa, and the Middle East, copies may be ordered from
American Psychological Association
3 Henrietta Street
Covent Garden, London
WC2E 8LU England

Typeset in Goudy by Circle Graphics, Inc., Columbia, MD

Printer: The Maple-Vail Book Manufacturing Group, York, PA
Cover Designer: Mercury Publishing Services, Rockville, MD

The opinions and statements published are the responsibility of the authors, and such opinions and statements do not necessarily represent the policies of the American Psychological Association.

Library of Congress Cataloging-in-Publication Data

Rehabilitating sexual offenders : a strength-based approach / William L. Marshall . . . [et al.]. — 1st ed.
   p. ; cm.
 Includes bibliographical references and index.
 ISBN-13: 978-1-4338-0942-2 (print)
 ISBN-10: 1-4338-0942-7 (print)
 1. Sex offenders—Rehabilitation. I. Marshall, William L. II. American Psychological Association.
   [DNLM: 1. Sex Offenses—prevention & control. 2. Sex Offenses—psychology.
3. Criminals—psychology. 4. Denial (Psychology) 5. Psychotherapy—methods.
6. Rehabilitation—methods. WM 610]

   RC560.S47R42 2011
   616.85'83—dc22

                                    2010038515

British Library Cataloguing-in-Publication Data

A CIP record is available from the British Library.

Printed in the United States of America
First Edition

doi:10.1037/12310-000

Many people wait throughout their whole lives for the chance to be good.
—*Friedrich Nietzsche, 1844–1900*

CONTENTS

FOREWORD

SHADD MARUNA

It is with tremendous pride that I introduce both an outstanding new book and what I hope will be an exciting new series for APA Books. *Rehabilitating Sexual Offenders: A Strength-Based Approach* is the first title in the new Psychology, Crime, and Justice Series, which was created to feature the best new research and theory on violence, crime, and criminal justice written from a psychological perspective. Inaugurating this series with Marshall and colleagues' provocative and thoroughly researched challenge to the field of sex offender treatment, then, could not be more appropriate. Drawing on the authors' own original research, rating scales, assessment measures, and (most importantly) their own successful program of treatment, this important book systematically outlines a "positive" approach to intervention that would reduce attrition rates through motivational engagement strategies.

In some ways, it was inevitable that this series would begin with the topic of sex offender interventions. Arguably, there is no other area of criminal justice work where psychology has played a more substantial, leading role than in this domain. My own research area does not primarily involve sex offender treatment issues, but I have often attended the annual meetings of groups like the Association for the Treatment of Sexual Abusers (in the United States) and the National Organisation for the Treatment of Abusers (in the United Kingdom) because I find the standard of discussion so high at these meetings. Whether the reason is the sheer size of the field, the amount of resources devoted to the topic by governments, or something intrinsic to the urgent nature of the issue being discussed, sex offender treatment research often appears to be a decade or so ahead of the debates in other areas of offender rehabilitation, where my own work tends to focus.

This book, by some of the leading thinkers in the sex offender treatment field, is certainly no exception. At the heart of the book is the simple but potentially groundbreaking idea that working positively with sexual offenders leads to positive outcomes—including reduced recidivism—for offenders and improves the quality of work life for practitioners as well. This idea, based on an emerging body of evidence, represents a direct challenge to confrontational treatment approaches, which insist on early disclosure of the offense and moral shaming. Indeed, the authors argue that of the factors that impede change, confrontation is the most pronounced. Marshall and colleagues provide a comprehensive vision for a different sort of therapy based on respect and trust.

Such a vision typically triggers one of two reactions from critics. The first response is to argue that these "soft" approaches sound nice, but they do not meet hard standards for evidence-based practice. Marshall et al. clearly discredit this objection, reviewing the empirical evidence demonstrating, for instance, that therapeutic alliance can account for as much as 30% of treatment-induced changes, compared with only 15% for specific treatment techniques.[1] The second, more savvy challenge to the authors' argument, then, is to concede the research findings but argue that, really, this approach is no different from what we have been doing all along anyway. Like the first objection, this one can also be discredited through simple research. For instance, a historian of correctional practice could content-analyze Marshall and colleagues' tremendous book and compare it with similar treatment manuals written only a few decades ago. Such a comparison would find that this book not only outlines a unique treatment approach, it also uses an entirely different vocabulary from that of the past. On every page of this text, one finds words and phrases like "acceptance of the client," "collaborative approach," "strengths," "relationships," "motivational interviewing," "therapists' style," "perceived warmth and empathy," "schema therapy," "emotional analyses," and "sincerity and respect." These are "only words," of course, but then any therapist who does not appreciate the importance of the language one uses in practice should probably consider a different line of work.

---

[1]Norcross, J. C. (2002). Empirically supported therapy relationships. In J. C. Norcross (Ed.), *Psychotherapy relationships that work: Therapist contributions and responsiveness to patient needs* (pp. 1–10). New York, NY: Oxford University Press.

Although the words that Marshall and colleagues use in this book might appear radical to some at the moment, my hunch is that in treatment litera-ture *following* this book, those words will become mainstream. That is, the rest of us working in the field will soon catch up with the positive approach. The label "paradigm shift" has become an overused cliché, but in this case, it is actually appropriate.

Rehabilitating Sexual Offenders: A Strength-Based Approach sets a very high standard for the titles forthcoming in the Psychology, Crime, and Justice Series. Yet, this is as it should be. Psychological perspectives represent a unique and underused vantage point for understanding the pressing issues faced in the criminal justice system. These perspectives should provoke new ways of thinking about the entrenched, difficult problems of crime and violence. Watch this series.

ACKNOWLEDGMENTS

We wish to acknowledge a number of people who contributed their support and assistance in our efforts to complete this book.

First, we are grateful to our families, who always offer us their encouragement and love. Without this we would find it difficult to do the clinical work that has led to the development of the ideas embodied in this book.

We want to thank Shadd Maruna, the series editor, for inviting us to write the book, for his support throughout the process, and for his helpful editorial feedback.

Dr. Tony Ward provided a series of suggestions that proved extremely valuable in revising our original draft. Tony's publications and the ideas he has exchanged with us over the years contributed significantly to our emerging notions that have come to fruition in the present book.

Our development editor at the American Psychological Association, Beth Hatch, gave us a significant number of detailed suggestions, as well as specific structural ideas, all of which vastly improved the book. We are extremely grateful to Beth for her guidance and help.

We thank Jean Webber for typing the manuscript and for correcting our grammatical errors. Most of all, we are grateful for the helpful and uncomplaining style Jean brings to all her work.

The settings in which we work are staffed by correctional officers, case managers, teachers, other treatment staff, psychologists, psychiatrists, and various administrators. These on-site staff offer encouragement to our clients and fully support our programs. To them we offer our heartfelt thanks. We also acknowledge the important contributions of parole officers across the country for helping our clients maintain an offense-free life after release from prison. Thanks are due to the Correctional Service of Canada for giving us the opportunity, over so many years, to engage in treatment and research with men who committed sexual offenses.

Finally, this book, and particularly the ideas in it about how best to deliver treatment, is primarily a product of our clinical work with the many men we have had in our treatment programs over the years. We are very grateful to them for providing us with so much information and feedback. We acknowledge and admire their courage in providing us with so many details of their lives. We wish them all a fulfilling life free of any further problems.

Rehabilitating
Sexual
Offenders

INTRODUCTION

Sexual offending is a serious social problem that negatively affects far too many innocent people and that has apparently been occurring since the beginning of recorded time (Licht, 1932; G. R. Taylor, 1954). Unfortunately, until the middle of the 20th century, neither scientists nor therapists gave much in the way of devoted attention to it. This meant that the resources of society were not directed toward ameliorating the problem. Growing interests among researchers and clinicians began in the late 1960s, although there were earlier sporadic academic attempts to understand and manage these behaviors. There is now available a wealth of information relevant to the understanding, management, and treatment of these offenders and their victims.

Although the *Diagnostic and Statistical Manual of Mental Disorders* (DSM) in all its iterations has identified, among its paraphilias, some of these offenses (e.g., pedophilia, exhibitionism, sexual sadism), other offenses, such as those against pubescent children and the rape of adults, are nowhere to be found in the manual, although consideration has been given to include the former in the forthcoming *DSM–V*. Even in the current *DSM–IV–TR* (4th ed., text rev.; American Psychiatric Association, 2000), the criteria for pedophilia would exclude a significant number of child molesters. Unfortunately, exclusion from the *DSM* restricts the capacity of mental health providers from providing services to sexual offenders that might reduce their risk to reoffend.

When treatment for the offenders is appropriately implemented, it markedly reduces the number of reoffenses (Hanson et al., 2002; Lösel & Schmucker, 2005) and thereby reduces the number of future victims. Effective intervention not only serves to reduce future victimization, it also saves considerable money that otherwise would be spent on police and judicial processes and on incarceration and victim costs (W. L. Marshall, 1992; Prentky & Burgess, 1990). Despite these obvious advantages, increased funding for both victims and offenders is desperately needed. Goode (1994) reported that funding for studies of depression by the U.S. National Institute of Mental Health amounted to $125.3 million annually, whereas only $1.2 million was made available for research on sexual offending.

This book, then, addresses the current state of knowledge on the treatment of sexual offenders and the issues that must be targeted for treatment to be effective. A consideration of this extensive information, as well as our own clinical experience, has led us to develop an approach to treating these offenders. Whereas most offender treatment approaches take an aggressive, confrontational approach that emphasizes admitting guilt, our approach emphasizes warmth, empathy, and support for the offenders— what we refer to as a *positive approach*. Obviously, the goal of this approach is not to condone sex offending; to the contrary, the goal is to prevent sex offenders from reoffending. Not only do we believe that this approach is most effective for changing offending behavior, but research also supports this conclusion.

The purpose of this book is to present a unified theoretical framework, drawing from offender treatment and positive psychology literature, for treating sexual offenders. Specifically, we discuss the theory and research on sexual offender treatment, demonstrating the empirical support for a positive approach. We also describe in detail the features of three treatment programs for sexual offenders, which we developed and provide in Canadian prisons.

The remainder of this chapter is organized as follows. First, we review the incidence and effects of sexual offending, followed by a brief history on the theory and research of sexual offender treatment. Next, we discuss problems with the dominant (negative) approach to treatment and the origins of our own positive approach. We then introduce positive psychology and explain how it has been applied to sexual offender treatment, with the goals of this positive approach being identified. Finally, we discuss the scope and organization of this book.

INCIDENCE AND EFFECTS OF SEXUAL OFFENDING

We now have available a wide range of data on the incidence of sexual offending (Calhoun, McCauley, & Crawford, 2006; Peters, Wyatt, & Finkelhor, 1986); however, it is well-known that most sexual assaults are not reported to the authorities (American Academy of Child and Adolescent Psychiatry, 2004; Canadian Centre for Justice Statistics, 1999).

Sexual Offenses Against Children

According to Bagley (1991), the majority (81%) of sexual offenses involving children are limited to unwanted sexual touching, whereas 19% represent more severe attacks. Bagley's survey revealed that up to 33% of males and 50% of females reported being sexually abused as children, with most of these assaults occurring before 12 years of age (Bagley, 1991).

In the United States in 2004, more than 84,000 children were verified by child protection services to be victims of sexual abuse, accounting for 10% of the total number of substantiated cases of child maltreatment (U.S. Department of Health and Human Services, 2006). A retrospective national telephone survey in the United States indicated that 32% of women and 14% of men suffered sexual victimization during childhood, with a reported mean age of onset of 9 years (Briere & Elliot, 2003). Reports of sexual abuse to child protection and law enforcement agencies are much more likely to involve female victims than male (U.S. Bureau of Justice Statistics, 2000); however, self-report and retrospective studies have indicated that boys are victimized far more often than official data indicate (Finkelhor, 1984, 1994). Finkelhor (1984) found that 16% of adult men reported sexual abuse as a child, and parents reported that 39% of the children who disclosed sexual abuse to them were boys.

Considerable research has documented the consequences of being a victim of childhood sexual abuse. Research has suggested that the effects of sexual abuse on young victims can be extensive, long-lasting, and damaging. However, the impact varies such that some victims experience extensive and damaging consequences, whereas others experience some but less severe effects, and some appear to suffer few, if any, negative sequelae (Conte & Schuerman, 1987). Paolucci, Genuis, and Violato (2001) conducted a meta-analysis of the published research on the effects of child sexual abuse, examining posttraumatic stress, depression, suicide, sexual promiscuity, victim–perpetrator cycle, and poor academic performance. They examined 37 studies published between 1981 and 1995 involving 25,367 participants. Paolucci et al.'s results demonstrated that child sexual abuse can in fact have serious mental health consequences. The most frequently reported effects include depression, anxiety, dissociation, conduct disorders, aggressiveness, and inappropriate or early sexual behavior and activity. Sexual maladjustment, interpersonal problems, educational difficulties, self-destructive behavior, somatic symptoms, low self-esteem, prostitution, and criminal behavior, and actual or attempted suicide have been reported (Bagley, 1991; Bagley & McDonald, 1984; A. Browne & Finkelhor, 1986; Conte & Schuerman, 1987; Mayall & Gold, 1995; Swanston, Tebbutt, O'Toole, & Oates, 1997; Widom & Ames, 1994). Posttraumatic stress disorder (PTSD) symptoms and sexualized behaviors are among the most frequently reported effects (A. Browne & Finkelhor, 1986; Kendall-Tackett, Williams, & Finkelhor, 1993).

Sexual Offenses Against Adult Women

An international survey revealed that across countries (European, Asian, and North and South Pacific nations), the rates of rape were disturbingly high (van Dijk & Mayhew, 1992). W. L. Marshall and Barrett (1990) extracted the number of rapes from official records in Canada during 1988. Taking a conservative stance, they multiplied this rate by four (the lower estimate of underreporting derived from surveys), which produced an estimated 75,000 adult female victims of rape for that year. This is consistent with other studies in which as many as 30% of women reported being sexually assaulted at some point in their adult lives (Russell, 1984).

The rape of adult women produces a range of negative effects. Burgess and Holstrom (1974) described what they called the *rape trauma syndrome*. This syndrome has most of the features in common with the effects of other types of trauma, such as the development of phobias, panics, flashbacks, obsessional ruminations, mood swings, irritability, and sleep disturbances. Among rape victims, problems with sexual functioning, a loss of trust in others, and hypervigilance are commonly observed sequelae, as are poor work and school performance and substance abuse (Calhoun & Wilson, 2000). More rape victims are classified as suffering from PTSD than any other group who have experienced trauma (Resick, 1993). It has been reported that fewer than 40% of rape victims have been able to recover sufficiently to function effectively within the several months after the attack (Burgess & Holstrom, 1974). In fact, rape victims appear to suffer immediate and long-term negative effects similar to those suffered by child victims of sexual abuse.

Ripple Effects of Sexual Abuse

Sexual abuse not only affects the victim but also has an impact on the family and friends of the victim and the abuser and his family, as well as various effects on society. Because sexual abuse interferes with the victim's intimate relationships, sexuality, work relationships, and friendships, then clearly these consequences affect other people within the victim's circle of family and friends. Research has suggested that many survivors of sexual abuse report fears about parenting, including their fear that they may themselves repeat the abuse or be unable to protect their children from abuse, or that they may overprotect their children (Westerlund, 1992). Interestingly, Bolen and Lamb (2004) found that following the disclosure of child sexual abuse, one third of nonoffending guardians expressed ambivalence toward the victim; 25% were clearly nonsupportive, 31% were only partially supportive, and only 46% were fully supportive. On the basis of the evidence, sexual offending has potentially traumatic effects that need to be addressed. Fortunately, treatment programs are available to victims of sexual abuse (Calhoun et al., 2006) as well as to the abusers (Levenson & Prescott, 2007), although in many jurisdictions these programs are quite limited.

A CHANGE IN THE APPROACH TO TREATMENT

Although many sexual offender treatment programs take an aggressive, confrontational approach that emphasizes admitting guilt, research has shown that this common approach does not alter actual criminogenic factors related to reoffending rates. That is, these programs, although satisfying the desire of some people to see offenders admit guilt, do not actually reduce recidivism. Offenders who receive treatment in such programs are no less likely to reoffend than those who receive no treatment. Furthermore, this approach can alienate and demoralize offenders, who often report "not getting anything out of it."

In contrast to these common confrontational approaches, a new trend is emerging in the treatment of sexual offenders. In this new style of treatment, therapists display, among other things, warmth, empathy, and support for the offenders—what we refer to as a *positive approach*. Backed by research, this approach does not ignore criminogenic factors but presents them to clients as targets for the development of strengths rather than as deficits to be overcome. Working positively with sexual offenders not only produces effective results, it also changes the way therapists feel about themselves and their jobs. Enhancing the enjoyment of doing the difficult task of being a therapist for sexual offenders inevitably creates greater enthusiasm for the job and reduces the likelihood of burnout. For all involved (clients, therapists, and the public), then, adopting a positive approach to treating sexual offenders seems a promising way to produce broad benefits.

Although we have previously published descriptions of a limited positive approach to treating sexual offenders (W. L. Marshall, Marshall, Serran, & Fernandez, 2006; W. L. Marshall et al., 2005), the current book provides a more detailed account of this approach and a more comprehensive framework that was not available for our previous reports. Primarily, this framework derives from the recent flourishing ideas of what has come to be called *positive psychology*. Positive psychology represents something of a paradigmatic shift away from focusing on people's deficits and onto researching strengths and building life-enhancing programs. In clinical applications of positive psychology, the emphasis is on assisting clients to recognize and enhance their strengths so they can increase their resilience in the face of future problems. In the context of sexual offending, positive psychology draws on personal strengths to replace abusive behavior with prosocial, life-enhancing alternatives.

In our work at Rockwood Psychological Services (RPS) in Ontario, Canada, we have used a positive psychology approach to run three group treatment programs in two Canadian prisons. In the Millhaven Institution (a maximum security prison), we provide our Preparatory Program, which engages offenders in the process of change before the main treatment program begins. In the Bath Institution (a medium security prison), we provide both our Primary Program, which targets actual criminogenic factors that are known to predict reoffense (problems with attitudes and cognitions, self-regulation, relationships, and sexual issues), and the Deniers' Program, which also targets criminogenic factors but is tailored to the specific needs of those who deny committing a sexual offense. All of these programs emphasize increasing self-esteem, decreasing shame, and building personal strengths and resilience to live a healthy, prosocial life. We have run the Preparatory Program since 1997, the Primary Program since 1991, and the Deniers' Program since 1998.

The RPS programs typically have eight to 10 clients in an open-ended group run by one (and occasionally two) therapists. The groups meet twice each week for 2.5 hr with each client remaining in the group until he meets satisfactory levels on the targets of treatment; this typically results in most clients achieving the goals of treatment after 4 or 5 months in treatment. It is important to note that all these offenders are also involved in various other programs (e.g., anger management, substance abuse, cognitive skills) as well as receiving educational upgrading and job-skills training where relevant. Since the original start-up date (1991) of our Primary Program, 950 sexual offenders have entered treatment in this program (up to the end of 2009), of whom 910 completed treatment. The Deniers' Program has had 102 participants since its inception (1998), all of whom completed the program, and the Preparatory Program has had 380 participants since its inception (1997), with again all of them completing treatment.

Each of the RPS programs has been evaluated by independent researchers and found to be effective. We provide details of these evaluations in a later section of the book (Chapter 5). For now, we briefly review the history of sexual offender research and theory.

A BRIEF HISTORY OF THEORY AND RESEARCH ON SEXUAL OFFENDERS

The first important comments on unusual sexual behaviors appeared in Richard von Krafft-Ebing's (1886) book *Psychopathia Sexualis*. This book described, among other unconventional sexual interests, the proclivity among some men to be sexually interested in children; Krafft-Ebing called this *paedophilia*. Later in the 19th century, Albert Moll also described child molestation in his book *Perversions of the Genital Instinct* (Moll, 1893). In the early part of the 20th century, both Havelock Ellis (1915) and Magnus Hirschfeld (1920) wrote about this behavior. Not surprisingly, Freud wrote extensively on the subject (Freud, 1905/1957), although he changed his initial theory in response to a hostile reception he received at a conference. All these authors saw the problem as a mental disorder that required treatment, and they offered accounts of the origins of such behaviors. More explicitly, both Von Schrenck-Notzing (1895/1956) and Norman (1892) offered explanations of the etiology of aberrant sexual interests that match more recent accounts. Norman, for example, suggested that deviant sexual interests were the product of repeated masturbation to sexual fantasies involving deviant acts, which foreshadowed the influential conditioning account of McGuire, Carlisle, and Young (1965).

These etiological explanations were accompanied in some cases by descriptions of learning-based treatment strategies that presaged more recent techniques (see Laws & Marshall, 2003, for details of this early history). For example, both Charcot and Magnan (1882) and Von Schrenk-Notzing (1895/1956) outlined a technique that is almost a perfect match for what Marquis (1970) called *orgasmic reconditioning*. A shaping procedure, akin to a treatment later proposed by Barlow and Agras (1973), was described much earlier by Moll (1911).

However, it was not until the 1960s that the modern approach to the treatment of these problematic behaviors was initiated (see W. L. Marshall & Laws, 2003, for details of this later history). The early modern attempts rested on the simple idea that deviant sexual activities were driven by previously developed sexual interests in the deviant acts. McGuire et al. (1965), for example, proposed that deviance resulted from the accidental pairing of sexual arousal with circumstances that matched the later enactment of the deviant behavior. They offered one illustration of this in which a young man found it necessary to urinate in a wooded location where he thought he was alone when suddenly there appeared a woman who saw him. Later reflections on this accidental exposure of his penis in the presence of the woman caused him to become sexually aroused. Subsequently, McGuire et al. suggested, the man recreated this experience in his imagination to deliberately generate sexual arousal. This repeated pairing of the original scene with masturbation was said to lead to the establishment of a sexual interest in exhibitionism, which sooner or later resulted in the man's actual and deliberate genital exposures to a woman.

This conditioning account of the etiology of deviant sexual acts was elaborated and extended by others (Abel & Blanchard, 1974; Laws & Marshall, 1990) to apply to other types of sexual offenders. These conditioning theories led to an early focus in treatment on simply modifying sexual interests, it being believed that changing these interests would automatically lead to the elimination of the deviant behavior and the emergence of appropriate sexual activity (Bond & Evans, 1967). W. L. Marshall (1971) was the first to point to deficiencies in this view of the necessary components of treatment. He pointed out that eliminating deviant sexual interests, and even adding a procedure to enhance appropriate sexual interests, did not guarantee the emergence of prosocial sexual behaviors. Marshall suggested that a child molester who had never previously had satisfactory sexual experiences with adults would, after a conditioning treatment program alone, not necessarily have the skills, attitudes, and self-confidence to successfully approach an adult for a sexual and romantic relationship. He proposed that effective treatment would require, in addition to changing sexual interests, components addressing the deficiencies in the offender's capacity to meet his needs in prosocial ways. This proposal by Marshall was followed by a process of research and treatment development that produced ever expanding targets in the treatment of sexual offenders, culminating in the present day range of comprehensive treatment programs.

The major changes in intervention approaches with sexual offenders during the 1970s, driven in large part by the seminal work of the American psychiatrist Gene Abel and his colleagues (Abel, Blanchard, & Becker, 1978), was the expansion of the issues addressed in treatment. Most of these changes derived from either clinical intuition or early research showing differences between sexual offenders and one of a variety of other groups (e.g., nonsex offenders, community samples). It was too early in the development of the field for the identification of what would later be called *criminogenic factors* (Andrews, Bonta, & Hoge, 1990); that is, deficits in functioning that are shown to be predictive of subsequent reoffending. These were to become the bases for establishing appropriate treatment targets for sexual offenders, but not until researchers identified the relationship between deficits and reoffending (Hanson, 2006b; Hanson, Bourgon, Helmus, & Hodgson, 2009; Hanson & Bussière, 1998; Hanson & Morton-Bourgon, 2005). Two of the earliest additions to the targets of treatment were deficiencies in empathy (Becker, Abel, Blanchard, Murphy, & Coleman, 1978) and distorted cognitions that justified offending (Brownell, 1980). In fact, by the early 1980s, treatment programs had expanded to include a broad range of targets (W. L. Marshall, Earls, Segal, & Darke, 1983).

The most important change in the 1980s was the adaptation (Marques, 1982) to the field of sexual offender treatment of Alan Marlatt's (1982) relapse prevention (RP) approach with addictive behaviors. A detailed description of this approach was provided by Pithers, Marques, Gibat, and Marlatt (1983), and RP soon became the dominant treatment approach, particularly in the United Stated (Laws, 1989). The enthusiastic acceptance of this logically sound treatment model was, unfortunately, not matched by a careful empirical examination until Ward and his colleagues published a series of critical appraisals of RP (Ward & Hudson, 1996; Ward, Hudson, & Marshall, 1994; Ward, Hudson, & Siegert, 1995). This culminated in a thorough reappraisal of the value of RP with sexual offenders (Laws, Hudson, & Ward, 2000) and its explicit rejection by Yates and Ward (P. M. Yates, 2007; P. M. Yates & Ward, 2009), although many still cling to the RP model (see Carich, Dobkowski, & Delehanty, 2009). These rejections of RP now seem justified given the clear failure of a well-designed evaluation of a model RP program (Marques, Weideranders, Day, Nelson, & van Ommeren, 2005).

The 1990s saw the introduction of empirically based risk-prediction instruments (Epperson, Kaul, & Hesselton, 1998; Hanson, 1997a; Hanson & Thornton, 1999; Harris, Rice, & Quinsey, 1993; Quinsey, Rice, & Harris, 1995), which were very useful in various decisions (e.g., allocation to treatment intensity, supervision on release) but did not, for the most part, contain modifiable treatment targets. It was not until later that potentially changeable risk predictors (so-called dynamic factors) were identified (Hanson & Harris, 2000b).

As a result of the serious questions regarding the value of RP, alternative models of sexual offender treatment were proposed. Ward and Hudson (2000), for example, introduced sexual offender treatment providers to the extensive literature on self-regulation (Baumeister & Heatherton, 1996; Carver & Scheier, 1990) and integrated this with their pathways model (S. M. Hudson, Ward, & McCormack, 1999) to provide a treatment approach (S. M. Hudson & Ward, 2000). In a later extension of this approach, Ward (Ward & Gannon, 2006; Ward & Marshall, 2004; Ward & Stewart, 2003a), again borrowing from the general psychological literature (Austin & Vancouver, 1996; Emmons, 1996; Rasmussen, 1999; Schmuck & Sheldon, 2001), suggested that sexual offender treatment should aim to identify and seek to achieve for each client a personalized good life. Ward called his development of this approach the *good lives model* (GLM), and he (Ward & Brown, 2003) suggested that it could complement the risk, needs, and responsivity model espoused by Andrews and Bonta (1994). The GLM (which is described in detail later in this book) enunciates a positive view of both the character and future possibilities of sexual offenders. As such, this model is in line with the recent movement in clinical psychology that has been characterized as positive psychology (Linley &

Joseph, 2004b; M. E. P. Seligman & Csikszentmihalyi, 2000; Snyder & Lopez, 2005). Consistent with this movement, we described a treatment approach for sexual offenders that emphasized dealing respectfully, optimistically, and motivationally with the offenders that we called "working positively" with sexual offenders (W. L. Marshall et al., 2005). This latter article has provided the basis on which the treatment described in the present book evolved. This book, then, details our current approach to the treatment of sexual offenders.

In conjunction with the expanding range of treatment targets, there are now comprehensive assessment batteries (Dougher, 1995b; Knight, Prentky, & Cerce, 1994; Mussack & Carich, 2001; Prentky & Edmunds, 1997), well-articulated theories of the etiology and maintenance of sexually aberrant behaviors (Stinson, Sales, & Becker, 2008; Ward, Polaschek, & Beech, 2006), and thorough postdischarge management strategies (Birgden, Owen, & Raymond, 2003; Cumming & McGrath, 2000; Kemshall & McIvor, 2004). Recent research, which is reviewed in detail in later chapters, has offered reasonably sound evidence for the effectiveness of these expanded treatment and management strategies.

PROBLEMS WITH THE DOMINANT TREATMENT APPROACH

As we have seen, the RP model, when introduced to the field of sexual offender treatment in the early 1980s, rapidly came to dominate the field. This approach was consistent with Finkelhor's (1984) four preconditions model of sexual offending behavior, a theory that was very popular in the 1980s. Finkelhor proposed that for men to sexually abuse children, sex with children must be emotionally satisfying to them, they must be sexually aroused by children, they must be unable to meet their sexual needs prosocially, and they must somehow overcome their inhibitions about having sex with a child. All of Finkelhor's ideas clearly represent a deficit model of the offenders. Programs modeled after the RP approach included the requirement that each offender had to produce an elaborate and detailed account of his offense, including the immediate precursors. These precursors were assumed to involve sexualized thoughts about a victim, careful preoffense planning, setting up the opportunity to access a victim, and possibly deliberately inducing intoxication to overcome any prohibitions against offending. Again, this is clearly a deficit model.

Strict applications of the RP model became quite common, and it was assumed that all sexual offenses followed the pattern outlined by this model. As a result, offenders were required to admit to having deviant fantasies and to planning their offenses. The account sexual offenders gave of their offenses had to include these details; otherwise, they were deemed to be noncompliant. There was less concern about the more distal issues in the offender's life that might have created a vulnerable state whereby sexual offending became acceptable. These more distal problems might result in a lack of the capacity in the offenders to meet their needs prosocially. As a result, little effort was made to explore the reasons why sexual offenders were unable to achieve satisfaction through appropriate means. Most RP programs routinely treated the same group of deficits for all offenders rather that tailoring treatment to individually identified difficulties. The focus was almost entirely restricted to eliminating deviance, confronting offense-supportive cognitions, identifying potential risks, and planning how to avoid these risks in the future.

Along with the requirement of outlining their assumed planning of the offense, sexual offenders were required to describe in detail what they actually did during the offense, with the requirement that this "offense account" match precisely the official record (i.e., the victim's report generated from the police interview). The veridicality of the official record was never questioned in the RP approach. The client's agreement with the official record of the offense was taken to mean he had accepted responsibility for the offense, which was seen as a necessary step to effectively engage in treatment. We (W. L. Marshall, Marshall, & Ware, 2009) have pointed to sound empirical reasons for being sceptical about the accuracy of victims' reports of sexual abuse, with errors being more likely when young children are the victims. Similarly, Maruna and Mann (2006) pointed to the impossibility of perfect accuracy for any retrospective account of an event, including the accounts of a sexual crime by either the perpetrator or the victim.

Most sexual offender programs not only require the offender at the start of treatment to give a detailed disclosure of his offense, they then immediately begin to focus on his deficits (which are all too often assumed to be present) across a range of areas of functioning. Such programs have little to say about each client's strengths, and this is true of those cognitive–behavioral programs that either preceded the introduction of the RP model or that have used RP concepts as adjuncts to their program. This seems strange in retrospect because on all measures of human functioning that have been applied to sexual offenders, considerable heterogeneity is evident, indicating that many of these men function normatively (i.e., they have significant strengths) on aspects of the behaviors, thoughts, and feelings that are typically targeted in treatment programs. Clearly, most sexual offenders have strengths within each of the typical targets of treatment, and these strengths can be recruited to facilitate the achievement of all other treatment targets. Attention has recently been given to a strengths-based approach to the treatment of various other presenting problems (Hodges & Clifton, 2004) in which the focus is not so much on eliminating deficits but rather on using the client's strengths to develop better ways of living (S. D. Miller, Duncan, & Hubble, 1997). These strength-based approaches have been shown to be effective across all types of problematic behaviors (Saleeby, 2002).

A failure to help sexual offenders identify their strengths ignores the fact that the processes of investigation, prosecution, and sentencing have created in most of them the belief that they are "bad" people, implying that they do not have the capacity to change. Indeed, one of the tenets of RP, which is commonly expressed in the majority of treatment programs for sexual offenders regardless of whether or not they are RP-based, is that the best sexual offenders can do is learn to control the overt expression of their deviant tendencies (see Seto, 2008, for a detailed expression of this view). Such a gloomy perspective is unlikely to elicit a strong commitment to treatment among these men and does not rest on solid evidence. Indeed, we (W. L. Marshall, 2008; W. L. Marshall, O'Brien, & Marshall, 2009) have shown that the deviant sexual interests of child molesters (which are said to underpin their deviant acts) can be significantly reduced to within normal limits and that these changes are enduring over many years. Apparently child molesters do not have to struggle for the rest of their lives to control an intractable desire to offend.

It has been shown that on arrival at a treatment facility, sexual offenders consistently score low on measures of self-esteem (W. L. Marshall, Anderson, & Champagne, 1997) and high on measures of shame (W. L. Marshall, Marshall, Serran, & O'Brien, 2009; Sparks, Bailey, Marshall, & Marshall, 2003). Both these features have been shown in the general psychological literature to be obstacles to engagement in change processes (Baumeister, 1993; Tangney & Dearing, 2002). Unfortunately, most treatment programs for sexual offenders either ignore these obstacles or give them limited attention. Our view is that a first step in treatment should be motivational and aimed at enhancing engagement, and that this should precede any attempt to address areas of difficulty. Part of this approach in our program involves increasing self-esteem and reducing shame so that clients can then more fully engage in treatment. Such procedures, when effective, also make clients more ready to believe they have strengths and that these strengths can be built on to ensure a better, offense-free future. It also increases their readiness to believe that they can develop strengths in areas in which they presently have deficits that are criminogenic in nature. Interestingly, all the criminogenic features that are potentially amenable to change (i.e., the so-called dynamic risk factors), are among the strengths sexual offenders need to develop to function more optimally in a way that will lead to an enhancement of their lives. Thus, developing strengths that will enable sexual offenders to have a better life will almost necessarily inhibit criminogenic features, a point Ward (Ward & Brown, 2003; Ward, Collie, & Bourke, 2009) has made in the context of discussing his GLM.

Finally, the essence of RP programs is expressed in the requirement that offenders identify a list (usually quite extensive) of all the situations, persons, and places, as well as feelings and thoughts, that might put them at risk to reoffend. Once this list is completed to the satisfaction of the therapist, the offenders are then required to identify how they will avoid such risks or escape from them should they occur inadvertently. In RP programs, this component of treatment occupies a significant amount of time and essentially frames the rest of treatment. It is drilled into the clients that unless they memorize this list of risks and their associated avoidance strategies, or carry the list with them at all times, they are bound to relapse. This seems to us to be a misplaced strategy. In the first place, this required vigilance to potential risks once the clients are back in the community is simply too burdensome to allow offenders to do much else, and strict adherence to it would seem to preclude a range of positive activities. Furthermore, it seems unrealistic to expect anyone to be able to generate a list of thoughts and feelings that actually occurred prior to their offense. As we will see, memory is a reconstructive process such that recall of actual events or circumstances may be distorted, then surely the recall of thoughts and feelings is likely to be even less accurate.

Pressing a client to generate a list of risks on the basis of what he recalls from his past offenses would seem certain to result in "created" factors. Having clients feel the need to produce something to simply meet the demands of treatment without believing that the product is genuine will encourage them to focus in treatment on gaining the approval of the therapist rather than actually addressing their important issues. We have all too often had offenders enter our program after completing an earlier program only to deny much of what they told the previous therapist. When questioned about this, they respond by saying that they were pressured to admit to behaviors, thoughts, and feelings that they either did not remember or actually did not believe happened. This is certainly not the approach to treatment we wish to encourage in our clients.

In a caricature of this aspect of the RP model, the parole board of an Australian state presented a logistical problem to us. They told us that they were required to place a restriction on child molesters released from prison such that these men were not allowed to live within 1 km of a school or day care center. The board members noted that, as a result of the proliferation of day care centers and the expansion of schools arising from significant population growth in their capital city, it had become impossible for child molesters to find accommodation that met these requirements anywhere in the city. The consequence was that the parole board had to order these offenders to relocate to a town unfamiliar to them where they knew no one and where there were no jobs suited to their skills. We did not have to point out to the parole board members that this was a problematic rule, the implementation of which would place the offenders under considerable stress and thereby increase their risk to reoffend.

Aside from such practical absurdities, the notion underlying this central aspect of the RP approach, that avoidance strategies are the appropriate solutions to reduce future risk, is contradicted by evidence. Research has clearly shown that avoidance goals are rarely maintained for any length of time and are all but certain to fail, whereas approach goals are persistently engaged and typically successful (Emmons, 1996; Gollwitzer & Bargh, 1996).

ORIGIN OF OUR APPROACH

Our own thinking about the treatment of sexual offenders is rooted in an early analysis of a set of diaries kept by a chronic child molester. These diaries revealed a picture that was far different from the public's image of such a man. This offender, John, admitted to, and recorded in his detailed diaries, having molested 420 boys over a 26-year period. When he was arrested in 1972, the police searched his house; they found the diaries and forwarded them to the treatment providers. W. L. Marshall (1996) reported some aspects of this case, but we provide a more in-depth description here.

In June 1973, Marshall and two researchers independently conducted a random but extensive content analysis of these diaries. What was found, to everyone's surprise, was that only 8% of John's recorded hours involved grooming or molesting boys. In 92% of his hours, he was involved in prosocial activities, most of which were mundane, such as healthful exercises, assisting an invalided neighbor, working diligently as an accountant, taking the bus to and from work, and conversing with people he met. Interviews with John revealed considerable remorse, a desire to do something restorative for the boys and their families, effective social skills, broad-ranging interests, and a good sense of humor. Focusing on these extensive strengths early in treatment led to a shift in John's view of himself from shame about his crimes to feelings of guilt; the former (i.e., shame) has, as we have noted, been shown to block attempts at change, whereas the latter (i.e., guilt) facilitates engagement in change processes (Tangney & Dearing, 2002). This focus on his strengths resulted in a positive mood change in John and an enthusiastic devotion to the treatment program. A more traditional approach to John might have seen him as a "monster" with extensive deficits, whereas the view of him generated from the analyses of his diaries was of an "everyman" who had many strengths and a remarkably resilient character. As a result of treatment, John had, as Maruna (2001) suggested, rewritten his shameful past into a strategy for a better life.

Our detailed examination of John led us to reconsider both the way we thought about sexual offenders and, more particularly, the way we approached our treatment. Research and clinical experience would later lead us to publish a paper (W. L. Marshall et al., 2005) that encapsulated what we described as our positive approach to the treatment of sexual offenders. This approach, although based on sexual offender research, would later be enriched conceptually from our growing familiarity with positive psychology.

POSITIVE PSYCHOLOGY: A CONCEPTUAL FRAMEWORK

Throughout history, numerous authors have discussed the human striving for the fulfillment of potentialities (Linley & Joseph, 2004b). Aristotle, for example, wrote a treatise on what he called *eudaimonia*; that is, "the state of being well and doing well in being well" (McIntyre, 1984, p. 148). William James (1902) was also interested in the processes that stimulate optimal human functioning, and Carl Jung (1933) examined procedures that might assist people in achieving their goal of fulfillment. This tradition of emphasizing the ways in which people can develop their strengths was continued in the writings of Maslow (1968) and his notion of *self-actualization* and more recently in Snyder's (1994, 2000; Snyder, Rand, & Sigmon, 2005) hope theory. Others have addressed related areas such as subjective well-being (Diener, Lucas, & Oishi, 2005; Eid & Larsen, 2008), life satisfaction (Diener & Diener, 1995), the development of resilience (T. M. Yates & Masten, 2004), and the generation of optimism (M. E. P. Seligman, 1991).

Perhaps the embodiment of these ideas is best represented by the recent focus on what has come to be known as the GLM, which Ward (2002; Ward & Gannon, 2006; Ward & Mann, 2004; Ward & Marshall, 2004) developed and which he derived from a diverse body of research devoted to examining how people thrive, achieve self-satisfaction, and succeed in meeting their goals (Deci & Ryan, 2000; Emmons, 1999; Kasser, 2004; Schmuck & Sheldon, 2001). The GLM proposes that humans, whether they are aware of it or not, strive toward the attainment of satisfaction in nine areas of functioning: (a) optimal mental, physical, and sexual health; (b) knowledge; (c) mastery in work and play; (d) autonomy; (e) inner peace; (f) relatedness; (g) creativity; (h) spirituality; and (i) happiness. Note that happiness, often thought of as the primary human pursuit, is but one of these nine areas of striving and likely is a product of at least a minimal degree of success in the pursuit of the other eight primary goods (Sheldon & Lyubomirsky, 2004).

As noted, this emerging focus in clinical psychology that integrates all these diverse issues has been referred to as positive psychology. M. E. P. Seligman (2002, 2003; M. E. P. Seligman & Csikszentmihalyi, 2000; M. E. P. Seligman & Peterson, 2003) was one of the first to point to an alternative to the focus in clinical psychology and psychiatry on disorders and pathologies.

This traditional approach primarily involves attempts to overcome deficits. Seligman noted the lack of concern with clients' strengths in this essentially disease model of human problems. Positive psychology, so Linley and Joseph (2004a) declared, aims at the fulfillment of potential in clients who come for treatment as well as the amelioration of their pathology. It is the facilitation of optimal functioning that is the concern of the positive psychology approach. In evaluating a client, positive psychology clinicians look to the individual's strengths, capacities, and resources to assist him or her in overcoming difficulties. This does not mean that these practitioners ignore the presenting problem; rather, it is the failure of most therapists to use the clients' strengths in dealing with their difficulties that concerns positive psychologists. Thus, it is a strength-based model of treatment.

Kasser and his colleagues (Kasser & Ahuvia, 2002; Kasser & Ryan, 1993, 1996) demonstrated that it was the centrality in people's lives of striving to achieve intrinsic goals (i.e., autonomy, relatedness, competence, and community) that was associated with well-being. A failure of self-actualization, Kasser observed, was associated with debilitating physical symptoms and depression. A mistaken assumption of the traditional approach to the problems people present at treatment, as Sheldon and King (2001) pointed out, is that ameliorating suffering, rather than increasing happiness, will lead to well-being. Contrary to this view, Thunedborg, Black, and Bech (1995) showed that it was scores on measures of the quality of life, rather than symptom ratings, that predicted the recurrence of depression. As Ryff and Singer (1996) observed, it is the absence of well-being that creates the vulnerability that leads to problems. They suggested that recovery is most likely to occur when the focus in treatment is on engendering positive behaviors and feelings rather than exclusively attending to the alleviation of negative symptoms.

In a similar vein, Fava and Rafenelli's (Fava et al., 2001; Rafanelli et al., 2000) well-being therapy focuses on enhancing environmental mastery, generating personal growth, identifying a purpose in life, increasing a sense of autonomy, accepting one's self, and developing positive relations with others. These targets are a match for the primary goals that have been identified in the GLM. Most important, Fava and his colleagues have shown their approach to be effective in alleviating affective disorders (Fava, Rafanelli, Cazzaro, Conti, & Grandi, 1998; Fava, Rafanelli, Grandi, Conti, & Belluardo, 1998) as well as in reducing generalized anxiety (Ruini & Fava, 2002). Ruini and Fava (2004) recommended including well-being therapy as part of a symptom-oriented, cognitive–behavioral program for all types of disorders.

Maddux, Snyder, and Lopez (2004) claimed that clinical psychology, particularly throughout the latter half of the 20th century, has been steeped in an illness ideology. Bandura (1998) similarly noted that clinical psychology is "more heavily invested in intricate theories of failure rather than in theories of success" (p. 3) when, in fact, most people attend clinics seeking help to function more effectively (Bandura, 1978). The traditional focus on dysfunctions, with its concerns for weaknesses, excludes any effort to evaluate and build on the strong and healthy aspects of clients. Maddux et al. viewed the established pathologically focused approach not as a scientifically based theory of human problems, but rather as a "socially constructed ideology." Positive psychology, on the other hand, "emphasizes goals, well-being, satisfaction, happiness, interpersonal skills, perseverance, talent, wisdom, and personal responsibility" (Maddux et al., 2004, p. 330).

Bernard (2006) reviewed a number of studies indicating the greater importance of resilience or positive protective factors over risk factors in helping children and families resolve problems. Even among children from deprived or dysfunctional families, the majority overcome these early obstacles (Rhodes & Brown, 1991). Thus, it is not so much vulnerabilities that need to be attended to in interventions but rather factors that provide resilience.

In his seminal study of the desistence of criminal behavior in males, Maruna (2001) observed that this occurs only when the man begins a fundamental shift in his sense of self and his place in society. Maruna (2001) spoke of *redemptive scripts* whereby a person rewrites "a shameful past into a necessary prelude to a worthy productive life" (p. 87). The focus of those offenders who are able to give up a life of crime (i.e., those who desist) is clearly on building or redirecting their strengths rather than giving in to their urges to offend (the persisters).

MODELS FOR APPLYING POSITIVE PSYCHOLOGY TO THE TREATMENT OF SEXUAL OFFENDERS

One of the major inferences we have drawn from the positive psychology movement for the treatment of sexual offenders concerns a shift in therapeutic attention (a) from a focus on the details of past offenses to the identification of areas of functioning that need to be enhanced; (b) from an exclusive concern about clients' deficits to a more strength-based emphasis; (c) from an elaborate detailing of potential future risks to the generation of future possibilities for a better life; and (d) from the production of an extensive list of situations, thoughts, feelings and behaviors to be avoided in the future to the development of approach behaviors that will enhance their life. All these shifts reflect a movement away from the RP approach.

The following models adopt an approach that fits with positive psychology specifically for the treatment of sexual offenders.

"Old Me" Versus "New Me"

One of the first examples of an incipient positive psychology approach to the treatment of sexual offenders was articulated by James Haaven (Haaven, Little, & Petri-Miller, 1990). Haaven assists his clients in distinguishing their "old me" (i.e., those features that allowed them to commit crimes) from a "new me," which involves goals and plans built around the clients' individual preferences and strengths. His whole program is based on an attempt to help clients develop an optimistic view of their potential to change and to develop a better life. The concept of their old me serves to help them recognize that they made choices they did not have to make, and Haaven emphasizes to his clients that they have the potential to change. Developing a new me is embedded in convincing the offenders that they have the capacity to make choices that will enable them to get what they want in ways that do not hurt others. Haaven's approach is in many ways akin to Ward's GLM, although it is not as comprehensively framed around the pursuit of self-fulfillment across the range of goals reflected in the GLM. Haaven's strength-based, positive-focused program, appears to be effective (Haaven & Coleman, 2000).

The GLM

Ward and his colleagues (Ward, 2002; Ward & Mann, 2004; Ward & Marshall, 2004; Ward & Stewart, 2003a; P. M. Yates & Ward, 2008) have outlined the potential application of the GLM to the treatment of offenders, including sexual offenders. In fact, sexual offenders appear to want a better life. Mann and Webster (2002), for example, found that many sexual offenders who admitted to offending, and who expressed a desire to change, nevertheless declined an offer of treatment. When questioned by Mann and Webster, these men said they did not want to enter a program that focused only on their deficits. They wanted treatment to help them lead a better life; that is, they wanted what the GLM offers.

Ward and Stewart (2003b) argued that applying treatment on the basis of the GLM can be effectively implemented in conjunction with Andrews and Bonta's (1994) risk, needs, and responsivity (RNR) approach. The RNR approach, which is based on an extensive meta-analysis of effective treatment programs with criminals, says among other things that interventions for offenders should target those problems that have been shown to predict future offending (i.e., criminogenic factors). Ward's position is that enhancing the skills, attitudes, and behaviors that lead to a good life will necessarily deal with the criminogenic problems. For example, providing the skills, attitudes, and self-confidence necessary to function effectively in adult intimate and sexual relationships will necessarily overcome the risk factor involving problems in adult relationships. Ward sees criminal behavior as a consequence of failing to achieve a good life. He has suggested that providing offenders with the skills, attitudes, and self-belief necessary to achieve greater satisfaction, through the process of identifying both individually specific goals and the steps needed to achieve those goals, will necessarily overcome the criminogenic factors. Essentially this means that following positive psychology's approach of dealing with deficits by enhancing appropriate strengths should result in effective treatment for sexual offenders. A focus on building strengths in the areas of criminogenic deficits should encourage a more hopeful disposition in sexual offenders than that which occurs when treatment simply targets deficits. Instilling hope in clients has been shown to increase treatment effectiveness for various problem behaviors (Snyder, 2000).

Motivational Interviewing

The motivational interviewing (MI) approach advocated by W. R. Miller and Rollnick (1991, 2002) fits well with positive psychology. In the second edition of their book, W. R. Miller and Rollnick (2002) wrote they that found many therapists were using the "techniques" of MI without understanding its "spirit." As a result, Miller and Rollnick placed greater emphasis in their most current book on this spirit. In their view, the essential features of the spirit of MI involve the following:

1. *Collaboration* between therapist and client. This partnership involves support rather than persuasion and is opposite to the confrontational approach so common in offender treatment programs. As Miller and Rollnick noted, the MI therapist creates an interpersonal atmosphere conducive to change that is noncoercive. Interestingly, Shingler and Mann (2006) described using a collaborative approach with sexual offenders not just in treatment but also in procedures designed to assess future risk. Tyron and Winograd (2001) demonstrated that clients who had been collaboratively involved in setting treatment goals had far better outcomes than did those clients for whom treatment goals were set by the therapist.
2. *Evocation*, which involves eliciting from the client (rather than imposing on him) insight and reality. The therapist's role is not to impart wisdom but rather to adopt a nonexpert role involving drawing out motivation from the client. It is the therapeutic process of engaging the client that allows this evocation of insight to occur. This is the opposite of a psychoeducational approach, which has been, and continues to be, popular in sexual offender treatment (Green, 1995).

3. *Autonomy*, in which the focus is on the client being responsible for change. MI therapists offer an invitation to treatment but it is the client's responsibility to accept it or not. This is directed at developing intrinsic motivation so that change will arise within the client rather than being imposed on him.

In addition to these three features of the spirit of MI, W. R. Miller and Rollnick (2002) described four guiding principles for therapists to follow:

1. Express empathy by responding to the client's perspectives as understandable and valid. Ambivalence by the client, they pointed out, is to be expected particularly within the context of a criminal justice system that is typically coercive.
2. Help the client see the discrepancy between his present situation (including his attitudes and behaviors) and his goals, such as wanting to be healthy, happy, and successful and to have good relationships and a positive self-image. In this sense, MI is intentionally directed toward the resolution of ambivalence.
3. Roll with the resistance clients typically have toward change. Attempting to overcome this by arguing with the client will not be successful and will likely increase resistance. Inviting the client to consider other perspectives, particularly about the personal value to him of effectively engaging in treatment, is more likely to overcome resistance.
4. Support and encourage the client's emerging self-efficacy. This will instil hope, and there is evidence that the development of hope is significantly related to effective treatment progress with offenders (Moulden & Marshall, 2005). Bandura (1977a) showed that clients must believe in their capacity to change for treatment to be effective. It is important that the therapist believes in the client's capacity for change; otherwise, this scepticism will inevitably be conveyed to the client.

Ginsberg, Mann, Rotgers, and Weekes (2002) described the application of MI to the treatment of offenders, including sexual offenders. They pointed to evidence indicating that a lack of motivation is the primary reason that offenders drop out of treatment (Stewart & Montplaisir, 1999). Others have also recommended using MI in treatment with sexual offenders (Garland & Dougher, 1991; Kear-Colwell & Pollack, 1997), and Mann (1996) described several case studies pointing to the value of an MI approach with these offenders. In one such case (Mann & Rollnick, 1996), she illustrated the successful application of MI with a reluctant sexual offender who was also denying he had committed an offense. A similar approach was effectively used with another sexual offender who claimed he was innocent despite overwhelming evidence to the contrary (Ware & Marshall, 2008).

Invitations to Responsibility

In his book *Invitations to Responsibility*, Jenkins (1990) outlined the way in which he gets men who have abused others to accept responsibility for the ways in which they allowed themselves to engage in abusive behavior and, most important, to accept responsibility for changing. In our approach, we are less concerned about the former and focus more on having the client accept responsibility for his future, a sentiment reflected in an article by Maruna and Mann (2006). Jenkins suggested that when abusers fail to take responsibility for their offenses, this failure is typically seen by most therapists as resistance and this view, Jenkins said, is a recipe for therapist frustration and failure. The challenge, Jenkins claimed, "is to derive an approach which will engage the man in a way that facilitates his taking responsibility for his participation in therapy and encourages an active interest and motivation in changing his own behavior" (p. 16). He said that all perpetrators seek explanations for their abusive behaviors but most of the explanations they offer are exculpatory. Jenkins attempts to guide them to explanations that help them take responsibility and that point to solutions that will lead to a cessation of abuse. He encourages abusers to ask themselves what is stopping them from taking responsibility to relate respectfully and sensitively to others.

Jenkins (1990) viewed abusive behavior as resulting from a set of restraints. These derive from sociocultural restraints (e.g., striving too much for status and entitlement), family restraints (e.g., failure to obtain satisfaction from marital relationships), and gender restraints (e.g., acceptance of gender stereotypes of male roles and privileges). These restraints are identified in sexual offender treatment as deficits in skills, attitudes, and self-belief so that in our program these restraints would identify areas in which to build strengths. Like us, Jenkins assumed that abusers "do not want to hurt or abuse others and that they do want caring and respectful relationships" (p. 57). Although Jenkins does ask the abuser what stops him from taking responsibility for his abuse, he is primarily concerned with what prevents the client from taking responsibility to develop sensitive and respectful relationships. We would ask what skills we can teach the client that will allow him to meet his needs in prosocial ways.

It is Jenkins's nonconfrontational, invitational style that we find most attractive about his approach. His approach is respectful toward the client, and he works at eliciting from the client the issues relevant to effective treatment. We see this as akin to Miller's motivational therapeutic style; both fit with our respectful and supportively challenging approach that attempts to build on our client's strengths.

Approach Goals

The typical strategy in RP approaches with sexual offenders is to require them to generate a list of situations, persons, and thoughts that they must avoid in the future. For many offenders, being bored has in the past been a significant factor in the cycle of events that led to the offender seeking out a victim. Avoidance of boredom would then be part of the offender's RP plans; for example, the client might be instructed to avoid spending hours watching television. A more realistic approach goal would be aimed at building a set of interests that would fill the client's idle time, thereby significantly reducing boredom.

In most RP programs, the clients are required to generate a long list of avoidance plans with little thought given to how they might expand their repertoire of behaviors that would give them enjoyment. Indeed, the focus on avoidance is often so strong in many programs that sexual offenders may readily conclude that their future life is to be spent focusing on what not to do, with little hope of having a reasonably full life. This, we believe, will lead the offenders to become dispirited and hopeless and to feel as if their punishment will never end. Hope is vital to recovery from any problematic behavior (Moulden & Marshall, 2005). Most important, evidence from the general field of psychological research has shown that avoidance goals are characteristically not maintained, whereas approach goals are (Emmons, 1996; Gollwitzer & Bargh, 1996).

Mann, Webster, Schofield, and Marshall (2004) compared groups of sexual offenders who had been treated in programs that either emphasized the RP approach (i.e., clients were required to generate elaborate avoidance plans) or were focused on generating individualized approach goals. Only those clients in the latter program were shown to be fully engaged in treatment, to have completed all their between-sessions practice, and to have willingly disclosed problem areas; these members of the positively focused group were also found to be genuinely motivated to remain offense free.

GOALS OF A POSITIVE APPROACH
TO TREATING SEXUAL OFFENDERS

Our programs at RPS (W. L. Marshall, Anderson, & Fernandez, 1999; W. L. Marshall & Barbaree, 1988; W. L. Marshall et al., 1983; W. L. Marshall et al., 2006; W. L. Marshall & Williams, 1975) have for many years stressed to our clients those personal strengths that could enable them to recognize their potential to develop a better life. As Ward, Mann, and Gannon (2007) suggested, the major aim of a positive approach to the treatment of sexual offenders should be to "equip the offenders with the skills, values, attitudes, and resources necessary to lead a different kind of life, one that is meaningful and satisfying and does not involve inflicting harm on children or adults" (p. 6). This emphasis has readily lent itself to the generation of approach goals that lead to a better life. More recently, we have explicitly outlined these positive features in two papers (W. L. Marshall, Marshall, Serran, & O'Brien, 2008; W. L. Marshall et al., 2005).

We have suggested, as a basis for this positive emphasis in treatment, that sexual offenders seek the same goals (i.e., those of the GLM) as do other people, but because they do not have the full range of requisite skills, they choose inappropriate pathways (i.e., sexual offending) to meet their needs (W. L. Marshall, 1989). Treatment, therefore, should develop or enhance the prosocial skills of sexual offenders so they will be equipped to pursue productive relationships and all the other features of a good life. To set our clients on the right course, we begin treatment by defining the goals for the program as helping them to achieve a fulfilling and satisfying life. In this approach, we tell our clients, the primary goal of our treatment is not simply the reduction of crime but rather the enhancement of well-being. We tell them that if they can meet their needs in prosocial ways and as a result feel fulfilled, they will be very unlikely to commit any further offenses. An examination of the list of dynamic risk factors (i.e., criminogenic needs) reveals that enhancing the skills necessary to function prosocially reciprocally deals with almost all criminogenic factors. As W. L. Marshall (1997) showed, even deviant sexual interests can be reduced to manageable levels by focusing treatment on building skills in the complete absence of addressing deviant fantasies. This attitude toward treatment demands that we offer concrete possibilities for living worthwhile lives that take into account each client's abilities, circumstances, interests, and opportunities.

SCOPE AND ORGANIZATION OF THIS BOOK

In the present book, we address a range of issues, and our focus is on work with adult male sexual offenders. The extant literature on adult male sexual offenders is unevenly distributed across the types of sexual misbehaviors. Very little, for example, is known about voyeurs and almost nothing about frotteurs (offenders who attempt to surreptitiously rub their genitals against a woman's body, typically in very crowded circumstances) or about men who engage in telephone scataolgia (obscene phone calling). Although much research focused on exhibitionists in the early days of the modern period (Cox & Daitzman,

1980), very little has appeared since the mid-1980s. What literature there is on sexual sadists is fraught with problems and abounds in unsubstantiated opinion (see W. L. Marshall & Kennedy, 2003, for a review). As a result, the majority of the literature we consider in this book, and the evidence on treatment that we review, necessarily concerns rapists and child molesters. This is what is known rather than what we would like to know.

This restricted focus, however, does not represent an overly serious limitation to the present book. The majority of sexual offenders in prisons, and the majority of these men who constitute a serious danger to society, have committed hands-on offenses against either children or adult women. Thus, restricting our focus to child molesters and rapists nevertheless deals with the most problematic sexual offenders. We should note that we are using the term *rapists* to describe all those men who sexually assault adults regardless of whether or not penile penetration took place. Fortunately, our treatment experience (collectively some 70 years) with sexual offenders in prison and hospital settings, and particularly in community-based programs, has suggested that other types of sexual offenders appear to respond well to a program similar to that offered to rapists and child molesters. In two excellent books edited by Laws and O'Donohue (1997, 2008), the authors for each of the chapters addressing the assessment and treatment of various sexual deviations, including the array of sexual offenders, make treatment recommendations that are all much the same despite the diversity in the type of offending behavior being considered.

The remainder of this book examines in greater detail some of the issues raised in this Introduction as well as covers additional topics. We begin Part I, which deals with research and theory, by considering the assessment of the offenders. In Chapter 1, we challenge the ways in which assessments are typically done in treatment programs for sexual offenders, although we emphasize the importance of risk assessments. Pretreatment assessments are presumably done to develop individual case formulations so that a standard treatment program can be adjusted accordingly. We reject the case formulation strategy typically advocated in general clinical psychology and suggest that in-treatment formulations are the most effective way to guide the adjustment of treatment to meet individual needs.

In Chapter 2, we consider the influence of various treatment procedural features on effective therapeutic implementation. Issues covered include appropriate allocation to treatment, use of manuals, group therapy, and open or closed groups, as well as such operating decisions as number and length of sessions, total treatment length, and the number of therapists and clients in each group.

Chapter 3 focuses on personal and interpersonal factors, identifying the most effective therapist characteristics, group climate, and therapeutic alliance for facilitating treatment engagement. We emphasize here the need to create a positive atmosphere for treatment.

Some additional problems with common cognitive–behavioral approaches to treating sexual offenders are identified in Chapter 4, in which we emphasize the need to integrate cognitions, behavior, and emotions. We illustrate our view of the appropriate use of cognitive strategies, behavioral enactments and practice, and the value of emotional expressiveness.

After covering these various issues, we end Part I by describing in Chapter 5 the ways in which treatment for sexual offenders has been evaluated and by outlining the major outcome evaluations, including evaluations of the RPS programs. This chapter demonstrates the effectiveness of RPS programs.

Part II provides clinical descriptions of the three RPS programs: the Preparatory Program (Chapter 6), the Primary Program (Chapter 7), and the Deniers' Program (Chapter 8).

Finally, in an afterword, we highlight the main points of the book and indicate what research and treatment needs to be done to advance the field.

I

RESEARCH AND
THEORY ON SEXUAL
OFFENDER TREATMENT

1

ASSESSMENT

This chapter identifies the reasons why assessment of sexual offenders is said to be necessary. Assessment is meant to serve at least four purposes: (a) to provide estimates of risk so that decision makers (e.g., parole boards, courts, prison-transfer committees), and later community supervisors, can make informed decisions and so that treatment providers can make appropriate decisions about allocation to levels of treatment intensity and duration; (b) to generate a basis for an individual case formulation so that specific treatment targets can be identified; (c) to evaluate each individual's treatment progress (i.e., pre- to posttreatment changes); and (d) to demonstrate that the treatment program in general (i.e., across a large number of clients) achieves its identified goals (e.g., enhancements in self-esteem, empathy, coping skills, and relationship skills, as well as decreases in deviant interests, reductions in sexual preoccupation, and finally the generation of sound plans for the future development of potentials). We consider each of these aims of assessments in turn.

RISK, NEEDS, AND TREATMENT ALLOCATION

Cortoni (2009) declared risk assessment to be "the central feature that influences all aspects of the management of sexual offenders" (p. 39). To this end, specific validated risk assessment instruments have been developed. The history of risk prediction has been summarized in several excellent articles (Beech, Fisher, & Thornton, 2003; Belanger & Earls, 1996; Craig, Beech, & Harkins, 2009; Doren, 2002; Hanson & Bussière, 1998; Hart, Laws, & Kropp, 2003; Quinsey et al., 1995; Thornton et al., 2003), and the reader is referred to these sources for more details.

Quinsey et al. (1995) generated a measure that derives from their earlier scale for predicting violence (i.e., the Violence Risk Appraisal Guide [VRAG]; Harris et al., 1993). This measure (the Sex Offense Risk Appraisal Guide [SORAG]) has been shown to accurately predict sexual reoffenses (Hanson, Morton, & Harris, 2003). Hanson and his colleagues have developed two measures of future risk: the Rapid Risk Assessment for Sexual Offence Recidivism (RRASOR; Hanson, 1997a) and the STATIC-99 (Hanson & Thornton, 2000). Both these measures have also been shown in independent studies to accurately predict risk (Barbaree, Seto, Langton, & Peacock, 2001). The Minnesota Sex Offender Screening Tool–Revised was developed by Epperson et al. (1998) and has also been shown by independent researchers (Barbaree et al., 2001) to accurately predict risk.

In terms of predicting the future likelihood of a sexual reoffense, any set of these measures is useful. In the settings where we work (Canadian federal prisons and an institution for mentally disordered sexual offenders), the typical instruments used are the RRASOR, STATIC-99, and SORAG for sexual reoffense risk; the VRAG for risk of future violence; and the Level of Service Inventory–Revised (Andrews & Bonta, 1995) for general recidivism. Scores on these various instruments provide not only information in terms of likely future risk but also the basis for allocation to the level of treatment needed.

The utility of the risk measures described previously for allocation to different levels of treatment intensity is based on Andrews and Bonta's (1994) principles of effective offender treatment. These principles have been generated by large-scale meta-analyses of treatment programs addressing the needs of various types of offenders. The three principles they identified were labelled the *risk, needs, and responsivity (RNR) principles*; it is only the first two we are concerned with here, with the responsivity principle taken up later when we discuss the actual application of treatment.

Andrews and Bonta (1994) found that those programs targeting high-risk offenders had the greatest effect in reducing long-term recidivism, as did those that provided the most intensive and extensive treatment to offenders with the greatest needs. Furthermore, when treatment targeted deficits that had been shown to predict future risk (so-called criminogenic needs), it was more effective than when noncriminogenic needs were the focus of treatment. Thus, risk assessments were said by Andrews and Bonta to be the proper bases for allocating offenders to the appropriate level of treatment intensity and for identifying appropriate treatment targets. Recently, Hanson et al. (2009) showed in a meta-analysis of the outcomes of sexual offender treatment programs that these same principles apply to effective interventions for these clients.

In large operations (e.g., prisons operated by the Correctional Service of Canada or Her Majesty's Prison Service in the United Kingdom) in which sexual offender treatment programs operate in numerous institutions across a wide geographical range, it is possible to have different interventions specifically for the high, moderate, and low risk/needs offenders. In smaller operations, the level of treatment intensity and duration must be adjusted to suit each offender's risk and need. This latter strategy is difficult to do unless the program operates on a rolling or open-ended principle, an approach we discuss in more detail later. In a closed group that has a mix of high, moderate, and low risk/needs offenders, it is necessary to spend more time on each issue with the higher risk/needs men, which means that those with lower risk/needs must spend more time on the same issues than is necessary. This means that low risk/needs offenders will be overtreated in these circumstances, which may lead to an increase in subsequent reoffending (Lovins, Lowenkamp, & Latessa, 2009). In a rolling program, in which each offender proceeds through treatment at his own pace, these problems of the differential allocation of treatment intensity are avoided.

In any event, Andrews and Bonta's (1994) findings for offenders in general, and their confirmation by Hanson et al. (2009) for sexual offenders, do indicate that the most effective application of the RNR principles will result in the most effective treatment. One problem with relying on the previously mentioned risk assessment instruments is that they contain primarily *static* factors; that is, factors that are not amenable to treatment-induced change. Fortunately, researchers have more recently turned their attention to the identification of risk factors that are potentially modifiable. These factors are referred to as *dynamic risks*. Hanson and his colleagues (Hanson, 2006b; Hanson & Harris, 2000b) have again been at the forefront in identifying dynamic (i.e., changeable) risk factors. Hanson distinguished between *stable* dynamic risk factors and *acute* dynamic risks. The former are the most relevant as treatment targets because they are characteristics that can be potentially changed. Acute factors are more transitory, and although treatment providers can help offenders anticipate these factors, they are more relevant to the management of the offenders after release into the community.

Exhibit 1.1 lists the stable dynamic factors that have so far been identified, although the reader should note that this is a growing list as researchers

EXHIBIT 1.1
Stable Dynamic Risk Factors

Deviant sexual interests
Sexual preoccupation
Sexual entitlement
Poor coping skills
Attitudes supportive of sexual offending:
   – tolerance of offending
   – adversarial sexual beliefs
   – hostility toward women
   – emotional congruence with children
Deficits in perspective taking
Intimacy deficits/emotional loneliness
Behavioral dysregulation
Emotional dysregulation

look for more of the changeable criminogenic factors. According to the RNR principles, these dynamic factors should be the primary targets of treatment, although there are some additional, apparently noncriminogenic targets that when properly addressed can facilitate engagement in treatment. There are now available several dynamic risk instruments designed to assess the deficits listed in Exhibit 1.1.

Thornton (2002) and Webster et al. (2006) described and validated the Structured Assessment of Risk and Need, and Hanson and Harris (2000a) developed the STABLE-2000. Both these measures identify criminogenic and changeable factors that can then be targeted in treatment. As such, these measures can provide the basis for generating individual case formulations, and the Correctional Service of Canada does indeed use the STABLE-2000 for this purpose.

CASE FORMULATION

Case formulation has been a part of, and a guide for, psychological treatment programs since such interventions began. Indeed, Kuyken (2006) declared case formulation to be the "cornerstone of evidence-based practice" (p. 12). In its more recent form, case formulation has become a clearly articulated approach and has emerged from, and is essentially a variant of, the earlier behavioral analysis approach. Behavioral analysis was first introduced by Kanfer and Saslow (1965) as behavior therapy was beginning to establish itself as an independent and unique approach to the treatment of psychological problems. With its focus on the uniqueness of the individual client, behavioral analysis denied the value of diagnoses because these were seen as categories that depended on shared (rather than unique) characteristics. In its most recent form, case formulation is a particular approach to determining the unique problems of each individual client and, as a result, shares many features in common with behavioral analyses.

Eells (1997) articulated a clear description of the case formulation approach. He viewed it as a way to formulate hypotheses "about the causes, precipitants, and maintaining influences of a person's psychological, interpersonal, and behavioral problems" (Eells, 1997, p. 1), the aim of which is to develop individually tailored interventions that will address the person's specific needs and goals. Ward and his colleagues (Collie, Ward, & Vess, 2008; Ward & Haig, 1997; Ward, Vertue, & Haig, 1999) have suggested the same goals for case formulation with sexual offenders, and they have repeatedly stressed the need to develop a theory about the origins of this problematic behavior. The goals Eells and Ward identified for their approach, however, might be seen by clinicians as somewhat overambitious and possibly not pertinent to designing treatment. For example, it may not be necessary for treatment purposes to identify the causes or etiology of a disorder. For most human problems, the factors that lead to the development of the disorder do, over time, become less relevant, whereas factors that maintain the behavior are more important for treatment purposes.

All advocates of case formulation have agreed that its essential characteristic is the testable nature of the formulation (Bruch & Bond, 1998; Persons, 1989; Tarrier & Calam, 2002). Tarrier (2006) said that this testing should be done with the client in a collaborative manner. The ideal place and time for this collaborative work to occur is throughout the early stages of the intervention. Case formulation should also include known vulnerabilities and risk factors derived from the body of literature relevant to the client's presenting problem (Tarrier & Calam, 2002). However, in our view, it should also emphasize the client's strengths, which in the bulk of sexual offender programs are all too often overlooked.

In practical terms, Persons (2008) indicated that a thorough assessment should be the basis on which a case formulation is generated. She noted that although assessment and treatment are supposed to be done independently, it is difficult in practice to make this distinction, and she pointed out that all aspects of case formulation should be responsive to new information, including information revealed in treatment. Unfortunately, throughout her book Persons (2008) failed to clearly distinguish between assessment and treatment, which makes it difficult to determine when it is that she recommends treatment should start and how much she sees treatment-derived information as influencing the case formulation. In our experience with sexual offenders, it is only after trust in the therapist has developed that these clients will be sufficiently forthcoming to provide a sound basis for developing a case formulation. Persons (2008) appeared to agree with this view for clients in general when she stated that "a complete and fully elaborated case formulation typically is available only after treatment has begun" (p. 6). Part of Persons's suggested assessment involves a series of interviews as well as various psychometric tests.

Persons (2008) pointed out that a noncase formulation approach to treatment simply applies a standardized (or manualized) program that assumes everyone with a particular problem shares in common the same mechanisms and precipitants and will therefore benefit from the application of the same treatment. This is the *nomothetic* approach. Persons's approach readily identifies the breadth of all of the client's problems. Faced with clients having multiple problems, to determine effective treatment the therapist will need to identify which problems are the ones most interfering with the client's quality of life or, in the case of sexual offenders, which ones place the client at risk to reoffend. Next, it will be necessary to determine whether it is best to treat these various problems simultaneously or sequentially. If a sequential approach is chosen, the therapist must decide which problem to target first. In making these decisions, the therapist should keep in mind that treating one problem may facilitate changes in the others.

Most treatment programs require sexual offenders to complete an extensive battery of tests (see Mussack & Carich, 2001), the results of which are meant to identify treatment needs and to provide a basis for case formulation. Exhibit 1.2 lists some of these tests, but unfortunately many of them do not appear likely to provide information about the problems that are known to be common among sexual offenders and that are established as predictors of recidivism.

As can be seen from an inspection of Exhibit 1.2, some of these tests assess personality dispositions and chronic mood disorders or aim to generate a *DSM* diagnosis, none of which have been shown to be related to reoffending. Some of these tests that do not identify criminogenic factors may, nevertheless, reveal problems that could interfere with treatment engagement. For example, there is evidence in the general psychological literature that both low self-esteem (Baumeister, 1993) and shame (Tangney & Dearing, 2002) prevent people from engaging in behavior change. However, far too many of the proposed tests have little relevance for designing treatment for sexual offenders or for generating each individual's case formulation. All too often it appears that pretreatment assessments have been assembled to cover too many possibilities and simply serve to overwhelm the clinician responsible for case formulation.

Of perhaps greater relevance in considering the value of extensive batteries of tests, particularly self-report questionnaires, is that the prosocial answers to many of the questions are all too obvious. Clearly sexual offenders have a vested interest in presenting themselves in the best possible light. In

EXHIBIT 1.2
Potential Problem Identification Assessments

Social Functioning
Rosenberg's Self-Esteem Measure (Rosenberg, 1965)
Social Self-Esteem Inventory (Lawson, Marshall, & McGrath, 1979)
Rathus Assertiveness Scale (Rathus, 1973)
Bass-Durkee Hostility Inventory (Buss & Durkee, 1957)
State-Trait Anger Expression Inventory (Spielberger, 1988)
State-Trait Anxiety Inventory (Spielberger, Gorsuch, & Lushene, 1970)
Fear of Negative Evaluations Scale (Watson & Friend, 1969)
UCLA Loneliness Scale (Russell, Peplau, & Cutrona, 1980)
Miller's Social Intimacy Scale (R. S. Miller & Lefcourt, 1982)
Relationship Questionnaire (Bartholomew & Horowitz, 1991)

Empathy
Interpersonal Reactivity Test (M. H. Davis, 1983)
Empathy for Children (Hanson & Scott, 1995)
Empathy for Women (Hanson & Scott, 1995)

Coping
Coping Inventory for Stressful Situations (Endler & Parker, 1999)
Sex as a Coping Strategy (Cortoni & Marshall, 2001)

Cognitive Distortions
Abel's Child Molester Cognitions Scale (Abel et al., 1989)
Molest Scale (Bumby, 1996)
Rape Scale (Bumby, 1996)
Justifications of Sex with Children (Mann, Webster, Wakeling, & Marshall, 2007)
Young's Schema Questionnaire (Young & Brown, 2001)

Sexual Interests
Multiphasic Sex Inventory (H. R. Nichols & Molinder, 1984)
Clarke Sexual History Questionnaire (Langevin, 1983)
Phallometry (W. D. Murphy & Barbaree, 1994)
Viewing Time (Abel, 1995)
Screening Scale for Pedophilic Interests (Seto & Lalumière, 2001)

General Axis I Disorders
Millon Clinical Multiaxial Inventory (Millon, Antoni, Millon, Meagher, & Grossman, 2001)

Substance Use
Michigan Alcoholism Screening Test (Selzer, 1971)
Drug Abuse Screening Test (H. A. Skinner, 1982)

Personality Disorders
Minnesota Multiphasic Personality Inventory (Hathaway, McKinley, & Butcher, 1990)
Psychopathy Checklist–Revised (Hare, 1991)

Criminality
Criminal Sentiments Scale (Simourd, 1997)
Measures of Criminal Attitudes and Associates (Mills & Kroner, 1999)

Relapse Prevention
Measures of Offence Chain (Beckett, Beech, Fisher, & Fordham, 1994)
Situational Competency Test (Miner, Day, & Nafpaktitis, 1989)

Social Desirability
Marlow-Crowne Social Desirability Scale (Crowne & Marlow, 1960)
Balanced Inventory of Desirable Responding (Paulhaus, 1991)

addition, the time required to complete all the tests tires the offender and renders his responses to the latter parts of testing of dubious value. Finally, these tests have to be scored to be of use, and this takes time and resources proportional to the number of tests and questions asked within each test. Scoring and interpreting the results of an extensive battery means treatment will have to be delayed or the results will play no part in the preintervention case formulation.

However, some tests that may be useful for this purpose are those listed in Exhibit 1.1, which identify dynamic risk factors. Large-scale meta-analyses (Hanson & Bussière, 1998; Hanson & Morton-Bourgon, 2005) have revealed an array of factors that reliably predict recidivism in sexual offenders. Many of the features identified in these particular studies, however, are unchangeable; that is, they are static factors. One factor among the otherwise static features identified in these studies is the offender's sexual arousal to deviant stimuli (e.g., his response to either forced sex or to sex with children). Such responses are at least potentially modifiable and are, therefore, relevant to case formulation. The recent attention given to dynamic risk factors (Hanson & Harris, 2000b; Thornton, 2002) has provided a broad basis for identifying for each client a set of problems that can be changed. The use of one or another of the scales measuring stable dynamic risks can provide an alternative to a large battery of tests that is likely to be a more accurate and less resource-demanding way to develop each client's case formulation.

As a way to start the case formulation, Persons (2008) suggested relying initially on a nomothetic approach that will describe the features common to all clients with a particular presenting problem. In the case of sexual offenders, this starting point would be a formulation describing the known common criminogenic features (i.e., deficits or problems that are established predictors of reoffending), such as deviant interests, sexual preoccupation, problems in behavioral and emotional self-regulation, intimacy and attachment difficulties, loneliness, and antisocial attitudes (Hanson, 2006b). The identification of the problems at this initial stage could, for sexual offenders, rely on measures of stable dynamic risks (e.g., STABLE-2000). Persons saw this as a first step that guides the case formulation but is then followed by the development of an idiographic case formulation. In this latter step, the client is evaluated on the nomothetically defined features to determine his strengths or weaknesses in any of the identified areas, as well as identifying any additional unique problems. As noted, Persons saw the case formulation as constantly being adjusted, as new information appears not only during the pretreatment stages of the formulation but also throughout treatment.

It is as well to note the point made by Nezu and Nezu (1989) that various sources of error can occur during the continuous process of case formulation, with the most important problem being a confirmatory bias that blocks recognition of any contrary information. Thus, the person doing the case formulation should not be blind to alternative hypotheses and should work in a truly collaborative way with clients because this is the best way to ensure that contradictory perspectives are not ignored. Mann and Shingler (2006) made a strong case for working collaboratively with sexual offenders both during assessment (including risk assessment) and in treatment.

Ward and his colleagues (Drake & Ward, 2003; Ward & Maruna, 2007; Ward, Nathan, Drake, Lee, & Pathé, 2000; Ward et al., 2000) are strong advocates for a case formulation approach with sexual offenders. In his writings on this issue, Ward embedded his formulations in his version of the good lives model (see Ward & Stewart, 2003a, for the application of this model). The resulting case formulation then guides the subsequent individually unique treatment interventions.

The first phase of Ward's approach involves a series of interviews and a comprehensive assessment battery. Two features of Ward's views on case formulation need comment. First, Thakker, Collie, Gannon, and Ward (2008) declared that part of the reason to do a thorough case formulation is to determine the client's amenability for treatment. Our view is that every effort should be made to encourage all sexual offenders to enter treatment given the threat they pose to the public, regardless of what a case formulation may reveal. Sexual offenders are, in this respect, different from clients with other Axis I disorders. Second, Collie et al. (2008) noted that as part of a thorough case formulation, some programs use polygraph testing to facilitate truthfulness. Unfortunately, the reader is left with the impression that Collie et al. support the use of this procedure when in fact they do not (Ward, personal communication, August 28, 2009). The fact is that thorough appraisals of the scientific bases of polygraphy have indicated quite clearly that there are no grounds for accepting this procedure as a lie detector or truth revealer (Iacono & Patrick, 1999; National Research Council, 2003).

It appears from Ward's descriptions, and from our observations of its application, that his particular version of case formulation involves a lengthy and resource-consuming endeavor prior to treatment. In terms of its length, Ward's case formulation appears to be consistent with that described by others. For example, I. M. Blackburn, James, and Flitcroft (2006) outlined 13 steps in case formulation, with each step involving considerable work, including extensive interviews and a battery of tests. K. M. Davidson (2006) required five sessions to arrive at a case formulation, Lavender and Schmidt (2006) targeted seven areas in assessment and 31 features that must be assessed to produce their case formulation, and Wells (2006) used behavioral tests and psychometric measures to evaluate nine potential maintenance processes. These lengthy processes and the resultant case formulation guide to treatment, however, do not enhance treatment effectiveness compared with a "one-size-fits-all" manualized approach (see Kuyken, 2006, for a summary of the relevant studies). The available evidence, it would seem, does not justify the substantial investment of resources required by the typical descriptions of case formulations, but can we save the value of an idiographic strategy by adjusting our approach to case formulation? It seems likely that overcomplicating a client's problems by these excessively detailed case formulation procedures may both overwhelm clients and induce pessimism about their potential for change. This would be particularly true for such formulations done prior to treatment. In addition, with recalcitrant clients such as sexual offenders, useful information may not emerge until the clinician has won their confidence. Reducing the complexity of the case formulation and delaying making inferences until the client–therapist relationship has been effectively developed seem likely to increase the utility of the formulation.

Sexual offenders tend to be quite distrustful of professionals when they first arrive at a treatment facility. Very few of these men are self-referred; most have gone through a lengthy process of being reported, investigated, charged with an offense, tried in court, sentenced, and then imprisoned or court-ordered to treatment. During this process, the courts routinely require the offender to be assessed to assist the judge at sentencing, and the subsequent reports are not usually favorable to the offender. In Canada, a probation officer also completes a presentence report, which likewise is usually not favorable. In these types of reports, an array of problematic issues (e.g., school and employment problems, family difficulties, Axis I and Axis II comorbid disorders, relationships issues, intellectual functioning) is raised that, when read by the offender, must seem overwhelming. These experiences cause sexual offenders to be guarded in what they say to professionals, and consequently they are not at all forthcoming in initial interviews and assessments. Prior to treatment, the offender's lack of confidence in professionals, and his understandable circumspection about revealing details that may make him appear more problematic, prevent the gathering of pertinent information or distort its presentation. It has been our experience that assessing sexual offenders too early in the process causes them to respond by attempting to present themselves in the best possible light. Thus, the data from pretreatment test batteries are likely to provide a distorted picture of the client's problems and can be quite misleading.

OUR APPROACH TO CASE FORMULATION

For the reasons outlined previously, we do not use extensive tests prior to treatment. We rely on the data produced by a completion of the STABLE-2000 as a starting point to frame our tentative idea of each individual client's potential problems. Once sexual offenders enter treatment, if the therapist adopts a motivational approach and displays the appropriate therapeutic style (see Chapter 3 of this volume for the relevant details), the clients develop trust in the therapist and progressively reveal far more relevant issues and more detailed life histories. From this position of greater confidence, the offender can generate the kind of information necessary for the case formulation to begin in earnest. Also, when the offender engages each target of treatment, it is readily apparent how skilled or deficient he is, allowing treatment to be adjusted accordingly. We find this treatment-based approach to case formulation to be better than the usually recommended course and far more economical of resources.

Our approach is to offer a treatment program that is based on nomothetic data that provide a set of criminogenic targets (i.e., factors that predict reoffending). Each offender addresses each target in the detail required by the extent of the strengths and weaknesses he displays. Because we operate treatment groups as open-ended (also called *rolling groups*), in which every client is at a different point in the program and progresses at his own pace, it is quite easy to adjust the dosage of treatment for each target to match each client's needs. How skilled an offender is at relationships, for example, can most effectively be determined by engaging him in the processes needed to address potential deficits in relationship skills. The same is true for all the targets of treatment. In addition, as treatment progresses, some problems emerge that have not been identified as criminogenic (e.g., serious Axis I disorders) but present as obstacles to effective engagement in treatment and must, therefore, be addressed. Equally important, as each client progresses in treatment, a broader range of his strengths becomes apparent. These positive features can be used to encourage optimism about the potential for change and hope for the future; these strengths can also be used to have the client assist other members of the treatment group. Assisting other clients enhances the sexual offender's sense of self-worth, which increases his capacity to engage in processes to overcome problems that might otherwise be seen by him as insurmountable. Thus, for us, case formulation is generated as an evolving concept that begins with a tentatively held, nomothetically based conceptualization and is continually modified throughout treatment to produce an idiographic intervention that will maximally influence the factors that led to the client's offending behavior.

EVALUATING INDIVIDUAL PROGRESS

All treatment programs are required to produce reports on each participant indicating the progress made and what further treatments, if any, are required. Some programs base these reports on pre- to posttreatment changes as assessed by a large battery of tests. As noted previously, we have reservations about this approach. In addition to the reservations we expressed, there are further problems with this approach. Although some of the measures provide normative data against which to compare the posttest results, very few reports in the literature, and very few reports we have read from various programs around the world, actually indicate the relative normative status of the offender's responses to the posttreatment evaluations. This is critical because the goal of treatment is, or should be, to move each offender to a position as close to normal as possible on as many indices as possible.

Another way of looking at this difficulty is to consider the magnitude of the treatment-induced changes. Although a change may be statistically significant, it may not be clinically meaningful (Garfield, 1993). For example, when we (W. L. Marshall, Bryce, Hudson, Ward, & Moth, 1996) evaluated the effectiveness of our program in instilling adequate intimacy skills and in overcoming chronic emotional loneliness, we found less than satisfactory results. On the loneliness measure we observed changes that were both statistically significant and well within the normative range. However, the clients' scores on intimacy, although reflecting statistically significant improvement, were still well below the normative mean. This meant they were still unlikely to be able to function effectively in a relationship. Thus, in this instance, statistically significant changes did not represent clinically meaningful changes.

Another problem with using a battery of tests at pre- and posttreatment to identify changes with treatment concerns the fact that sexual offenders respond heterogeneously on all measures that have been applied to them. At pretreatment testing, for example, some of these men score well within the normative range on some of the measures. As a result, these offenders will appear at posttreatment assessments to have not profited from some aspects of treatment when, in fact, they may not have needed treatment for the issue in question.

OUR APPROACH TO EVALUATING INDIVIDUAL PROGRESS

Faced with these dilemmas, we decided to develop a rating scale that therapists could use to estimate how close each offender's functioning was to normal on each of the targets of treatment. Other researchers had previously developed similar scales. Hogue (1994), for example, designed a goal attainment scale that provided an estimate of the changes produced by the treatment of sexual offenders, and R. D. Anderson, Gibeau, and D'Amora (1995) described a similar measure of sexual offenders' progress in treatment. Langton, Barbaree, Seto, Harkins, and Peacock (2002) revised an earlier scale (Seto & Barbaree, 1999) that had failed to predict long-term benefits from treatment.

Langton et al. first demonstrated that their revised scale could be completed reliably across raters, and they then showed that it accurately predicted long-term recidivism. There are, therefore, grounds for assuming that it is possible to produce therapist rating scales that are both reliable and accurate predictors of future behavior. On the basis of these observations, we designed our Therapist Rating Scale (W. L. Marshall et al., 2006).

In an attempt to reduce therapists' biases (e.g., wanting to rate all offenders positively or allowing their personal likes or dislikes to corrupt their judgements), our rating scale distinguishes the offender's intellectual grasp of the issue separately from his emotional and behavioral displays regarding the issue. The latter are derived from the therapist's direct observations as well as from reports from other staff and from other offenders. These ratings of emotional and behavioral displays reflect the offender's commitment to the issue or his internalization of his intellectual understanding. The scale also provides an extensive list of phrases describing each of four levels of functioning (i.e., inadequate, some grasp of the issue, normative level, and optimal functioning) for each of the two categories of intellectual understanding and emotional/behavioral commitment. Instructions to the raters indicate that heterogeneity of ratings across the targets of treatment and between the two categories of ratings (i.e., intellectual grasp and emotional/behavioral commitment) is to be expected. In fact, the instructions suggest that if the total ratings are all given the same score, then in all likelihood the rater has not been sufficiently objective. We have recently extracted long-term follow-up (8.4 years at risk for 534 offenders) data from our files showing that therapists' estimates of progress in treatment were the most accurate predictors of long-term successes or failures after release to the community. In contrast, pretreatment actuarial risk measures were not valuable predictors of postrelease recidivism among the treated subjects. These data have strengthened our confidence in our Therapist Rating Scale. However, feedback we have received from therapists in various countries who adopted our measure has indicated that it was too complex and laborious for routine use. As a result of detailed feedback and our own observations of its utility, we have produced a shortened version. This shortened version has 10 targets, and the instructions for rating each target have been abbreviated. We have attached the new Therapist Rating Scale (TRS-2) as an appendix.

EVALUATION OF PROGRAM GOALS

The question here, which, unfortunately, is rarely addressed, is how effective is the treatment program in achieving its stated goals? For example, most programs for sexual offenders target a range of issues. For the best programs, these goals are the modification of those problems that have been shown to be criminogenic factors. The general array of issues targeted in sexual offender programs are listed in Exhibit 1.1—that is, the stable, dynamic, criminogenic factors.

Although there are numerous reports of pre- and posttreatment evaluations showing that deviant sexual interests can be changed (see W. L. Marshall, O'Brien, & Marshall, 2009, for a review), very few studies have reported effective changes in the other typical treatment-targeted problems. W. L. Marshall, Bryce, Hudson, Ward, and Moth (1996) demonstrated that their programs were effective at increasing intimacy skills and in reducing emotional loneliness, and Serran, Firestone, Marshall, and Moulden (2007) showed that their strategies for addressing deficits in coping skills were effective. There are also a limited number of reports of the effective modification of other problems, such as increases in general empathy (Pithers, 1994) and victim-specific empathy (W. L. Marshall, O'Sullivan, & Fernandez, 1996), as well as reductions in denial and minimizations concerning their offending (W. L. Marshall, 1994) and enhancements of self-esteem (W. L. Marshall, Champagne, Sturgeon, & Bryce, 1997). However, although these latter factors were all, at one time, thought to be important treatment targets, subsequent research has shown they are not criminogenic (Hanson & Bussière, 1998; Hanson & Morton-Bourgon, 2005).

The evaluation of the attainment of appropriate (i.e., criminogenic) treatment targets by particular procedures needs to be demonstrated. One possible strategy, and the one that we have found to be best, is to follow the approach of the previously mentioned studies of evaluating the effectiveness of each target in a series of discrete studies. This generates a circumscribed evaluation of the effectiveness of procedures that target specific issues rather than the effects of the overall program. This also allows the possibility of comparing two or more procedures for each target. For example, Webster, Bowers, Mann, and Marshall (2005) compared two procedures for developing victim empathy in sexual offenders. One procedure included offense reenactments, a strategy that is fraught with problems (see Pithers, 1997), whereas the other was an exact match except for the absence of the enactment. Results of this study showed that both procedures were effective but the enactments added nothing.

Most researchers, however, rather than assessing the effectiveness of each component of treatment choose to evaluate the overall effectiveness of the program in terms of modifying all of the targets (Beckett, Beech, Fisher, & Fordham, 1994; Beech, Fisher, & Beckett, 1999). These studies used an extensive battery of tests covering detailed aspects of each of the targets of treatment, with these tests being administered before and immediately after treatment. Aside from the problems mentioned earlier about the transparency of such measures, and the inclinations of sexual offenders to present themselves in an overly positive way, the amount of resources required to implement such studies has markedly limited their application.

Whatever strategy is used to do such evaluations, there is presently a dearth of studies showing that specific treatment procedures aimed at modifying criminogenic features (other than those designed to alter deviant interests) actually achieve the sought-after goals. The modification of the appropriate targets is essential because it is assumed, on the basis of the evidence demonstrating such targets to be criminogenic, that changing these dispositions will reduce reoffending. Simply showing that a program reduces reoffending, although very important, does not demonstrate that the program has effectively changed the targets of treatment. A program that is effective in reducing recidivism may, nevertheless, include irrelevant targets, or it may be that changing just one or a few of the criminogenic problems is enough to produce a reduction in reoffending. There is, then, an urgent need for more thorough detailed evaluations of the effectiveness of treatment to change specific criminogenic features across most clients and to determine which of these changes is essential to reduce future reoffending.

CONCLUSION

In this chapter, we have considered the value of various approaches to the assessment of sexual offenders. Satisfactory measures have been developed that identify factors predictive of reoffending. Some of these factors are historical and therefore static and as a result are essentially unchangeable. However, they do indicate the level of treatment required. Other factors are potentially modifiable (so-called dynamic factors) and should be the focus of treatment. We also considered various recommended ways to generate individualized case formulations that can be used to adjust generic treatment programs so that each client's strengths and specific needs can be properly addressed. Our approach to individualized case formulations relies on adjusting the way we address each criminogenic dynamic factor on the basis of information derived during treatment. We suggest that evaluating each client's progress in treatment is best determined not by repeating a battery of tests at posttreatment, but rather by using our posttreatment Therapist Rating Scale. Finally, we considered the best way to determine whether a treatment program actually achieves its stated goals (i.e., produces change in criminogenic targets). More research, we believe, is required on all these issues.

In Chapter 2, we turn our attention to the influence on outcome of various features of treatment procedures.

2

PROCEDURAL FEATURES
OF TREATMENT

Procedural features are necessarily decided on in all treatment programs and seem likely to have significant effects on the achievement of treatment targets. Yet, little or no attention has been given to them in the literature. In this chapter, we consider the influence of allocating clients to different levels of treatment intensity, the utility of manuals or guides, and whether treatment should be conducted in groups or individually. We question whether rolling (i.e., open-ended) groups are more effective than closed (i.e., with pre-determined start and end dates) groups, and we consider the potential influence of various operating choices (i.e., number of sessions per week, length of each session, total length of treatment, and the number of therapists and clients in each group).

ALLOCATION TO TREATMENT

The first decision to be made in planning treatment concerns the appropriate allocation of sexual offenders to programs. In large-scale systems, such as the Correctional Service of Canada's (CSC) penitentiary system, which has programs in several prisons across the country, or Her Majesty's Prison Service (HMPS) in the United Kingdom, which has programs in 25 prisons, there is the opportunity to have separate programs aimed at addressing sexual offenders with different needs. For example, in such settings it would seem sensible to have specialized programs for low-functioning offenders, and there are established models to follow in providing treatment to these men (Haaven et al., 1990; Lindsay, Steele, Smith, Quinn, & Allan, 2006; G. Murphy & Sinclair, 2009). HMPS has an adapted program specifically for such offenders, but CSC does not. However, CSC does have specialized programs for aboriginal offenders, and there are similar programs in other countries (Cull & Wehner, 1998; Ertz, 1997; J. Larsen, Robertson, Hillman, & Hudson, 1998). Indeed, there are now specialized programs for sexual offenders with a variety of unique needs (see W. L. Marshall, Fernandez, Hudson, & Ward, 1998, for a description of these various programs).

Aside from programs catering to unique needs, some authors have suggested that particular types of sexual offenders (e.g., child molesters, rapists, incest offenders) should be allocated to separate groups to direct appropriate attention to their different individual needs (Allam, Middleton, & Browne, 1997). The majority of the programs entering the extensive meta-analyses of Hanson et al. (2002) and Lösel & Schmucker (2005) were mixed for offender type and yet produced satisfactory outcomes.

In an attempt to examine the possibility that the presumed distinctive features of the different types of offenders would affect the group's functioning, Harkins and Beech (2007b) evaluated the group climate of several programs using Moos's (1986) Group Environment Scale (GES). They compared two rapist-only groups with three child-molester-only groups and 15 groups mixed for the type of offender. Previous research (Beech & Fordham, 1997; Beech & Hamilton-Giachritsis, 2005) has demonstrated that groups scoring high on the Cohesiveness and Expressiveness subscales of the GES were the most effective groups in attaining the goals of treatment. In Harkins and Beech's (2007b) study, all 20 groups scored high on these subscales, although the mixed groups did score somewhat lower on Expressiveness, which the authors attributed to the possibility that in groups containing rapists, the child molesters might have felt inhibited in discussing their issues. Harkins and Beech saw this latter effect as resulting from the way the therapists ran the groups, and they suggested that therapists should emphasize the similarities between group members as a way of eliminating this problem. It is important to note that all groups were equally effective in lowering recidivism, so the observed lower scores in Expressiveness in the mixed groups may be irrelevant. We have always run mixed groups, and our outcome data reveal (see Chapter 5) equal reductions in recidivism rates for nonfamilial child molesters, rapists, and incest offenders. As Ware, Mann, and Wakeling (2009) pointed out, "greater heterogeneity enhances opportunities for the development of perspective-taking, relationships, and coping skills" (p. 17).

Having settled on a solution to the offender-type issue, it is necessary to decide on the group composition regarding the risk and needs of the offenders. With the development of actuarial risk-assessment instruments (see Craig, Browne, & Beech, 2008), it is now possible to determine the risk group to which each client belongs and to determine each individual's criminogenic needs. The meta-analyses of a vast range of offender treatment programs conducted by Andrews and his colleagues (Andrews, Bonta, & Hogue, 1990; Andrews, Zinger, et al., 1990) demonstrated that three principles characterized effective offender programming: risk, needs, and responsivity. The risk principle indicates that the greatest reduction in recidivism is achieved by targeting the high-risk offenders; the need principle directs treatment providers to target those modifiable factors that have been shown to predict recidivism (i.e., the so-called criminogenic features); and the responsivity principle demands that treatment be, among other things, attentive to the unique features of each individual and to the day-to-day fluctuations in each client's mood and functioning. Hanson et al. (2009) showed in a meta-analysis of 23 programs that these same principles of effective treatment also apply to sexual offenders. Interestingly, they also demonstrated that the risk principle alone was associated with the lowest (although still significant) effect size, as did Andrews, Dowden, and Gendreau (1999). Hanson et al. took this to mean that this principle should be seen as an administrative indicator guiding allocation to treatment intensity rather than guiding the selection of treatment targets (the need principle) or indicating how treatment should be delivered (the responsivity principle). We speak more about the application of the responsivity principle in Chapter 3.

Both the risk and need principles are relevant to the allocation of offenders to groups. Where resources are available, and when there are sufficient numbers of referrals, it would appear to be best to have three levels of programs: one for the high risk/needs offenders, one for the moderate risk/needs clients, and one for the low risk/needs men. The intensity and duration of treatment should differ for each of these groups, although there are no clear guidelines on what these levels of treatment should be. CSC has established specialized sexual offender programs for each of the three risk/needs levels. These programs operate in prisons in which the security level matches the offenders' risk. Once an offender has completed the high risk/needs program, he will cascade to a lower level of security where he might receive further treatment before release.

MANUALS OR GUIDES

Those responsible for designing treatment programs, particularly when these programs are to be run in several different locations or when several different groups will be run by different therapists, have typically designed detailed treatment manuals to guide therapists. The goal of such manuals is to ensure that each group will address the same issues, in the same order, and follow the same approach. This is meant to ensure the integrity (or internal validity) of the program delivery to facilitate replication, although this requires the additional burden of close supervision of the delivery of treatment. A debate concerning the merits of requiring sexual offender treatment providers to follow a detailed manual was recently covered in a special topic section of the *Journal of Sexual Aggression* (Hollin, 2009; Mann, 2009; W. L. Marshall, 2009), and the interested reader is referred to those sources. Our position is that requiring adherence to a detailed manual can have the effect of reducing compliance with the responsivity principle and of diminishing the role of important process variables such as therapists' warmth, empathy, and rewardingness, as well as the forming of an effective therapeutic alliance and the creation of an appropriate group climate. These process variables, as we show in Chapter 3, have powerful effects.

Adherence to a detailed manual tends to be associated with an unbending attention to only the targets specified in the manual while ignoring any individually unique and appropriate targets (W. L. Marshall, 2009). A manual may increase the likelihood that only the specified procedure(s) for modifying each target will be used, when in fact there are many alternatives that might better suit some clients. Furthermore, in their most detailed form, manuals reduce treatment to psychoeducation rather than psychotherapy. It is only in a psychotherapeutic approach that the important process variables can be implemented. Also, overly manualizing necessarily leads to dealing with each treatment target within a module in which each and every client essentially goes over the same material one after another. This, we believe, leads to boredom and a loss of motivation on the part of both the therapists and the clients. Similarly, the choice of a detailed manual reduces, although it does not eliminate, opportunities to engage in collaborative work with the clients. Shingler and Mann (2006) made a strong case for the value of collaboration with sexual offenders in both generating treatment targets and working together to learn new skills. As they noted, this is one of the essential aspects of W. R. Miller and Rollnick`s (2002) motivational interviewing.

In the appraisal of the value of manuals, the choice of a manual should not be viewed as categorical, but rather as dimensional, with the location on the dimension being the result of the degree of details and the range of choices specified in the manual (W. L. Marshall, 2009). The chosen location

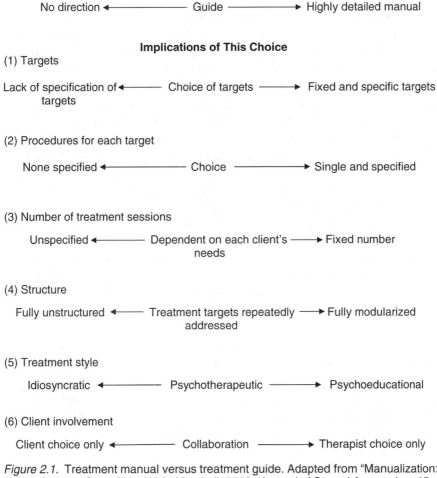

Degree of Manualization

No direction ◄——————— Guide ——————► Highly detailed manual

Implications of This Choice

(1) Targets

Lack of specification of ◄——— Choice of targets ———► Fixed and specific targets
     targets

(2) Procedures for each target

None specified ◄——————— Choice ——————► Single and specified

(3) Number of treatment sessions

Unspecified ◄——— Dependent on each client's ———► Fixed number
                  needs

(4) Structure

Fully unstructured ◄——— Treatment targets repeatedly ———► Fully modularized
                  addressed

(5) Treatment style

Idiosyncratic ◄——————— Psychotherapeutic ——————► Psychoeducational

(6) Client involvement

Client choice only ◄——————— Collaboration ——————► Therapist choice only

Figure 2.1. Treatment manual versus treatment guide. Adapted from "Manualization: A Blessing or a Curse?" by W. L. Marshall, 2009, *Journal of Sexual Aggression, 15,* p. 111. Copyright 2009 by Taylor & Francis. Adapted with permission.

along the continuum of detail in the manual has implications for other important aspects of treatment, with each of these aspects also lying along a continuum (W. L. Marshall, 2009). Figure 2.1 describes the continuum of manual choice as well as the implied location of this choice on six other dimensions.

    As can be seen, selecting a highly detailed manual is associated with (a) a set of fixed specific treatment targets, (b) a specified procedure for each of these targets, (c) a fixed number of treatment sessions for the program, (d) a fully modularized approach, (e) a structured psychoeducational approach, and (f) little or no collaboration with the client because everything is preordained by the manual. In contrast, selecting a less detailed "guide" implies that an array of targets could fit with the unique range and degree of problems displayed by each client. Because sexual offenders display heterogeneity on all criminogenic factors, and most have additional unique problems, effective treatment should reflect this variability. Although a range of procedures has not yet been generated for all treatment targets (but perhaps they should be), one target illustrates the possibility of providing such a range. As we discuss in Chapter 7, several procedures appear to effectively modify sexual interests, and it is appropriate for therapists to collaborate with each client in the choice among these procedures. A guide lends itself to this approach. The use of a guide also allows the number of sessions to be determined by each individual's rate of progress. This is more likely to encourage a psychotherapeutic approach that, as we discuss in Chapter 3, is far more likely to be effective than a psychoeducational approach. Finally, a guide encourages collaboration between therapists and clients on all issues.

The complete absence of any guide would readily lead to therapists taking a variety of idiosyncratic approaches to treatment, some of which may not be empirically sound, such as addressing irrelevant targets and using unsound procedures (W. L. Marshall, 2009). As an alternative, a guide should specify criminogenic targets, offer suggested procedures for modifying these targets, and emphasize the importance of therapeutic processes (W. L. Marshall, 2009). However, in her article in this special topic issue, Mann (2009) made a strong case for the merits of a detailed manual in guiding treatment when such treatment is applied across a wide range of variable settings. She noted that the use of manuals needs to be associated with careful supervision and monitoring. It appears that our suggested approach is perhaps better suited to small operations where on-site supervision is continuous, whereas some variant of Mann's model is perhaps necessary for large-scale, multisite operations.

GROUP OR INDIVIDUAL TREATMENT

Another question of importance that has to be resolved concerns whether programs should be run in groups or offered as individual therapy or whether a combination of these two approaches is best. A survey of North American sexual offender programs revealed that group therapy was by far the most popular choice (89.9%; McGrath, Cumming, & Burchard, 2003), and this appears to be particularly true in correctional services (Morgan, Winterowd, & Ferrell, 1999). The two large-scale meta-analyses (appraising in total 112 reports) of treatment outcome with sexual offenders (Hanson et al., 2002; Lösel & Schmucker, 2005) found that only eight used individual therapy alone, whereas another eight used "mainly" individual treatment. In an edited book devoted to describing treatment programs within various settings and covering specialized programs for sexual offenders with specific associated difficulties or features (W. L. Marshall et al., 1998), 15 of the 28 programs offered group therapy, but nine had additional individual treatment.

Abracen and Looman (2004) claimed that individual treatment is as effective as group therapy and that it should be seen as essential for some clients. Ware et al. (2009) indicated that in their experience, some sexual offenders express a strong preference for the individual approach. They suggested that some offenders worry about confidentiality in groups or complain that they are unlike other offenders (usually meaning that they see their crimes as "not really offenses") or that they indicate they cannot function within a group setting (e.g., they say that they are socially anxious or shy). In our experience, so long as the rules of confidentiality are made clear and are enforced, this issue quickly disappears as do concerns about not being seen as a "sexual offender." As for social anxiety, the group setting provides an excellent opportunity for the therapist and the other group members to assist the shy client to overcome his inhibitions and anxieties. Social fear should be seen as a collateral and important, although noncriminogenic, problem that treatment must address if the client is to function effectively in group and in other prosocial relations. So rather than anxiety being grounds for offering individual treatment, shyness should be seen as a strong reason for entering a group program.

Di Fazio, Abracen, and Looman (2001) described treatment options for high-risk sexual offenders within a prison-based specialized program. Individual treatment was offered to offenders suffering from either severe Axis I disorders or significant cognitive deficits, whereas all other offenders were treated in groups. Those participating in either program all equally met the goals of treatment, suggesting that either approach may be effective. Of course, offenders in each approach were not matched on a variety of important variables, and the actual content of treatment also differed, so it is difficult to know how to interpret these results. Furthermore, those in the group program also received three individual sessions per week. The total number of hours for those receiving only individual treatment was just 1 hr more of individual work than for those in the group program. These differing features also restrict the inferences that can be drawn from DiFazio et al.'s report.

Another way to appraise the relative value of these alternatives is to ask the clients for their experience of each. Garrett, Oliver, Wilcox, and Middleton (2003) provided some interesting comments by sexual offenders about their participation in group treatment. Forty-six percent said they had a positive experience in group and that they preferred it to the option of individual therapy, whereas another 34% said they would accept either alternative. Although few offenders in this study had ever had individual therapy, they listed numerous positive features of groups, including the sharing of experiences among group members as well as challenges or alternative perspectives offered by others.

In the broader general clinical literature, some meta-analyses seem to have favored individual treatment (Dush, Hirt, Schroeder, 1983; Nietzel, Russell, Hemmings, & Gretter, 1987), although other meta-analyses have suggested equivalent effects (Hoag & Burlingame, 1997; McRoberts, Burlingame, & Hoag, 1998). More recent studies have found greater effectiveness for group approaches. For example, Renjilian et al. (2001) randomly assigned obese adults to either their preferred choice (i.e., group vs. individual) or to their nonpreferred choice. The results revealed an unequivocal advantage for group treatment in terms of weight loss. For the most part, however, comparisons of these alternatives across a range of disorders have revealed essentially equivalent results (Bastien, Morin, Ouellet, Blais, & Bouchard, 2004; Lockwood, Page, & Conroy-Hiller, 2004).

It appears that the presently available evidence, limited though it is, indicates that there may be no strong differences in the effects of group therapy alone, individual therapy alone, or a combination of the two. Which alternative is chosen seems to rely more on either the particular therapist's preference or on concerns about efficiency. For example, Sawyer (2002) pointed out that group treatment is far more resource efficient than individual therapy; that is, group treatment can deal with far more clients within any time period, and it is cost-effective.

Because sexual offenders have numerous interpersonal skills deficits, there are obvious advantages to having them participate in group treatment in which they can practice these skills in role-plays and in therapeutic interaction with others. Groups, when properly run, also produce cohesiveness among the participants (Beech & Fordham, 1997; Beech & Hamilton-Giachritsis, 2005), which not only involves active participation with others but also invokes supportive and empathic behaviors, skills that are typically absent in sexual offenders. As Ward, Vess, Collie, and Gannon (2006) pointed out, group therapy "can act as a catalyst for the development of a whole range of treatment related competencies" (p. 389). An additional important feature of group therapy is the opportunity for, and perhaps the inevitability of, vicarious learning. Bandura (1977b) pointed to the importance of this type of learning in humans and indeed in other animals. D. Glaser and Frosh (1993) noted that group treatment allows offenders to recognize that they are not alone in having sexually abused others, and it helps them overcome the secrecy they had previously found necessary to survive. When a sexual offender challenges another member of the group, this challenge not only offers insight to the person being challenged, it also frequently clarifies the challenger's own issues (W. L. Marshall & Barbaree, 1990).

In an examination of these various proposed advantages, Fuhriman and Burlingame (1990) found that group treatment had a number of unique features that were absent in individual work. Within groups, vicarious learning was clearly evident, as was role flexibility (being able to be both a help seeker and a help provider), the clear realization by clients that their problems were not unique, altruistic behavior, and significant interpersonal learning. Brown (2005), on the other hand, pointed to the possibility that group work with sexual offenders might allow them to set up networks to facilitate subsequent offending and that it might encourage a worsening of deviant fantasies after hearing the offense details of others. First, there is no evidence that either of these possibilities happens, and the latter could only occur if treatment inappropriately required the offenders to provide details of what they did sexually during their crimes. There are very good reasons to not have offenders provide these offense details (see W. L. Marshall, Marshall, & Ware, 2009), so this would only be a possible problem if the therapist was to ignore the evidence. Finally, Schwartz (1995) pointed out that adding individual treatment to group work may allow the offender to form a bond with the therapist that may undermine participation in group.

CLOSED OR ROLLING GROUPS

If treatment providers decide to use group therapy, they must decide whether to run closed or open (often called *rolling*) groups. A closed group is one in which all participants start and finish the program at the same time. This usually involves going through, in a fixed sequence, a series of components that address the targets of treatment. This means that each client in turn completes each component in turn so that the exercises are repeated in essentially the same way for each participant. Although this allows for both direct and vicarious learning of the issue, it also has the danger of boring both the clients and the therapists with each issue. An open-ended approach involves continuous intake such that as one participant completes all the targets and is discharged, a new client takes his place. As a consequence, each of the eight or 10 clients will be at a different point of progress through the program. This means that boredom with any one target or exercise will be reduced, because each target will be addressed intermittently. This also provides the opportunity for the more senior group members to assist the newer clients. An open-ended approach also allows each client repeated opportunities to challenge and support newer members on the same issue. These repeated opportunities, when the more senior clients have continued to assimilate more and more of the program, allow for more sophisticated challenges and continuous vicarious learning. These opportunities for nurturing the newer group members are greater in open-ended programs than in closed groups.

Ware et al. (2009) pointed to additional advantages derived from open-ended groups. Each group member can proceed at his own pace without having to keep up with, or wait for, other participants who may move more quickly or more slowly through each component. This, of course, allows the therapist to pay particular attention to the responsivity principle; that is, it allows attention by the therapist to the unique features or learning styles of each client. In this respect, an open-ended group offers some of the benefits of individual treatment, which in a closed group is more difficult to achieve. As Ware et al. also pointed out, an open-ended group allows difficult clients, or clients with transitory problems, to be temporarily suspended from the program and to reenter when they are deemed to be ready, without upsetting the flow of the group and without having the suspended client have to start all over again. A really important point made by Ware et al. is that an open-ended group can take in emergency referrals, such as offenders with short sentences, who might otherwise not be able to complete the program.

Ware and Bright (2008) reported changing their program from a closed format to an open-ended approach, so they took the opportunity to compare the two approaches. Apparently the offenders found the open-ended group more appealing, as all the spaces were consistently filled in this group, whereas only 50% of treatment places were filled in the closed group. Equally important, the attrition rate dropped dramatically when the program switched from a closed to an open-ended format; in addition, therapists reported feeling more effective and expressed more positive attitudes toward treatment in the rolling group. Staff also said the open-ended group made them feel more at ease, and they felt less pressure to achieve changes at specific points in the program. These therapists noted that with the closed format, they always felt under stress about getting each client to the same point on each target, particularly when there was a disparity between clients in their capacity to grasp the essentials of the component.

Consistent with these observed benefits, Hoffman, Gedanken, and Zim (1993) found that compared with a closed group, an open-ended approach achieved group cohesiveness more rapidly, increased clients' motivation and engagement, and produced increases in self-esteem. It is important that the dropout rate was lower in the open-ended than in the closed group. L. E. Marshall, Serran, and Marshall (2008) used the same experienced therapist to run a series of both closed and open-ended groups during the same period (one in the morning, the other in the afternoon); the therapist followed the same treatment guide. There were no differences in the style of delivery or in the content of the two groups, nor were there differences in the offense variables or offense types of the participants between the two groups. Marshall et al. found that the open-ended format achieved group cohesiveness more rapidly than did the closed group, and on several other subscales of Moos's (1986) GES, the open-ended program was superior, although by the latter stages of the closed group the two approaches were essentially equal. Apparently, closed groups can attain the same levels of the important features of group treatment as open-ended groups, but they take longer and make more demands on the therapists, at least until they achieve the appropriate levels of operating. A. J. Davis, Marshall, Bradford, and Marshall (2008) demonstrated that even with mentally disordered sexual offenders, the same high levels of cohesiveness and expressiveness can be obtained in an open-ended group format. In both groups (L. E. Marshall et al., 2008; A. J. Davis et al., 2008) described previously, the scores on almost all the subscales were better than the standard scores that Moos reported for any of the groups he studied. Because Beech and his colleagues (Beech & Fordham, 1997; Beech & Hamilton-Giachritsis, 2005) have shown that scores on the subscales of Moos's measure are highly correlated with changes on treatment targets with sexual offenders, our findings are quite important and certainly support the idea that open-ended groups function very effectively.

It is clear that more studies are required before firm conclusions can be made about the advantages of either an open-ended or closed group, but the evidence to date does seem to favor the former. In conducting therapist training, we have found that some therapists whose experience has been entirely with the closed-group format appear reluctant to try an open-ended approach, but as seen in Ware and Bright's (2008) study, when they can be persuaded to do so, they are typically enthusiastic about the change. We choose to run open-ended groups and have done so for the past 19 years.

OPERATING PRINCIPLES

The final issues that require decisions involve what might be thought of as a number of operating principles. These include how many sessions per week is optimal, how long each session should be, the total length of treatment (or how many total hours of treatment), and the number of therapists and clients per group. However, there is little in the way of empirical direction on any of these issues.

Across various programs, the number of sessions per week and the duration of each session vary considerably. Very intensive programs tend to have at least one session each day of the working week, and in some of these programs each session can be as long as 5 hr. There is a subsection of the literature on human learning concerning the optimal frequency and duration of training sessions. In this research, a comparison is made between what is called *massed practice*, in which the whole topic is studied in one long session, and *spaced practice*, in which the same material is broken up into smaller segments that are studied, each segment at a time, for a relatively short duration and in which there are significant delays between the study of each segment (Dellarosa & Bourne, 1985; Dempster, 1988; Underwood, 1961). Results of this research consistently showed an advantage for spaced practice in terms of long-term retention of the material. For example, Keppel (1964), in an examination of the retention of paired-associate learning, showed that subjects learning under spaced-practice conditions recalled much more material 29 days later than did those who learned under massed-practice conditions. The subjects who underwent massed practice recalled, immediately after the learning sessions, as much material as did the spaced-practice subjects at the end of their learning sessions. However, for the massed-practice subjects, almost all the material was lost by the recall day (29 days after learning was terminated), whereas the spaced-practice subjects still retained all their learning. Bloom and Shuell (1981) and Krug, Davis, and Glover (1990) found similar results under more naturalistic circumstances of classroom learning, and Baddeley and Longman (1978) found the same advantages for spaced practice in teaching typing to government employees.

It appears that these discrepant effects for spaced versus massed practice are due to the way in which people in the different conditions process the information. Dellarosa and Bourne (1985) suggested that in massed practice the subjects are not able to fully process the material because they are overwhelmed. What people under massed practice conditions of learning do is superficially process the material retaining only the gist of the issue without any of the details. This does not allow them to deeply process the material and integrate all aspects of the topic. When encoding trials are sufficiently separated, as in spaced practice, this permits forgetting to occur so the subjects must more thoroughly process the material at each session, and between sessions, if they are to retain it. As a result, repeated full processing entrenches the material. This literature revealed that massed practice may accelerate the speed of acquiring new information at least at a superficial level but does not lead to the long-term retention of what is learned, particularly in terms of detail. Spaced practice, on the other hand, results in slower acquisition but is more likely to lead to long-term detailed retention.

These all but forgotten principles (e.g., we could not find any references to spaced/massed practice in textbooks on learning published in the past 20 years) of human learning ought to serve as guidelines for deciding the frequency and duration of treatment sessions. Unfortunately, this is not a literature that is familiar to most cognitive–behavioral therapists working with sexual offenders, despite the fact that cognitive–behavioral therapy's origins were derived from basic research in human and animal learning (Eysenck, 1959; Kazdin, 1978; Ullmann & Krasner, 1965). The most exaggerated example of massed practice applied to treatment is marathon therapy (Bach, 1966; E. E. Mintz, 1967), which was popular in the 1960s and 1970s. Evaluations of marathon therapy do indeed suggest rapid learning (Chambers & Ficek, 1970; Kilmann & Auerbach, 1974), but like massed practice, the evidence has indicated that these effects are not retained over time (Dinges & Weigel, 1971; Guinan, Foulds, & Wright, 1973).

The intensive sexual offender programs mentioned previously that have 3- to -5-hr sessions 5 days per week are also an example of massed learning. When we sat in on these intensive programs, we observed that both clients and therapists seem exhausted by Friday's session and often before that; the therapists also told us that between-sessions work by the clients typically fades toward the end of each week, and almost nothing is done by the offenders over the weekend. Our guess is that such massed treatment will not produce enduring changes in offenders.

On the basis of these observations, limited though they are, we suggest that therapists limit the number of sessions to a maximum of three per week, each of no more than 3-hr duration with a short break near the middle of each session. Our experience has been that under these conditions, both the therapists' and the offenders' enthusiasm is maintained, and the clients typically complete the between-sessions work.

The dosage of treatment refers to the total number of hours that need to be completed for the goals of the program to be secured. Actually, whatever this is determined to be (and there are no clear empirical guidelines), the suggested number of hours ought to serve as a guide rather than a fixed amount of time. Because sexual offenders can be expected to be as heterogeneous as other people in terms of how fast they learn to entrench concepts, we can expect some to get to the goals of treatment quicker than others. Flexibility on how much time is spent in treatment, dependent on each individual's rate of assimilating the ideas and the speed with which he learns the skills, can readily be attained in open-ended groups, whereas in closed groups, clients have to complete each module at the same rate as do the other group members—another advantage of the open-ended group format.

Large systems (e.g., CSC, HMPS) have established rules for treatment dosage that vary across the programs. These rules, however, are arbitrary because there is little in the way of sound evidence indicating the required hours necessary to achieve the goals of treatment. CSC's operating rules (Correctional Service of Canada, 2000) state that high risk/needs offenders should have between 360 to 540 hr of sexual offender specific treatment, with most having to complete additional programs (e.g., anger management, substance abuse, and prosocial attitudes and lifestyle programs), which would result in an additional 350 to 500 hr of treatment; that is, a total of 700 to 1,500 hr. This seems to us to markedly overestimate their needs and perhaps result in overtreatment, which can reduce treatment effectiveness. For example, when intensive interventions are applied to low-risk offenders, their recidivism rates increase (Andrews, Zinger, et al., 1990; Lowenkamp & Latessa, 2002; Lowenkamp, Latessa, & Holsinger, 2006). Examining sexual offenders specifically, Lovins et al. (2009) found that the same program increased reoffending in low-risk men but decreased these rates significantly in all other risk groups. In fact, untreated low-risk sexual offenders "fared 27% better than [those] who were exposed to . . . treatment" (Lovins et al., 2009, p. 353).

For moderate risk/needs sexual offenders, CSC rules indicate 160 to 200 hr of specialized treatment and possibly an additional 80 to 100 hr for other programs. Low risk/needs sexual offenders, according to CSC, should receive 24 to 50 hr of specialized treatment and a further 20 to 30 hr of additional programming. Although these guidelines seem clear, counts of the actual hours of treatment delivered by CSC programs have generated disagreements (see Abracen, Looman, Mailloux, Serin, & Malcolm, 2005; Mailloux et al., 2003; W. L. Marshall & Yates, 2005). In fact, in the Rockwood Psychological Services Primary Program, which we operate under contract to CSC in a medium security prison, sexual offenders with a distribution of risk levels receive 80 hr of specialized treatment and a further 100 hr (approximately) of other programming. This is well below CSC's rules, yet this program's long-term outcome (see Chapter 5) reveals the greatest reductions in recidivism reported by any evaluation of other CSC programs. So perhaps CSC's rules, arbitrarily decided on, represent an overtreatment strategy that may be one of the causes of their generally lower success rate than our program.

Finally, treatment managers have to decide how many therapists (and their gender) are needed for each group and how many clients are optimal. Most programs appear to prefer two therapists (although HMPS frequently has three), with one male and one female therapist being considered optimal. Groups typically include eight to 10 offenders, but new therapists might find it easier to start with just six. Any less than six would make it hard to generate the kind of consistent feedback from all group members that is needed, and cohesiveness may not be generated in such a small group if one or more members are uncooperative. When there are more than 10 group members, it will be difficult for even an experienced therapist to ensure that all participants are actively involved, and it will be hard to keep in mind the dynamics of each client. There is no available evidence that might provide direction for decisions about the number and gender of therapists or the ideal number of clients per group, so each program will have to make these decisions on the basis of reasoned judgements.

CONCLUSION

Sexual offenders should be allocated to treatment according to the risk and needs principles of effective offender therapy (Andrews & Bonta, 1994). The responsivity principle demands flexibility in the delivery of treatment according to each client's unique features, and this appears to be most readily achieved with group treatment that operates as an open-ended (i.e., rolling) format. Some balance in providing guidance to therapists via a manual or guidebook is necessary so that treatment is not overly prescribed in so much detail that the therapist cannot function flexibly. An aspect to the manual or guide needs to specify the therapeutic style that is most effective with sexual offenders, the form of the therapeutic alliance, and the way to facilitate group cohesiveness and expressiveness. Group treatment appears to offer the best format for achieving the goals of treatment, and treatment groups appear to function effectively when different types of sexual offenders (i.e., rapists, child molesters, and incest offenders) are included in the same group. Three sessions per week of 3 hr each appears to strike the balance suggested by the evidence on spaced versus massed practice. Groups with one or two therapists treating eight to 10 sexual offenders seem sensible, but as with the total number of hours of required treatment, there is no evidence to guide us.

Chapter 3 examines the various factors in treatment that have been described as process issues; that is, the characteristics of the therapist, the therapeutic alliance between the therapist and the clients, and the climate of the group.

3

PERSONAL AND INTERPERSONAL FACTORS

In any profession, it is apparent that some people are more effective than others. In the case of psychological treatment, this fact seems obvious. Effective therapists need to have a strong foundation in the empirical literature as well as to possess a specific set of characteristics that have been found to embody a good therapist. Over the past decade, we have emphasized the importance of therapist characteristics and other personal and interpersonal factors—such as client perceptions of treatment, therapeutic alliance, and group climate—in the treatment of sexual offenders (W. L. Marshall, Marshall, Serran, & O'Brien, 2008; Serran, Fernandez, Marshall, & Mann, 2003; Serran & Marshall, 2010). Concern about personal factors has a long history in the general clinical literature (Frank, 1971; L. S. Greenberg & Pinsof, 1986; Orlinsky & Howard, 1986; Rogers, 1957; Schaap, Bennun, Schindler, & Hoogduin, 1993; Strupp & Hadley, 1979), and it was this literature that initially led to our interest in these issues (W. L. Marshall, Fernandez et al., 2003).

Psychotherapists from a broad range of therapeutic orientations have accepted the crucial role that personal and interpersonal factors play in successfully treating clients. In fact, the general clinical literature has indicated that treatment effectiveness is significantly influenced by the therapist's style, the client's perception of the therapist, and the therapeutic alliance (Luborsky,

Crits-Christoph, Mintz, & Auerbach, 1988). The quality of the therapist–client relationship accounts for a significant amount of the variance in treatment effectiveness (Morgan, Luborsky, Crits-Christoph, Curtis, & Solomon, 1982). Successful therapeutic outcomes depend, therefore, on both the therapist's interpersonal skills as well as specific techniques, but clearly the relationship features are the strongest factors in generating treatment benefits.

As discussed previously, we have avoided the aggressively confrontational approach that some authors claim is essential in the treatment of sexual offenders (Salter, 1988; Wyre, 1989). Adopting this approach to treatment disregards the convincing evidence on good therapeutic personal and interpersonal factors and serves to reduce treatment gains. The evidence has clearly indicated that a therapist who embodies the positive characteristics identified as relevant in the process literature, and who delivers a program that is empirically sound, will provide the most effective and successful treatment, thus reducing recidivism to the lowest possible rates. In this chapter, we rely on the general clinical literature, the general offender literature, and the sexual offender literature to suggest how therapist characteristics, the therapeutic alliance, client perceptions of treatment, and group climate affect therapeutic outcome. We are convinced that these personal and interpersonal factors of treatment account for a more substantial amount of the changes induced in sexual offender treatment than is true of the various procedures used to address treatment targets.

GENERAL CLINICAL LITERATURE

In this section, we provide a brief view of the relevant sections of the general literature on process issues. First, we consider the importance of the therapeutic alliance, then we focus on the evidence concerning the characteristics of effective therapists, and finally we describe the evidence on the point of view of the clients.

The Therapeutic Alliance

Numerous studies have demonstrated that the therapeutic alliance predicts psychotherapeutic outcome (D. J. Martin, Garske, & Davis, 2000). The relationship between client and therapist is considered the foundation of therapeutic work and is viewed as one of the main tools for achieving client change (Klerman, Weissman, Rounsville, & Chevron, 1984; Luborsky, 1994). Several meta-analyses have demonstrated an effect between alliance and outcome. Horvath and Symonds (1991) reported an average effect size (ES = 0.26) for the influence of the therapeutic alliance, whereas D. J. Martin et al. (2000)

reported similar effects (ES = 0.22). In fact, Norcross (2002) showed that the application of specific therapeutic techniques or procedures accounted for only 15% of the treatment-induced changes, whereas the therapeutic relationship generated 30% of the benefits derived from treatment.

The quality of the therapeutic relationship also serves to decrease dropouts (Beckham, 1992; Piper et al., 1999; Samstag, Batchelder, Muran, Safran, & Winston, 1998; Tyron & Kane, 1990, 1993). Failure to create an effective therapeutic alliance leads to client noncompliance (Eisenthal, Emery, Lazare, & Udin, 1979), which is the typical reason given for removing clients from treatment. Eisenthal et al. (1979) demonstrated that if the quality of the therapeutic relationship is positive, the dropout rate is markedly reduced.

The therapeutic alliance is a function of both the manner in which the therapist presents himself or herself and the way in which the client perceives the therapist. Therapists' perceptions of their own style do not always match the way they are seen by clients (Bachelor, 1995; Free, Green, Grace, Chermus, & Whitman, 1985; Orlinsky, Grawe, & Parks, 1994), so it is essential to consider these two features independently.

Because group treatment is the most popular approach with sexual offenders, and there is evidence that it can be more effective than individual therapy (Bednar & Kaul, 1994; McRoberts et al., 1998), we also consider the role the group therapist plays in producing this effectiveness. Karterud (1988) found that among the six group programs he examined, the highest functioning group had supportive leaders who were nonaggressive and who encouraged clients to interact with each other in a supportive way. Similarly, M. Nichols and Taylor (1975) demonstrated that the most important factor in group treatment involved the leader facilitating active participation by all group members; this includes what is referred to as *cohesiveness*. It has been shown that group cohesiveness predicts the amount of between-session work as well as the degree of participation within sessions (Budman, Soldz, Demby, Davis, & Merry, 1993).

Therapist Characteristics

The general literature indicates that some of the features therapists display facilitate changes in the clients while others impede the clients' acquisition of the skills necessary to effective treatment. We examine the literature bearing on these issues in this section.

Characteristics That Facilitate Change

Exhibit 3.1 lists the essential therapist qualities for forming the type of therapeutic relationship that leads to benefits. For example, empathy, warmth, and genuineness have been shown to influence outcome in the treatment of

EXHIBIT 3.1
Therapist Features That Facilitate Change

Empathy
Warmth
Genuineness
Respectfulness
Support
Confidence
Emotional responsivity/expressiveness
Self-disclosure
Asks open-ended questions
Directiveness
Flexibility
Encourages active participation
Is rewarding/encouraging
Uses humor
Supportively challenging
Sincerity
Honesty
Interest

various psychological disorders (Keijsers, Schaap, & Hoogduin, 2000). In fact, Beutler et al. (2004) examined a range of factors (e.g., gender, age, ethnicity, years of training, behaviors in therapy) and found that the factor most predictive of beneficial outcomes was positive therapist qualities, whereas the other factors exerted minimal influence. Displays of empathy by the therapist were a positive predictor of both abstinence and controlled drinking in clients with alcohol addiction (W. R. Miller, Taylor, & West, 1980) and were related to improved coping in patients with panic disorder (Mathews et al., 1976) as well as reductions in depression (Burns & Auerbach, 1996). Warmth is displayed as acceptance, caring, and support and serves to encourage clients to examine their problem behavior (Safran & Segal, 1990). Orlinsky and Howard (1986), in their comprehensive review, concluded that warmth displayed by the therapist was a significant predictor of positive outcome and was associated with positive client ratings. Lambert (1989) also showed that warm and affirming therapists were the most effective. Genuineness, which has been shown to increase positive outcome (Keijsers et al., 2000), is defined by the therapist being himself or herself and is associated with sincerity, consistency, non-defensiveness, comfort, honesty, and a clear display of interest (Egan, 1998). Both sincerity and respect have been linked to beneficial treatment outcome (Rabavilas, Boulougouris, & Perissaki, 1979).

Adopting a reinforcing or encouraging approach increases clients' self-efficacy and enhances their expectations about the likely benefits of treatment (W. R. Miller & Rollnick, 2002), and it also reduces resistance and aggression among clients (Bandura, Lipsher, & Miller, 1960). The recommended strategy is to reward clients for small steps early in treatment and then gradually move encouragement to more extended chains of appropriate behavior (G. Martin & Pear, 1992). Therapist support and encouragement increases client self-efficacy, enhances positive expectations about treatment (W. R. Miller & Rollnick, 2002), and reduces aggression and resistance (Bandura et al., 1960).

Some degree of directiveness is important in establishing a constructive working relationship with the client and results in better outcome (J. F. Alexander, Barton, Schiavo, & Parsons, 1976; Beutler, Dunbar, & Baer, 1980; Schindler, Revenstorf, Hahlweg, & Brenglemann, 1983). Being directive does not require the therapist to tell the client what he should do, but rather simply to offer suggestions so that a collaborative approach can be maintained. Adopting a directive approach includes encouraging clients to practice skills outside of the treatment session (Schaap et al., 1993) and helps more concrete-thinking clients develop flexible problem-solving skills (Elliott, Barker, Caskey, & Pistrang, 1982). Being directive with clients provides structure, helps establish an effective working relationship, and leads to improved therapeutic outcome (J. Mintz, Luborsky, & Auerbach, 1971). However, it is important to balance directiveness with reflectiveness, as overly directive therapists may increase negativity and resistance with some clients. Ashby, Ford, Guerney, and Guerney (1957) found that a reflective style was more successful with angry and aggressive clients, whereas a directive approach was found to be effective with submissive or defensive clients (Beutler, Pollack, & Jobe, 1978). Clearly, flexibility is critical because some clients require more structure, whereas others might feel overly controlled when the structure is too pronounced. Various researchers (e.g., Cooley & LaJoy, 1980; Klein, Mathieu-Coughlan, & Kiesler, 1986; Orlinsky & Howard, 1986) have found that the degree of emotional expression in treatment (at least up to a point) is significantly predictive of beneficial outcomes. In addition, the expression of feelings by clients determines the impact of treatment sessions (Saunders, 1999).

Other important skills, which are emphasized less frequently in the literature but are nonetheless important, include encouragement of active participation, use of humor, and some degree of self-disclosure. Encouraging active participation is associated with both successful completion of treatment and positive outcomes (Garfield & Bergin, 1986). Although Keijsers et al. (2000) claimed that self-disclosure by therapists is not helpful, the evidence does not support this. Although excessive or irrelevant self-disclosure may undermine client confidence in the therapist (Curtis, 1982), appropriate self-disclosure increases trust (Braaten, Otto, & Handelsman, 1993). Therapists who disclose their thoughts and feelings appropriately are modeling to the clients appropriate behavior and by so doing display a coping rather than a mastery model. As Mahoney and Norcross (1993) suggested, if therapists present themselves as perfectly adjusted, clients will find it difficult to identify with them and will be unlikely or unable to emulate the therapist. Although little research has been conducted on the use of humor, Rutherford (1994) concluded that its appropriate use increases clients' interest and helps them adopt a more tolerant perspective. Humor creates a positive and open atmosphere (Greenwald, 1987) and helps relieve tension (Falk & Hill, 1992). Of course, humor needs to be appropriate and should not be derogatory.

A flexible approach that is adapted to each individual client is more effective than rigidly adhering to the same agenda for all clients (Ringler, 1977). Therapists who can adjust their style and tailor their approach to suit individual clients generate more positive results (Kottler, Sexton, & Whiston, 1994). Effective therapists are sensitive to clients' responses and are able to change their interactions based on this feedback (Duncan, Miller, & Sparks, 2004). L. Seligman (1990), after examining various psychotherapeutic orientations, noted that positive outcomes were significantly related to an emphasis on client support, interest in the client, and acceptance of the client, regardless of the therapist's orientation. Confident therapists typically display more positive therapeutic skills than do therapists who lack confidence (J. F. Alexander et al., 1976), and therapist confidence is related to beneficial changes (L. Seligman, 1990). However, this is true only if the clients perceive the therapists to be confident (McGuff, Gitlin, & Enderlin, 1996; V. L. Ryan & Gizynski, 1971).

Questioning clients, rather than simply accepting what they say, helps them develop greater insight (Schaap et al., 1993), but only when the questions are open-ended (Barkham & Shapiro, 1986; Hill, Carter, & O'Farrell, 1983). Asking closed questions, which typically lead to yes or no responses, appears to be ineffective. Problematic reactions by clients frequently result from closed questions, whereas open-ended questions, which demand elaborate answers, reduce the frequency and intensity of such reactions (Wiseman, 1992).

As we see in the next section, confrontation by the therapist is not a useful approach, whereas supportively challenging clients is both effective (W. R. Miller & Sovereign, 1989) and desired by the clients (Drapeau, 2005).

Features That Impede Change

Of the factors that impede change, confrontation is the most clearly demonstrated problematic approach. Harsh confrontation from therapists has the most damaging effects on clients (Lieberman, Yalom, & Miles, 1973). Harsh confrontation is defined by aggressive, critical, hostile, and sarcastic behavior. Such confrontational styles have been particularly popular in programs targeting substance abuse (W. R. Miller & Rollnick, 2002) and in the treatment of sexual offenders (Salter, 1988; Wyre, 1989). This approach is in conflict with evidence suggesting that confrontation is especially harmful to clients in the precontemplation stage, where many of our clients are initially (Prochaska & DiClemente, 1994).

Patterson and Forgatch (1985) showed that increased noncompliance with treatment is significantly related to the degree of confrontation in therapy, and M. Nichols and Taylor (1975) found that therapists who adopted a confrontational style had less effective outcomes compared with supportive group leaders. In the substance abuse field, W. R. Miller, Benefield, and Tonigan (1993) reported that a confrontational style was predictive of client relapse at 1-year follow-up. Similarly, W. R. Miller and Sovereign (1989) found increased resistance, denial, and greater alcohol consumption in clients who were exposed to an aggressively confrontational therapist. Cormier and Cormier (1991) found that clients who perceive the therapist as confrontational either discredit or forcefully challenge the therapist, devalue the issues, or agree on the surface but fail to make appropriate changes. Overall, a confrontational approach is clearly countertherapeutic and ineffective (Lieberman et al., 1973).

Some therapists have been found to engage in treatment primarily for the purpose of meeting their own needs. Such therapists have been found to produce negative effects rather than beneficial outcomes (Lambert, 1983). Other therapists have a hostile style, and it is not surprising that this has been shown to be a major characteristic of poor outcome (Cullari, 1996; Strupp, 1980).

Numerous other therapist features (e.g., sarcasm, excessively critical responses, coldness, and discomfort with silences) have been suggested to either impede change or generate negative outcomes, but research on these features is limited or nonexistent.

Client Perceptions of Treatment

Horvath (2000) pointed out that the client's perception of treatment significantly influences outcome, which is noteworthy given that M. H. Davis (1983) found that clients regard the use of procedures or techniques as of secondary importance to the influence of the therapist. McLeod (1990) observed that those therapists who were judged by clients to be most helpful were seen as displaying interest, encouragement, and reassurance. Clients' perceptions of the therapist's confidence, involvement, focus, and emotional engagement, as well as his or her display of positive feelings toward them, determined the clients' view of the value of treatment and the degree to which they were willing to engage in the therapeutic process (Saunders, 1999). When clients see therapists as directive (Schindler et al., 1983), confident and persuasive (V. L. Ryan & Gizynski, 1971), and sincere (Ford, 1978), then greater treatment benefits are generated than is true with therapists who are perceived to not possess these qualities.

Bachelor (1995) also examined the therapeutic relationship from the perspective of the clients. He noted that the manner in which clinicians and clients view the alliance often differs, emphasizing how important it is for therapists to consider their clients' view of the relationship and address these issues. More specifically, Free et al. (1985) showed that therapists were inaccurate in estimating client perceptions of their empathy, and yet it was the client ratings of therapist empathy that predicted treatment benefits. Similarly, Orlinsky et al. (1994) reviewed various studies and found that in the majority, it was the clients' estimate of therapist features that correlated with indices of beneficial treatment outcome. Fortunately, there are available measures for clients to report their perception of specific therapist features (see Burns & Auerbach, 1996).

GENERAL OFFENDER LITERATURE

There has been some interest in the influence of the therapist working with general offender populations (Carroll, 2001; Cooke & Philip, 2001; Cordess, 2002; Hodge & Renwick, 2002; Maier & Fulton, 1998; McMurran, 2001). Hemphill and Hart (2002) particularly emphasized the importance of a positive therapeutic alliance when working with psychopathic offenders. Advocates of a motivational approach with all types of offenders (W. R. Miller & Rollnick, 2002; C. M. Murphy & Baxter, 1997) have stressed the importance of respect and support by the therapist. In a particularly important finding, Dahle (1997) reported that offenders' trust in the intention of treatment providers was predictive of treatment readiness and commitment. Offenders typically experience difficulties trusting authority and often describe a more general distrust that commenced at a young age. Given the childhood histories of many offenders (Bandura, 1973; McCord & McCord, 1964), including sexual offenders (W. L. Marshall & Marshall, 2000; Starzyk & Marshall, 2003), this is perhaps no surprise. In our experience, the majority of offenders are at least initially suspicious of the motives of professionals, including treatment providers, which makes it critical to establish trust by being genuine and forthcoming.

Given these observations indicating that offenders have difficulty trusting others, it is no surprise to find that an aggressive confrontational approach is ineffective in engaging these clients. H. M. Annis and Chan (1983) found that a confrontational style by therapists led to a failure to achieve the changes sought in treatment. In fact, both H. M. Annis and Chan (1983) and Beech and Fordham (1997) showed that aggressively confronting offenders who had low self-esteem had the effect of further diminishing their sense of self-worth. Because low self-esteem is common in offenders (Gibbs, Potter, Liau, Schock, & Wightkin, 2001), including sexual offenders (W. L. Marshall, Anderson, & Champagne, 1997), and is related to resistance to change (Baumeister, 1993), confrontational approaches should be assiduously avoided.

An important caveat needs to be noted concerning self-esteem among offenders. Whereas most offenders have low self-esteem, some have been shown to have high self-esteem. Baumeister, Bushman, and Campbell (2000), for instance, reported high self-esteem among various offender types that they say manifests as "malignant narcissism," and there is evidence that narcissists in general have high, but false, self-esteem (Logan, 2009). More specifically, R. Blackburn (2009) found that one of his subgroups of psychopaths (those who are defensive and controlled) display high levels of self-esteem. In an early unpublished study, we found that whereas child molesters almost all scored very low on a measure of self-esteem (their mean was 1 SD below the normative mean and the variance was small), rapists showed a bimodal distribution of scores. Two thirds of the rapists had scores that matched those of the child molesters, whereas the other third had a mean score that was 0.5 SD above the normative mean. Consistent with Blackburn's report, these high self-esteem rapists also scored high on a measure of psychopathy. Thus, although most sexual offenders have low self-esteem, some have high, but apparently falsely based, self-esteem. In either case, efforts should be made early in treatment to normalize self-esteem, as falsely high self-esteem will serve as much of a block to treatment engagement, as will low self-esteem.

As noted earlier, Andrews, Bonta, and Hoge (1990), in their meta-analysis of offender treatment outcomes, generated a set of principles of effective offender treatment. Of these, the responsivity principle is most relevant to process issues. This principle includes a specific responsivity factor that directs therapists to adjust their approach to each client's unique learning style and personality. Dowden and Andrews (2004) showed that unless therapists had the skills necessary for specific responsivity (i.e., warmth, empathy, respectfulness), treatment benefits were diminished. Andrews (2001) reported that in the treatment of offenders, when the staff are not selected on the basis of therapeutic skills, the effect size for treatment is vanishingly small (0.05), whereas when there is evidence that therapists have the requisite qualities, the effect sizes are substantially greater (0.25–0.36).

In the treatment of domestic violence perpetrators, Babcock, Green, and Robie (2004) found significant overall treatment effects for the Duluth model (Pence & Paymar, 1993), although effect sizes varied considerably across programs from negative to negligible to quite powerful. A. Fisher (2008) reanalyzed these data, finding that the variance in outcome was largely accounted for by therapeutic process variables. Programs that adopted a more psychotherapeutic approach, emphasizing the therapeutic alliance, were by far the most effective, with effect sizes approaching 1.0. Taft and Murphy (2007) also examined treatment for batterers and found that a positive therapeutic alliance resulted in greater treatment compliance and lower reoffense rates.

Evidence on factors that impede treatment progress with offenders has indicated that when therapists are confrontational, defensive, and inconsistent, an increased number of offenders drop out of treatment, whereas when the therapist is supportive, empathic, warm, and genuine, almost all offenders complete treatment and achieve the desired goals (Simons, Tyler, & Lins, 2005). These observations are quite important because it has been found that sexual offenders who drop out of, or who are removed from, treatment have higher subsequent reoffense rates than do those who refuse to enter treatment (Abel, Mittelman, Becker, Rathner, & Rouleau, 1988; K. D. Browne, Foreman, & Middleton, 1998; Marques, Day, Nelson, & West, 1994). Preston (2001) reported that therapists with poor relationship skills failed to reduce offenders' resistance to treatment, whereas Stewart, Hill, and Cripps (2001) found the most positive effects from treatment with offenders occurred when therapists formed a warm and supportive bond with offenders.

SEXUAL OFFENDER LITERATURE

Beech and Mann (2002) pointed out that, at that time, little had been written about the qualities of an effective sexual offender therapist and even less about how to effectively train these therapists. Fortunately, there has been a recent growing interest in process issues among those who work with sexual offenders. Beech and Fordham (1997), for example, examined the influence of the group climate on an extensive set of indices of behavior change among sexual offenders. Group climate, it should be noted, is largely created by the therapist's style. Using Moos's (1986) Group Environment Scale, Beech and Fordham scored 12 prison-based sexual offender treatment groups in terms of the 10 subscales of this measure. Measuring treatment-induced changes across groups, Beech and Fordham found that the groups with the highest scores on the Cohesiveness and Expressiveness subscales generated the greatest degree of change across all measures. The groups with the lowest cohesiveness and expressiveness scores displayed minimal change. In Moos's measure, cohesiveness refers to the degree to which members of the group work together, support and challenge one another, and form bonds with each other. Expressiveness describes the degree to which clients express themselves; enter the discussions; and most important, display emotions in the group. Beech and Hamilton-Giachritsis (2005) repeated this study with seven community-based programs and again found that group cohesiveness and expressiveness predicted treatment-induced benefits.

Pfäfflin, Böhmer, Cornehl, and Mergenthaler (2005) also demonstrated that the expression of emotion during sexual offender therapy sessions was a significant predictor of treatment-induced change. These benefits, Pfäfflin et al. showed, were greatest when emotional expression was associated with an intellectual understanding of the issue at hand. Pfäfflin and his colleagues (Huter, Pfäfflin, & Ross, 2007) have replicated these findings in a further, more detailed and more comprehensive analysis of the influence of emotional expression in treatment.

Thornton, Mann, and Williams (2000) compared prison-based groups led by warm and supportive therapists with groups led by therapists who were confrontational toward the clients. Although both groups improved on measures of cognitive distortions, only the group with the warm and supportive therapist showed changes across all measures. K. Hudson (2005) asked sexual offenders about their experiences in treatment. These offenders reported that when the therapist was confrontational and pressured them to conform, they simply learned to say what they perceived the therapist wanted to hear rather than participating effectively in treatment. Similarly, Williams (2004) found that a coercive approach by the therapist reduced the effective participation of offenders in treatment, and Harkins and Beech (2007b) demonstrated that confrontation by the therapist reduced the positive quality of the group climate, which they had shown to be crucial to generating effective changes in sexual offenders.

Our research involved two studies examining the influence of the therapist's behavior and style on treatment change with sexual offenders. We were fortunate to have access to extensive data on treatment changes across a variety of treatment programs operated by Her Majesty's Prison Service in the United Kingdom as well as to have access to the video-taped recordings of every treatment session. These programs were run by different therapists who nevertheless all followed a detailed treatment manual and were monitored for compliance to the manual. The therapists received extensive training in running this manualized program, and as a result, treatment was standardized across programs. Furthermore, all these programs used the same extensive pre- and posttreatment assessment battery. Thus, the only factor that could vary, and then only in limited ways, was the therapists' style of delivery.

Initially, we established that therapist behaviors and qualities could be reliably identified from the videotapes. We had three experienced clinicians independently rate the videotapes for the presence of 27 therapist features.

Eighteen of these 27 features occurred frequently enough to be rated and were reliably identified, with interrater agreement ranging from kappa = 0.57 to 1.00 (W. L. Marshall, Serran, Moulden, et al., 2002). Two studies (W. L. Marshall, Serran, Moulden, et al., 2002; W. L. Marshall, Serran, Fernandez, et al., 2003) evaluated the influence of these therapist features on the indices of behavior change. Correlational analyses between the ratings of the therapists and behavior change scores revealed significant relationships on measures of a variety of coping skills, various indices of perspective-taking ability, several measures of cognitive distortions, and aspects of relationship skills.

The four most important therapist features to emerge were warmth, empathy, rewardingness, and directiveness. Most important, confrontation by the therapists was negatively correlated ($r = -0.31$) with various indices of behavior change. The combination of empathy, warmth, rewardingness, and directiveness accounted for between 30% and 60% of the changes observed in the positive benefits of treatment as measured by the various indices of change. This is considerably more than the effects of therapist features in the general literature, which typically range from 20% to 30%. Apparently therapist characteristics are more influential with sexual offender clients than with clients who have other Axis I disorders. No doubt this is due to both lack of trust among sexual offenders about the intentions of professionals as well as the offenders' understandable reluctance to disclose anything about themselves for fear it will cause them even more problems.

More recently, Drapeau and his colleagues (Drapeau, 2005; Drapeau, Korner, Brunet, & Granger, 2004) conducted two studies combining qualitative and quantitative approaches to the issue of sexual offenders' perceptions of their therapists. They found that sexual offenders judged the role of the therapist to be crucial to any benefits they derived from treatment, although these offenders also acknowledged some value for the procedures that were used to help them change. Effective therapists were those who were seen to be honest and respectful, caring, noncritical, and nonjudgmental. Therapists who were viewed as confrontational led clients to withdraw, whereas those therapists who challenged the clients in a supportive manner, elicited their full engagement. According to Drapeau, child molester clients struggled the most when working with a therapist who was overly controlling. It is important that offenders disengaged from treatment if they perceived the therapist to be unsupportive or lacking in therapeutic skills. These clients also expressed a desire to work collaboratively with the therapists in the identification of their problematic issues and on setting goals for treatment. Shingler and Mann (2006) emphasized the importance of working collaboratively with sexual offenders, not only in treatment but also in conducting risk assessments.

CONCLUSION

As has been made clear throughout this chapter, the therapist is key to producing changes (Simon, 2006). The client–therapist relationship provides the best explanation of why treatment does or does not work. All of the reviews and research outlined throughout this chapter provide directives for therapists working with sexual offenders. Most important, Hanson et al. (2009) found that the same effective correctional features reported by Andrews, Zinger, et al. (1990) also applied to sexual offender treatment. Not surprisingly, it was the responsivity principle that was most powerfully predictive of both positive treatment change and subsequent reductions in sexual recidivism.

The overall goal of treatment for sexual offenders is to prevent reoffending, and recent evidence has suggested treatment can reduce long-term recidivism (Hanson et al., 2002). W. L. Marshall and Serran (2000) proposed a number of ways to improve treatment efficacy with sexual offenders, specifically by enhancing therapeutic skills. As we have seen, an effective alliance between therapist and client plays a major role in generating treatment benefits. In view of these observations, therapists who work with sexual offenders should be carefully chosen on the basis of their ability to display the positive characteristics described in this chapter. Training programs for these therapists should incorporate these features.

Sexual offenders can be a challenging population to work with, not only because of the many issues they often have but also because they are characteristically unmotivated or reluctant to address their problem areas. This reluctance appears to be one of the reasons some therapists advocate a confrontational approach with sexual offenders. W. R. Miller and Rollnick (2002) reported that because resistance is increased by a confrontational approach, therapists should adopt a motivational stance that, as they have shown, enhances client involvement in treatment sessions. Motivational therapists encourage change by expressing empathy, avoiding argument, rolling with resistance, creating dissonance between the clients' view of themselves and their behavior, and encouraging the emergence of self-efficacy in the clients (W. R. Miller & Rollnick, 2002). This approach fits well with the literature we have reviewed in this chapter, and it is part of the approach we have adopted.

It is encouraging that more research targeting sexual offender treatment is being devoted to exploring personal and interpersonal factors such as therapist characteristics, the group climate, and the clients' views of treatment. These avenues of sexual offender work are exciting and the results will only serve to improve our interventions. It is clear, even at this early stage in these investigations, that personal and interpersonal factors are very important and appear to be more important than are the procedures designed to change behaviors. In both the treatment of clients with other Axis I disorders and the treatment of sexual offenders, it is clear that personal and interpersonal factors are far more influential in the achievement of treatment goals than are the procedures designed to change behaviors. As we noted, with other disorders, personal and interpersonal factors account for 20% to 30% of the changes induced by treatment, whereas procedures produce just 15% of these changes. These differences are apparently the same for the treatment of sexual offenders except that these features account for an even greater amount of treatment successes. We encourage sexual offender therapists and researchers to pay closer attention to these critical features of effective treatment.

4

PROBLEMS WITH CURRENT COGNITIVE–BEHAVIORAL APPROACHES

We have already noted, in the Introduction to this book, the rather negative focus of many cognitive–behavioral therapy (CBT) programs for sexual offenders. Our particular concern in that section of the book was with those treatment approaches that fully adhere to the early version of the relapse prevention model, although even later modifications of this model still seem to us to place too much emphasis on avoidance goals. In this chapter, we draw attention to behavioral and cognitive aspects of most CBT programs that we have concerns about. We then describe how our own treatment programs integrate cognitions, behaviors, and emotions in treatment and are modeled after the treatment programs that embody a positive psychology approach.

BEHAVIORAL ISSUES

It has been pointed out (Fernandez, Shingler, & Marshall, 2006) that the way in which most sexual offender programs are delivered is predominantly cognitive despite being described as cognitive–behavioral. Behavioral techniques such as role-play, behavioral rehearsal, the appropriate use of reinforcement, and between-sessions practice are often absent from CBT programs, and when they are present, they do not seem to be systematically or extensively used.

We have shown that a reinforcing style is crucial for facilitating the changes (i.e., reductions in criminogenic features) needed to reduce sexual offenders' future risk (W. L. Marshall, Serran, Fernandez, et al., 2003; W. L. Marshall, Serran, Moulden, et al., 2002). Fernandez et al. (2006) pointed out that for reinforcement to be maximally effective, it must be immediately contingent on the behavior, and the therapist must make it clear exactly what is being rewarded. Simply saying "that is good" will not be meaningful without specifying what is good. Making comments at the end of a session such as "You all did well today" is similarly not sufficiently specific. In the context of therapy, reinforcement should take the form of encouraging remarks by the therapist as well as body language (including facial expressions) that reflects these remarks.

However, some other features of reinforcement need to be kept in mind. Early in treatment, when change is just beginning, small steps in the desired direction should be immediately reinforced. For example, any sign that the client is beginning to feel comfortable, such as mentioning some aspect of a problem he may have had in one of his adult relationships, should be immediately reinforced by pointing to it and saying something like, "Well done. It's good that you indicated some difficulty in your relationship because relationship problems are one of the issues we will take up later. Remember to bring this up when we get to that topic." These remarks should be accompanied by the therapist's body language indicating his interest and pleasure at the client's comment. As the client develops his skills, reinforcement should only be given for larger changes (e.g., indicating broader relationship difficulties), otherwise the client might not be able to expand his repertoire. Similarly, the magnitude of praise should be greater for the early small steps but progressively reduced as progress is made.

However, reinforcement that only occurs within the group will almost guarantee that the behavior will be enacted in, and only in, the treatment room (Spiegler & Guevremont, 1998). Evidence from controlled studies reported in the general literature has indicated that generalization of behavior from one setting to another is not guaranteed (G. Martin & Pear, 1992). Generalization only occurs in a predictable way when it is programmed into training, so procedures and processes aimed at changing attitudes or behavior need to be practiced both within sessions (role-plays or behavioral rehearsals) and, most important, between sessions in the client's daily living circumstances.

As we have seen, generalization of behavior does not occur automatically; it only results from programmed practice. Although it is comforting to the therapist, and an essential first step in changing behavior, to see appropriate behavior and hear appropriate expressions of thoughts and beliefs within the treatment sessions, for treatment to reduce risk these changes must be maintained during the rest of the client's life. Practicing between sessions those positive behaviors that have been elicited in groups is an essential feature of good treatment and increases the likelihood that treatment-induced changes will be entrenched in the offender's life once treatment is over. However, it is essential, in the early stages of developing behavior, that the external circumstances in which between-sessions practice occurs are those that are most likely to lead to positive consequences from others. So when directing an offender to practice his newly developing skills between sessions, the therapist should assist him in selecting circumstances that are likely to maximize positive results. Of course, as the client's confidence grows, he should be expected to try out his new found skills in progressively more difficult circumstances with the understanding that prosocial behavior does not always realize positive returns.

Role-plays and behavioral rehearsals of these circumstances within treatment can be very useful if properly employed. Once these features are identified, behavioral practice within therapy can serve to identify and develop the skills necessary to ensure the success of between-sessions practice. In these role-plays, the client should at first play himself, with another group member playing the role of the other person. After this initial practice, the roles should be reversed so that the target client can view his behavior from the perspective of the other person. This, along with feedback from all other group members, helps the client to adjust his behaviors until they reach the point at which the likelihood of external success is maximized.

Some treatment programs have used role-plays of the client's actual offense; presumably this is meant to help the offender realize the impact of his crime and to assist in him taking responsibility. Such role-plays, however, are fraught with dangers. Pithers (1997) illustrated the potential consequences of misguided attempts to role-play enactments of sexual offenses. As a consequence of having poorly supervised role-plays, in which the enactments involved unacceptably close physical contacts, Pithers's program was challenged in a lawsuit and significant changes were required. Webster et al. (2005) demonstrated that including these types of role-plays added nothing to the effectiveness of treatment.

For other issues, however, these role-play techniques can be very helpful. For offenders with anger management difficulties or who are underassertive, having the client role-play specific interactions prior to the event can help him recognize the advantages or disadvantages of various strategies. As we noted, using one of the other group members to role-play the person the client will be approaching, and then reversing the roles, maximizes the value of these behavioral procedures. These procedures can also usefully be applied with offenders who have difficulty being empathic, or whose coping strategies are poor, or whose relationship skills are limited. Behavioral practice at expressing positive statements about themselves can help promote self-esteem and self-efficacy. There are, of course, numerous other issues for which role-plays or behavioral rehearsals can be helpful. Learning to integrate relevant emotions, as well as thoughts about what is appropriate with the behavioral enactments, is the most effective way to change behavior. These role-plays can serve to reduce anxiety or anger that may be associated with the issue of concern (e.g., being assertive). All actions involve a coordination of thoughts, feelings, and behavior, with the goal of role-plays being to generate the smooth and comfortable unified expression of these three features. It is only the imagination of the therapist that might limit the application of behavioral enactments to a variety of problem areas.

Contingent responses by therapists for the expression of various attitudes serve to either increase or decrease these expressions; that is, the therapist's responses function as rewards or punishers. There is a considerable body of knowledge on the nature of effective rewards and punishers that serve to increase or decrease the frequency of behaviors. What is important to note is that whether the therapist does so intentionally to modify specific behaviors, whatever he or she does or says contingent on a client's behavior exerts an influence on the frequency of the behavior. Therapists must, therefore, consciously monitor their own behavior and utilize their responses to deliberately shape the client's responses in the desired direction. Even noncontingent responses by the therapist can serve to influence the client's behavior as a result of modeling (Bandura, 1977b). If the therapist has won the client's confidence and respect, then the therapist's behavior will more likely be modeled by the client. Being aware of this, therapists can shape the client's behaviors and the expression of his attitudes by deliberately modeling appropriate actions and by deliberately expressing appropriate views.

Generally speaking, contingently rewarding behaviors is a more effective way of increasing appropriate actions and attitudes than is punishing these responses. Punishment or condemnatory responses to the expression of negative attitude can all too often produce an increase in the expression of the undesirable views. These responses to punishment are described as oppositional behaviors and can become easily entrenched.

When an offender expresses inappropriate attitudes, the therapist's response is critical. Responding with a confrontational response or a negative evaluation of the remark (i.e., punishing the remark) is unlikely to reduce its frequency. Confrontation has been clearly shown to reduce the likelihood of obtaining positive changes in sexual offenders (W. L. Marshall, Serran, Fernandez, et al., 2003). In any case, such a response by the therapist models inappropriately aggressive behavior, which can be expected to produce similar behaviors in the clients (Bandura, 1977b). Confrontational responses by the therapist can be viewed as forms of punishment and among offenders punishment has been shown to increase oppositional and uncooperative behaviors (Schmauk, 1970). Where possible, the best response to the expression of inappropriate attitudes is to ignore them. For example, if an offender is describing a failed relationship with a woman and another group member interjects a comment that expresses a negative attitude toward women or an inappropriately collusive remark, then the therapist should carry on as if the comment had not been made. This will avoid reinforcing, by attention, the inappropriate remark. Repeatedly ignoring such remarks over time should lead to the extinction of these unhelpful responses (Falls, 1998). However, extinction is not simply the passive loss of a response; it is also the active acquisition of an alternative behavior. The therapist, therefore, must remember to reinforce alternative prosocial remarks made by the collusive offender at the first and every subsequent opportunity.

Participatory learning, in which the client is actively involved in treatment by entering all discussions, has been shown (Spiegler & Guevremont, 1998) to be far more effective than passive learning (i.e., silently listening). Allowing clients to sit passively observing treatment should not be permitted. Asking silent clients to offer a comment, however brief their comments may be early in treatment, will, when steadfastly applied and rewarded, increase their active involvement in treatment.

Procedures meant to modify deviant sexual interests have been described as behavior modification techniques, and yet there are clearly cognitive and emotional components to these methods. In that sense, these techniques could be thought as exemplars for all strategies aimed at changing behaviors. All human actions seamlessly combine behaviors, thoughts, and feelings. Thus, for change strategies to be maximally effective, these strategies should all explicitly specify or explicitly integrate these three features of functioning.

Because the so-called behavior-modification techniques appear to be effective (W. L. Marshall, O'Brien, & Marshall, 2009), and a significant number of sexual offenders have deviant interests, it is surprising that only a limited number of programs (63%) report utilizing these techniques (McGrath, Cumming, & Burchard, 2003). Also, in our experience in providing training to even experienced therapists, it appears that few treatment providers have a sound understanding of the empirical and theoretical bases of these behavior-modification procedures. This lack of a thorough understanding all too often results in these procedures being inappropriately applied, resulting in failures to produce the desired changes. For a detailed description of the appropriate way to apply these procedures, the reader is referred to W. L. Marshall, O'Brien, and Marshall (2009). Perhaps this failure to truly understand these procedures and to implement them effectively explains the reluctance of some programs to use these techniques.

In conclusion, then, behavioral strategies of the various kinds we have listed previously should, in our view, be utilized as major components in treatment programs for sexual offenders.

COGNITIVE ISSUES

The main issue we wish to address is not only the general failure to fully use behavioral strategies but also the excessive (as we see it) focus on cognitions. In the sexual offender literature, there are numerous articles dating from the 1980s describing an extensive list of so-called distorted cognitions that are said to characterize sexual offenders (Abel, Becker, & Cunningham-Rathner, 1984; Beech & Fisher, 2004; Brake & Shannon, 1997; Carich, Michael, & Stone, 1992; Hanson, Gizzarelli, & Scott, 1994; Hartley, 1998; Howitt, 1995; W. D. Murphy & Carich, 2001; Quinsey, 1986; Sefarbi, 1990). These distortions include thoughts, beliefs, perceptions, and attitudes as well as what are said to be minimizations concerning the nature and details of the offense. Such distortions serve to diminish the offender's responsibility for the offense and to implicate the victim's role in supposedly provoking the offense. In addition, when an offender denies he committed an offense, this too is said to be a cognitive distortion. Given the evidence on false convictions, clearly some offenders who deny they offended must be telling the truth, although we cannot know who is lying.

Salter (1988) viewed these distortions as deliberate lies that must be vigorously challenged and overcome if treatment is to be effective. Consistent with this view, some authors (Feelgood, Cortoni, & Thompson, 2005) have suggested that these distortions facilitate and maintain sexual offending, and Ward, Keown, and Gannon (2007) concluded that this is a commonly held view in the field. Others see these distortions as ways to either justify, minimize, or rationalize offending (Bumby, 1996) or as a means to protect the offender's self-image and deflect public criticism (Gannon & Polaschek, 2005). Almost all sexual offender program providers, however they view the role of these distortions, agree with Salter that they must be changed if treatment is to be successful. But is this true?

In a study of ex-prisoners, Maruna (2001) found that those individuals in his sample who offered excuses for their crimes were less likely to reoffend than those who readily admitted to being "offenders." Consistent with Maruna's findings, other researchers have also shown that offenders who offer excuses for their crimes are less likely to reoffend than are those who accept full responsibility (Hanson & Wallace-Capretta, 2000; Hood, Shute, Feilzer, & Wilcox, 2002; Maruna, 2001, 2004; G. Ryan & Miyoshi, 1990; Smith & Monastersky, 1986). In addition, Maruna and Mann (2006) reviewed evidence showing that excuse making is not only a universal human disposition, as is lying (Bok, 1978), but is also typically related to good mental and physical health (Dodge, 1993; Schlenker, Pontari, & Christopher, 2001; M. E. P. Seligman, 1991). It appears that taking full responsibility for problematic behaviors places people at risk for problems such as mood disorders (Abramson, Seligman, & Teasdale, 1978). Making excuses helps maintain the person's reputation, prevents the loss of self-esteem, and avoids feelings of shame (W. L. Marshall & Marshall, 2010a). Feelings of shame have been shown to increase an interest in crime (Braithwaite & Braithwaite, 2001). Most important, the majority of the cognitive distortions displayed by sexual offenders are not criminogenic (W. L. Marshall, Marshall, & Ware 2009); that is, they do not predict reoffending (Hanson & Bussière, 1998; Hanson & Harris, 2000b; Hanson & Morton-Bourgon, 2005). In fact, it appears that only a limited set of cognitions, including the expression of attitudes reflecting a tolerance of sexual abuse and child molesters' emotional identification with children, are predictive of recidivism. When people offer excuses or justifications for their behavior they are, at least implicitly, acknowledging that they know their actions were wrong.

One set of responses that are assumed to be distortions, and that are a particular focus of most sexual offender treatment programs, are those aspects of the offender's account of the offense that disagree with the victim's descriptions. It is assumed in most programs that the victim's account represents an accurate version of the event, including the offender's behaviors. On the basis of this assumption, any deviation by the offender of this putative veridical account is identified as a distortion. In fact, there are numerous grounds for concluding that any description of a past event is likely to include numerous factual errors. The extensive body of literature on eyewitness testimony casts serious doubts about the validity of crime scene reports by those involved (Castelli et al., 2006; Eisen, Quas, & Goodman, 2002; D. F. Ross, Read, & Toglia, 1994; Sporer, Malpass, & Koehnken, 1996). Police interviews typically provide victims with information that produces distortions (Ceci, Ross, & Toglia, 1987; Warren, Woodall, Hunt, & Perry, 1996), and in any case, research in memory has demonstrated that the recall of any event is not the identification of actual details but rather a process of reconstruction that is flawed (J. R. Anderson, 1995; Reder, 1982). Finally, research has shown that events experienced in traumatic circumstances are the most susceptible to distorted recall (S. Taylor, 2006), and these distortions are particularly evident among sexual abuse victims (Tromp, Koss, Figueredo, & Tharan, 1995). On the basis of this body of evidence, it would be unwise to assume that the discrepancies between the victim's and the offender's account of an offense reflects deliberate falsification by the offender. The fact is that all accounts of past events contain errors, and no one can know the truth of the matter.

Despite the fact that this evidence has been available for some years, the majority of sexual offender treatment providers follow Salter's dictum that all assumed distortions must be aggressively confronted and changed. From the evidence mentioned previously, it is clear that a good deal of the cognitive restructuring (W. D. Murphy, 1990) that characterizes sexual offender treatment addresses empirically unsound targets, but many therapists appear to be either unaware of this evidence or simply loath to acknowledge the evidence, and as a result, they are reluctant to cease targeting these noncriminogenic cognitions.

In addition, as we have pointed out previously, most targets in treatment, including the genuinely criminogenic issues, tend to be addressed in most programs in an exclusively rational (i.e., cognitive) way to the exclusion of utilizing behavioral and emotionally based strategies. We realize the appeal of conducting therapy in a strictly rational way given the focus of the training therapists typically receive during their undergraduate and graduate years. But this does not make this practice the best choice. The Western intellectual heritage from Plato through the Enlightenment to the present day has been characterized in part by an attempt to free rational thought from the distractions of emotion (Saul, 1992), and this tradition is apparent in some treatment programs. For example, Mann and Thornton (1998), in describing the sexual offender programs of Her Majesty's Prison Service, extolled the virtues of what they call the "Socratic" method, which their therapists are trained to adopt in challenging the offenders. On the basis of Socrates' approach (actually Plato's account of Socrates' approach) to inquiry, this dialectic method is strictly rational, and in the dialogues Socrates in fact trips up his adversaries when they stray away from this rational discourse by allowing their emotions to "cloud" their vision. Adopting such an approach with clients who generally have limited, and often unpleasant, educational experiences seems unlikely to succeed. In fact, given that these clients are either emotionally detached or overly emotionally expressive, perhaps it is their emotional responsivity that is more problematic than their way of intellectually appraising their world.

The previous discussion does not imply that cognitions can be ignored or that a rational analysis is without value. Of course, behaviors are driven, at least in part, by the person's thoughts, and these thoughts are expressed as verbal behaviors that can and should be challenged. But a strictly rational analysis alone does not change behavior. Pfäfflin et al. (2005) showed that in the treatment of sexual offenders, it is only when a rational understanding is accompanied by an emotional response that behavior begins to change. Expressions of understanding unaccompanied by emotional expressions do not initiate the desired changes in sexual offenders' behaviors. It is interesting to note that B. F. Skinner (1957) long ago demonstrated that verbal expressions (including attitudes) can be brought under control by the contingent verbal responses of another person (in this case, a therapist). Thus, perhaps the most useful way to modify problematic cognitions is by contingent verbal behavior rather than by the exclusive use of cognitive restructuring, although even this rational strategy may not be effective in the absence of an accompanying emotional response.

In recent years, some researchers working with sexual offenders have begun to focus on the important role of not just the overt expression of problematic cognitions but also the schema that underlies these expressions (see Mann & Shingler, 2006, for a discussion). *Schemas* are said to guide "every human action, reaction, and interaction" (Freeman & Freeman, 2005, p. 421). They are templates of personal, cultural, and gender ideas that have developed throughout the person's life. Langton and Marshall (2000, 2001) described a model of information processing relevant to understanding the inappropriate cognitions of sexual offenders. Within this model, schemas are viewed as structures with cognitive contents where these structures influence and direct the processing of information. For example, a rapist may express a variety of specific inappropriate views of women (see Bumby, 1996) as a result of having a broadly entrenched negative view of women (i.e., the schema), which he is unlikely to be aware of. A child molester might indicate that he finds adults threatening and children accepting (see Howells, 1979) as a result of entrenched schemas about women and children. In both cases, these schemas not only direct the rapists' and child molesters' expressed views (described in the literature as cognitive distortions) but also direct their perceptions and their behaviors. To change these problematic schemas, it is necessary to modify each and every overt expression of the schemas, to assist the clients in recognizing the commonality of the cognitions, and to help them see the likely origins of the schemas.

We suggest that Young's (1999) schema therapy might provide a useful approach to attempts at changing the dysfunctional beliefs of sexual offenders. As we have noted, B. F. Skinner's (1957) method of contingent verbal responses can also change the specific expressions of problematic attitudes, but changes induced by that method seems unlikely to produce a generalized change in the underlying schema. So far, insufficient attention has been given to schemas by researchers and clinicians working with sexual offenders, although a start has been made (Hanson, 1998; Mann, 2004; Mann & Beech, 2003; Mann & Hollin, 2001; Myers, 2000; Serran, Looman, & Dickie, 2004). Ward and Keenan's (1999) work on implicit theories addresses essentially the same issues as a schema approach, and so does Myers's (2000) notion of "life maps." Drake, Ward, Nathan, and Lee (2001) offered suggestions for addressing dysfunctional schemas (or implicit theories) in treatment, as did Mann and Shingler (2006).

One set of schemas that presents a block to engagement in treatment are those about the self. People low in self-esteem hold an array of attitudes about themselves (e.g., "I am a failure," "I am unable to do anything success-fully," "Other people do not like me") that result in their being afraid to try to change. This resistance to change arises from a fear that they will fail, which they are sure will make them feel even worse (Baumeister, 1993). The schema driving these negative attitudes toward the self is typically well-entrenched, but among sexual offenders it is exacerbated by the processes associated with their arrest, investigation, prosecution, and incarceration. Clearly this lack of self-esteem must be overcome before treatment progress can be made. Low self-esteem is typically associated with shame, which also blocks any attempts at change (Tangney & Dearing, 2002). We (W. L. Marshall, Champagne, Sturgeon, & Bryce, 1997) have developed strategies to enhance self-esteem that form a combination of cognitive procedures involving assisting our clients to identify their strengths and behavioral procedures requiring them to expand the range and frequency of social and pleasurable interactions. However, the emotional attachment to all types of maladaptive schemas (including those associated with the person's view of himself) needs to be severed if the cognitive and behavioral changes are to endure.

EMOTIONAL ISSUES

Much has recently been made in the sexual offender literature of offenders' inability to regulate their behavior (Ward & Hudson, 2000). Self-regulation of behavior enables one to delay gratification in the pursuit of personal goals (Thompson, 1994). Obviously, sexual offenders have deficits in self-regulatory processes, and poor self-regulation predicts the likelihood of recidivism among these offenders (Hanson, 2006b). As Bless and Forgas (2000) noted, affective states influence behavior and cognition and as a result underpin all self-regulatory processes. Similarly, Baumeister, Zell, and Tice (2007) pointed out that stress and unpleasant emotions cause self-regulation to break down. Distressing emotions increase eating in overweight people (Greeno & Wing, 1994), cause smokers to smoke more (Ashton & Stepney, 1982), and markedly increase relapses in people attempting to quit a variety of behaviors (Brownell, Marlatt, Lichtenstein, & Wilson, 1986). All manner of problematic behaviors emerge when people are emotionally distressed, including excessive drinking (Sayette, 1993), gambling (Peck, 1986), and com-pulsive shopping (O'Guinn & Faber, 1989), and emotional distress appears to underpin the compulsive sexual behaviors of sexually preoccupied sexual offenders (L. E. Marshall & Marshall, 2006; L. E. Marshall, Marshall, Moulden, & Serran, 2008). Attempts to delay gratification fail when people are sad, angry, or anxious (Fry, 1975; Wertheim & Schwartz, 1983). Even the suppression of emotions can lead to impulsive actions (Baumeister et al., 2007).

Thus, to properly self-regulate their behavior, people must learn to self-regulate (i.e., express appropriately) their emotions. It is impossible to learn to regulate emotions unless treatment providers allow and encourage the expression of emotions during treatment. This does not mean allowing the completely unrestrained expression of feelings; obviously, out-of-control emotions present serious disruptions to treatment, and in such heightened emotional states little learning takes place. Encouragement of emotional expressions must be accompanied by some degree of restraint.

Emotional responsivity on the part of the therapist is essential to the generation of the client's emotional expressiveness, which is becoming an increasingly important target with a range of disorders (L. S. Greenberg, Rice, & Elliott, 1993; Kennedy-Moore & Watson, 1999). Emotional experiences during treatment, including encouraging clients to be emotionally expressive, is related to successful outcome with various disorders (Cooley & LaJoy, 1980; Orlinsky & Howard, 1986). This is because processing information while in an emotional state leads to change, whereas intellectualizing and analyzing issues is less likely to do so (Klein et al., 1986). In fact, Lietaer (1992) noted that little progress occurs when therapists are excessively rational. Research has supported this contention. For example, Saunders (1999) found that the expression of feelings by clients determined the impact of treatment sessions and that clients' emotional expression was facilitated by the emotional expressiveness of the therapist. However, although McClure and Hodge (1987) found that therapists' emotional expressiveness generally strengthened the alliance, when these emotional expressions became too strong the alliance was damaged, and this reduced treatment benefits.

Research has suggested that successful treatment outcome is related to the degree to which clients are given the opportunity to be emotionally expressive (Cooley & LaJoy, 1980; Orlinsky & Howard, 1986). Empathy and acceptance by the therapist contribute to affect regulation by providing interpersonal soothing and encourage the ability to regulate emotion. A validating relationship is viewed as crucial to affect regulation; people with underregulated affect have been shown to benefit from interpersonal validation as much as they do from specific techniques aimed directly at emotion regulation and distress tolerance skills (Linehan, 1993). The therapist's communication of emotion (through facial and verbal expression) creates the emotional climate. Providing a safe and responsive emotional climate facilitates emotional processing. Other researchers have also found that encouraging emotional expression facilitates treatment change (Klein et al., 1986; Orlinsky & Howard, 1986). Saunders (1999) demonstrated that the expression of feelings by clients determines the impact that each treatment session has, and he found that these expressions were best facilitated by the emotional expressiveness of the therapist. These various studies have indicated that attitudes, beliefs, and behaviors are affected by emotional states and that interpersonal schemas, which are often strongly held by clients, are typically only accessed and ultimately changed when activated through emotional expression.

Emotions are essential to learning new and more advantageous behaviors, and it has been found that sexual offenders are poor at identifying emotions in other people (S. M. Hudson et al., 1993). This failure to recognize emotional expressions interferes with effective communication with others and presents a problem limiting the capacity to build effective relationships. People who are poor at emotional recognition are usually poor at identifying their own emotions. Thus, a target in treatment for sexual offenders will be the acquisition of skilled emotional identification both in themselves and in others. This can only happen if emotional expression is encouraged.

In addition, research focusing on the effective features of sexual offender treatment has indicated that the appropriate expression of emotions is crucial to any benefits that may be derived from the program. As we have seen, Pfäfflin et al. (2005) found that it was only when emotions accompanied an understanding of the issues addressed in treatment that appropriate changes occurred. Beech and his colleagues (Beech & Fordham, 1997; Beech & Hamilton-Giachritsis, 2005) demonstrated that scores on the Expressiveness subscale of Moos's (1986) Group Climate Scale were significantly associated with beneficial changes across 19 different programs for sexual offenders. This subscale includes, very importantly, the expression of emotions. The appropriate expression of emotions, therefore, needs to be enhanced in sexual offenders, and such expressions need to be encouraged within treatment sessions if benefits are to be obtained.

This idea is expressed in other forms of treatment for various types of disorders (Bohart & Tolman, 1998; Goldfried, 1982; L. S. Greenberg & Pavio, 1997; Safran & Segal, 1990) in which it has been shown that appropriate emotional expression leads to greater self-understanding and increased self-acceptance (Roemer & Borkovec, 1994). As we (W. L. Marshall et al., 2006) noted in an earlier book, "therapists need to move clients beyond the easy route of rational and emotionally disengaged analyses . . . to move to active emotional analyses" (p. 33).

CONCLUSION

In this chapter, we have pointed to what we see as the failure of most so-called cognitive–behavioral programs for sexual offenders to integrate behaviors, cognitions, and emotions despite the obvious fact that this integration characterizes all human functioning. Essentially we view most CBT programs for sexual offenders as being predominantly cognitive in nature at least in so far as they are described in the literature.

In our approach, we attempt to integrate cognitions, behaviors, and emotions in treatment. This is how humans function in their daily lives, so it seems appropriate to do so in treatment. The integration of these issues requires the therapist to move away from the comfort zone of engaging clients in an exclusively rationale discourse. Arranging behavioral enactments both within and between sessions is not difficult, although it sometimes takes creative imagination within a prison setting. Perhaps the most difficult task for those therapists who have followed a traditional CBT approach is to facilitate the expression of emotions while limiting their intensity so that the group does not spin out of control. However, with a bit of practice it becomes a natural part of the group process. Without it, learning will either not take place or be easily lost once treatment is over.

Before we describe our treatment programs in Chapters 6, 7, and 8, we provide our view of the treatment outcome literature with sexual offenders. In the next chapter, then, we consider how best to evaluate treatment and what we see as a body of literature that encourages optimism about the benefits of sexual offender treatment programs.

5

EVALUATION OF SEXUAL OFFENDER TREATMENT PROGRAMS

In evaluating treatment for sexual offenders, two issues need to be addressed. First, the program must demonstrate that it actually achieves its goal of changing the clients on the relevant issues; this requires a determination of the degree to which the clients profited from treatment in terms of changes on the treatment targets, particularly the criminogenic targets. Of course, an ideal evaluation would appraise the clients on all issues addressed in treatment, including those (e.g., self-esteem and shame) that facilitate treatment engagement as well as the adequacy of the client's good lives model goals and plans, the appropriateness of both his support groups and his release plans, and how well he understands his risk factors.

The second—and perhaps the more important—aspect of treatment evaluation concerns a determination of the effectiveness of the program in reducing reoffense rates. Unlike the first issue in treatment evaluation, which can be addressed within a manageable time frame, outcome evaluations require large numbers of treated clients to be examined for recidivism over many years postrelease. Barbaree (1997) provided guidelines indicating the required number of clients evaluated over specified time periods that are necessary for adequate evaluations to be completed. He also pointed out that these issues are dependent on the expected base rate of the clients in the study. For example, because the base rate of reoffending (i.e., the rate among untreated offenders) is, ipso facto, high among a group of high-risk sexual offenders, then an evaluation of a program for these offenders requires fewer offenders to be examined over a shorter period of postrelease than would be true for a program focusing on low-risk sexual offenders. Indeed, it may be all but impossible to evaluate the long-term impact of a program for low-risk sexual offenders given their very low base rate.

What the treatment outcome literature with sexual offenders clearly reveals is that some programs have not been able to produce clear benefits; it would be, in our view, very surprising if all programs that have been applied to the treatment of sexual offenders were uniformly effective. Indeed, if the early attempts at interventions with these offenders, when we knew nothing about which factors were criminogenic, had been effective, there would be no grounds for the evolution of broad-based programs that has been evident from the early 1970s onward. The fact that many of the early programs were ineffective and that some more recent treatment models have also been shown to be ineffective does not justify abandoning treatment with sexual offenders, but rather justifies changing our approaches. Our interpretation of the literature is that when programs target problems that are obstacles to treatment, and then focus on changing known criminogenic features by taking a positive, respectful, and process-oriented approach, the reoffense rates of the sexual offenders treated in this way are likely to be significantly reduced. We believe that the following review supports this point of view.

In this chapter, we identify the aims of treatment evaluations with sexual offenders. First we focus on evaluations of the ability of treatment to produce changes in the criminogenic features of the offenders (i.e., within-treatment goals). Then we consider different approaches to the evaluation of the overall effectiveness of treatment in reducing reoffending (i.e., long-term outcome). Finally, we describe positive evaluations of Rockwood Psychological Services (RPS) program outcomes.

EVALUATION OF WITHIN-TREATMENT GOALS

Surprisingly, very few sexual offender programs have reported their effectiveness in achieving the goals of changing clients on the various targets addressed in treatment. Presumably, each program believes that if treatment corrects the clients' functioning on the treatment targets, then the likelihood that they will reoffend will be reduced. If so, then it ought to be mandatory for each program to demonstrate that it is effective in achieving these treatment goals. Unfortunately, as noted, most programs have not attempted this, but some have at least for some of the treatment targets.

Her Majesty's Prison Service's (HMPS) program in the United Kingdom (see Mann & Thornton, 1998, for a description) is the largest scale application of interventions for sexual offenders in the world, involving treatment delivered in 25 prisons for offenders at all levels of risk. Unlike most other programs, HMPS has undertaken a series of independent studies examining the effectiveness of these programs in producing the sought-after changes on the various targets of treatment (Beech et al., 1999; Beech, Oliver, Fisher, & Beckett, 2006). The British Home Office has also used independent researchers to conduct a similar evaluation of their probation-based community programs (Beckett et al., 1994; K. D. Browne et al., 1998).

Beech et al. (1999) conducted pre- and posttreatment assessments of an array of treatment targets in HMPS prisons and found that 67% of the clients showed significant changes on most of the main themes addressed in the programs. Similar appraisals of community probation programs revealed that 81% of the sexual offenders improved (K. D. Browne et al., 1998), which was consistent with the findings of an earlier study (Beech, Fisher, Beckett, & Fordham, 1996). More specifically, Mandeville-Norden, Beech, and Hayes (2008) evaluated changes in 341 child molesters that were produced by a community probation program. They assessed these clients prior to and after treatment on eight measures of attitudes and socioaffective states and found not only that there were significant changes on all measures but also that the posttreatment scores were within the normative range. This latter reported finding is quite important because, unlike these HMPS studies, other studies simply reported that posttreatment scores reflected significant improvements without indicating whether these scores were, or were not, within normative limits. Although changes in the right direction are desired, unless the clients are functioning at least close to the normative average on the criminogenic features prior to discharge, they will likely have difficulty achieving much in the way of a fulfilling life. The HMPS studies noted here represent the most comprehensive evaluations of the ability of sexual offender treatment programs to attain their stated goals. It is clear, then, that HMPS programs, both in prisons and in community settings, consistently achieve the broad range of targets they set out as the goals of their treatment. Now that researchers have generated these data, there is no longer any need for HMPS to repeat these studies. The next step should involve an examination of the relationship between these detailed changes and long-term outcome. We look forward to reading the results of this next step.

Unlike the HMPS's comprehensive studies, most evaluations have been restricted to only one or two of the within-treatment targets. Pithers (1994), for example, demonstrated that his program's goal of enhancing clients' empathy was effective. He showed that the sexual offenders in his program were deficient in empathy prior to treatment but that after treatment, their scores on his measure reflected a significant improvement in empathic responding. Insofar as empathy enhancement was seen as a crucial target in Pithers's sexual offender program, then his demonstration that this goal was achieved was necessary to validate the integrity of the program. However, there were many other unassessed targets in Pithers's program. Similarly, Webster et al. (2005) showed that HMPS programs were effective in increasing empathy, and we (W. L. Marshall, O'Sullivan, & Fernandez, 1996) have also demonstrated the effectiveness of the RPS programs' victim empathy component.

As we have seen, most sexual offender programs consider distorted cognitions to be a critical treatment target. Mann, Webster, Wakeling, and Marshall (2007) provided evidence that the component of HMPS programs aimed at modifying the distortions child molesters hold about sex with children was effective in moving their expressed attitudes in the right direction. Thornton and Shingler (2001) also showed that focusing on modifying the broadly dysfunctional schemas expressed by sexual offenders in HMPS programs was successful. In an examination of the effects of treatment on the denial and minimizations that sexual offenders displayed toward their offenses, W. L. Marshall (1994) demonstrated that categorical denial ("I did not commit an offense") was all but eliminated and that the few minimizations that remained after treatment were minor and not strongly held.

Self-esteem enhancement and shame reduction are parts of that aspect of RPS programs that serves to facilitate engagement in treatment. If this phase of treatment is to be successful in engaging the offenders, it must be demonstrated that these obstacles are overcome. In addition, low self-esteem appears to be a potential risk factor (Thornton, Beech, & Marshall, 2004); if these early data hold true, then enhancing self-esteem will be vital to reducing the tendency to reoffend. As a result, we have assessed the RPS programs' capacity to normalize our clients' functioning on these two features. W. L. Marshall, Champagne, Sturgeon, and Bryce (1997) found significant improvements in self-esteem among sexual offenders after treatment such that their confidence levels were equivalent to well-functioning nonoffenders. More recently, L. E. Marshall, Bailey, Mailet, and Marshall (2009) reported reductions in shame expressed by sexual offenders as a result of treatment.

Roger and Masters (1997) and Feelgood, Golias, Shaw, and Bright (2000) evaluated the effects of their program on the clients' abilities to cope effectively with various problematic issues in their lives. Both these studies revealed markedly improved use of effective coping strategies among sexual offenders and a change in their use of an effective coping style. Although Serran, Firestone, Marshall, and Moulden (2007) found rather small changes in overall coping style, the offenders showed a marked improvement in their capacity to cope with a range of specific problems. This latter study also demonstrated a marked improvement in the offenders' identification and sensible use of their support group.

Numerous studies have shown various specific procedures to be effective in normalizing sexual interests (see W. L. Marshall, O'Brien, & Marshall, 2009, for a review). However, many of these studies are single-case designs with few being experimentally controlled studies. In addition, a number of the group studies are with juvenile sexual offenders. Larger group studies are still needed to evaluate the efficacy of each of the various procedures aimed at correcting sexual interests. Evaluations have also indicated that various pharmacological treatments can be effective in reducing deviant sexual interests (see Saleh, 2009, for a review), but again, controlled studies using large numbers are needed.

Finally, we have shown that the RPS programs effectively increase intimacy and reduces loneliness in sexual offending clients (W. L. Marshall, Bryce, Hudson, Ward, & Moth, 1996) and that the RPS programs' motivational component enhances hope, improves self-efficacy, and moves clients along the dimension of Prochaska and Di Clemente's (1994) Stages of Change measure (L. E. Marshall, Marshall, Fernandez, Malcolm, & Moulden, 2008).

With the exception of the HMPS series of studies, all other sexual offender treatment programs have so far failed to conduct comprehensive evaluations of the success or otherwise of their program's efficacy in achieving positive changes on the targeted criminogenic features. Clearly more studies are needed to convincingly demonstrate that the criminogenic targets of treatment are attained and that such changes are, indeed, related to reduced recidivism. Most programs that have attempted to determine effectiveness have focused on evaluating long-term reductions in recidivism, and it is to that body of research that we now turn.

EVALUATION OF LONG-TERM OUTCOME

This is perhaps the most contentious area of research in the field of sexual offender treatment. There are disagreements about the best way to evaluate programs, particularly given factors relevant to sexual offender treatment that are unique to this field, an issue we take up later in this chapter. There are also quite strong disagreements about what the available evidence tells us about the effectiveness of sexual offender treatment. Claims have been made that the evidence has indicated that treatment is ineffective (Breiling, 2005; Rice, Quinsey, & Harris, 1991). Others (Seto, 2005) have claimed that the evidence is insufficiently convincing to declare treatment to be effective, whereas others (W. L. Marshall, 1993b; W. L. Marshall & Pithers, 1994) have concluded that there is evidence suggesting that treatment does work. This latter claim, it should be made clear, is not that any or all programs are effective but that at least some programs appear to effectively reduce recidivism. Much of these disagreements depend on what criteria a reviewer sets as the standard for designing treatment evaluations.

Approaches to Evaluation

The view most commonly expressed about the appropriate way to evaluate sexual offender treatment is to use the randomized controlled trial (RCT). Advocates of this view (Quinsey, Harris, Rice, & Lalumière, 1993; Rice & Harris, 2003; Seto et al., 2008) have dismissed all other designs as inadequate to the proper appraisal of treatment while at the same time acknowledging the practical obstacles to implementing an RCT study (Seto et al., 2008). We (W. L. Marshall, 1993b; W. L. Marshall & Marshall, 2007; W. L. Marshall & Pithers, 1994) have repeatedly pointed to the reluctance (in many cases, downright refusal) of most institutional systems, or other treatment funding agencies, to allow researchers to implement an RCT study. It may be that these agencies or institutions are ill-informed about the nature of good science, but the fact remains that proposing such a study is very likely to be turned down. These agencies, it must be kept in mind, are the ones that will face the wrath of a public response to a reoffending client when the resources were available for him to access treatment but these resources were deliberately withheld to scientifically answer the question of treatment effectiveness. An argument in support of the implementation of an RCT designed study may well be lauded in the scientific literature but perhaps not in the domain of public opinion.

In addition, W. L. Marshall and Marshall (2007) noted at least two potential flaws with the RCT approach. First, to get approval to implement a study evaluating effectiveness of any treatment program, ethics committees typically demand that the untreated group (or the group given a placebo treatment) be offered effective treatment at the earliest possible date after the evaluation is completed. With most Axis I disorders, this could be implemented within a reasonable time because the effectiveness of treatment for these disorders can be determined within a relatively short time after treatment termination. For sexual offenders, relapses occur over many years posttreatment, making it all but impossible to locate and then offer subsequent intervention to the untreated offenders. Second, there is also a potential design flaw with the RCT study when implemented to evaluate prison-based programs. Those volunteers who are allocated to the no-treatment group are unlikely to be viewed as positively by decision makers (e.g., parole boards or other release decision makers, or by prison transfer committees) as those who received treatment. For example, the Canadian National Parole Board rarely gives early release to untreated sexual offenders but does so with treated offenders, and they are unlikely to modify their decision making for the sake of science. This will mean that the untreated clients will suffer as a result of the nature of the RCT demands and are, therefore, likely to be in a very different frame of mind on release than are the treated men. This introduces a potentially serious confound. Given these likely consequences for the untreated sexual offenders, an ethics committee considering an RCT study with sexual offenders may well reject the proposal out of concern for the welfare of those who are allocated to the no-treatment group. Of course, advocates of the RCT approach to treatment appraisal insist, despite these and other problems, that evaluations not using the RCT design have little or nothing to tell us about the value of sexual offender treatment (Seto et al., 2008).

This same debate is engaged in the general clinical literature (Persons & Silberschaltz, 1998) as well as in the treatment of nonsexual offenders (Hollin, 2006). M. E. P. Seligman and Levant (1998) noted that there is little value in outcome studies that do not evaluate "therapy as it is actually delivered" (p. 211). Both in general clinical work (D. J. Martin et al., 2000; Schaap et al., 1993) and in the treatment of sexual offenders (W. L. Marshall, 2005), there is clear evidence that the therapist's characteristics (e.g., warmth, empathy) and the therapeutic alliance are critical to the effectiveness of treatment. These process issues account for some 30% of the variance in measures of effectiveness with most Axis I disorders (Norcross, 2002) and well over 30% of some measures of change with sexual offenders (W. L. Marshall, Serran, Moulden, et al., 2002). In addition, flexibility is required to adjust treatment to the uniqueness of individual clients in order for treatment to be maximally effective for Axis I disorders (Kottler et al., 1994; Schaap et al., 1993). This is also true for the treatment of offenders in which this feature is described as *responsivity* (Andrews & Bonta, 1994; Hanson et al., 2009).

Because the RCT design requires that the integrity of treatment (i.e., its internal validity) be assured, RCT studies demand that therapists in the study follow a detailed treatment manual. The use of such overly precise manuals markedly reduces the capacity of therapists to flexibly respond to each client's uniqueness and tends to stifle the implementation of good therapist qualities (W. L. Marshall, 2009). G. T. Wilson (1996) suggested that the use of detailed manuals contradicts the principles of cognitive–behavioral therapy (CBT) in that these manuals prescribe the same treatment for all clients and deny the utility of idiographic case formulations. Goldfried and Wolfe (1996) described this approach as a "straitjacket" and provided evidence showing that therapists who adhere closely to a manual compromise their effectiveness.

There are many other issues that we (W. L. Marshall & Marshall, 2007) have drawn attention to that express our concerns about the implementation of the RCT design to evaluate sexual offender treatment; we refer the interested reader to our article, as well as to the response by Seto et al. (2008) and our repost to their paper (W. L. Marshall & Marshall, 2008). In our view, it is reasonable to accept studies that have provided a reasonably well-matched comparison group of untreated sexual offenders (referred to as *incidental assignment designs*). This view is reflected in the standards for acceptable studies in two large-scale meta-analyses of sexual offender treatment outcome (Hanson et al., 2002; Lösel & Schmucker, 2005).

Of course, not all sexual offender treatment programs have access to untreated subjects. Indeed, programs with a strong motivational disposition to offers of treatment are the ones most likely to have few refusers and therefore little in the way of available untreated clients. Programs with such positive invitational strategies and motivational styles seem the very ones that are most likely to have the greatest effects. It is ironic that these programs are, in the eyes of advocates of the RCT design, the very ones that will be unable to demonstrate their effectiveness. We consider that allowing such programs to compare the recidivism rates of their treated subjects with the expected rates of reoffending, derived from sound risk assessment instruments, is an acceptable strategy. In the following review of outcome studies, we consider studies that used either the RCT design or the incidental assignment design and those that compared treated clients with their expected reoffense rates.

General Outcome Studies

There have been a number of meta-analyses of the available literature on treatment outcome with sexual offenders. Of course, the strength of any conclusions derived from meta-analyses is a function of the standards set for studies to enter the analyses. Unfortunately, attention to selection standards has not always been adequate in these reports. We are not referring here to the two alternatives to the RCT design that we listed previously, but rather to studies in which it was difficult to determine exactly what treatment involved or where recidivism was determined in unacceptable ways (e.g., clients' reports that they did not reoffend). Three meta-analyses have received widespread acceptance primarily because they specified standards for acceptance of the reports and also because the authors conducted more detailed analyses revealing important features related to outcome. In our descriptions of the outcome of the following meta-analyses, as well as for the individual outcome studies we describe, the differences between the recidivism rates for the treated subjects and comparison groups (or expected outcomes) are all statistically significant unless otherwise stated.

Hanson et al. (2002) entered 43 studies into their analyses. They required each program report entering the study to have used either random assignment of offenders to treatment or no-treatment (RCT designs) or what they called an incidental assignment design. This latter design attempts to create equivalent groups by having the treated subjects matched with untreated subjects on various risk-related variables. The untreated subjects in these incidental designs had to be from the same setting as the treated group but could come from an earlier time when treatment was not available, with corrections made for time at risk. All studies were also required to have relied on official data on offenses (e.g., police records or national databases) as their index of recidivism. Although it is well-established that official data underestimate true reoffending (Bagley & Pritchard, 2000; Friendship, Beech, & Browne, 2002; Koss, 1992; Lees, 1996; Myhill & Allen, 2002; Russell, 1984), we (W. L. Marshall & Barbaree, 1988) showed that official figures can, nevertheless, provide a sound basis for determining treatment effects. W. L. Marshall and Barbaree (1988) were able to access extensive unofficial reports of the sexual abuse of children held by police and child protection agencies when they were evaluating their community-based program. In this study, matched untreated subjects who attended the clinic for evaluation only were available as the comparison group. For both groups, unofficial and official data were available. Comparing the unofficial data with official information revealed that the proportionate difference between these two data sets was the same for both treated and untreated offenders, although in both data sets the untreated offenders had significantly higher reoffense rates (W. L. Marshall & Barbaree, 1988). We believe these findings indicate that official recidivism data (when derived from an adequate national database) can serve effectively as an index of outcome in studies of treatment effectiveness. The majority of researchers appear to agree with this view.

Hanson et al. (2002) pointed out that it is necessary not only to distinguish different types of research designs but also to distinguish different types of treatment. As a result, they compared the observed outcomes "between older and current treatments" (Hanson et al., 2002, p. 173) in which current meant "any treatment still being offered, or any cognitive–behavioral treatment (CBT) delivered after 1980" (p. 173). Although we appreciate the difficulties these reviewers faced, it is clear that programs described as CBT show considerable variability. For example, W. L. Marshall and Anderson (2000) examined the outcome of CBT programs that were described as relapse prevention (RP) based. Each of the programs we identified in the literature varied from each other on several important features, both with respect to the CBT elements and with respect to the degree to which the program actually had RP features. Thus, Hanson et al.'s (2002) report on the relative effectiveness of CBT versus earlier approaches did not rely on a uniform set of CBT programs. If so-called CBT programs differ on important treatment features, then there would be no reason to suppose they would produce uniform results. In this sense, treatment outcomes studies in the sexual offender field may not yet be ready for meta-analytic studies, but for the moment we set aside this concern and report what three meta-analyses have revealed.

Hanson et al. (2002) found that across all the studies ($k = 43$) in this analysis, the average recidivism rates for sexual offenses, over an approximately 5-year risk period, was 12.3% for the treated group and 16.8% for the untreated group. Similar differences were observed for general (i.e., nonsexual) recidivism, where 27.9% of the treated and 39.2% of the untreated sexual offender subjects reoffended. This latter observation is a quite welcome but unexpected effect of sexual offender specific treatment, suggesting that many features of such treatment programs may be applicable to other types of offenders.

When Hanson et al. (2002) compared CBT programs ($k = 13$) with earlier approaches, they found the older programs to have negligible benefits. The CBT programs resulted in 9.9% sexual recidivism and 32.0% nonsexual recidivism versus 17.4% and 51.0%, respectively, for the untreated group. Interestingly, the untreated rate of 17.4% sexual recidivism turns out to be an approximately consistent observation across the three meta-analyses we describe. This is much lower than the public expects based on media reports, which of course focus almost entirely on the highest risk offenders.

Lösel and Schmucker (2005) had access to more reports ($k = 80$) than did Hanson et al. (2002), although they used essentially the same standards for entry into their meta-analysis. They reported results similar to those found by Hanson et al. Once again, the average sexual recidivism rate for the untreated men over a 5-year follow-up was 17.5%, whereas of the treated subjects, only 11.1% reoffended. Lösel and Schmucker also observed benefits for sexual offender treatment on the propensity of these clients to commit nonsexual crimes; the treated subjects reoffended nonsexually at a rate of 22.4%, compared with 32.5% for the untreated sexual offenders. In particular, they noted a reduction in nonsexual violent offenses: 11.8% of the untreated sexual offenders committed violent offenses over the follow-up period as against 6.6% of the treated clients.

More recently, Hanson et al. (2009) reported a further meta-analysis. In this study of 23 outcome reports, the authors were interested not only in treatment effects but also in the influence of Andrews's (Andrews, Bonta, & Hoge, 1990) principles of effective offender treatment. As noted earlier in this book, Andrews and his colleagues have identified three principles, each of which (they have shown) exerts a positive influence on treatment effectiveness. Hanson et al. (2009) again found that treatment for sexual offenders reduced sexual recidivism rates, this time from 19.2% to 10.9%, with the familiar spillover effect on these clients' nonsexual reoffending propensities; 48.3% for the untreated group versus 31.8% for the treated group committed further nonsexual offenses. They also demonstrated that those programs that adhered to Andrews's risk, needs, and responsivity principles produced the greatest effects. However, the risk principle, which indicates treatment is most effectively applied to high-risk offenders, generated the weakest effect, whereas the responsivity principle generated the greatest effect. This latter observation is consistent with our claim that the way in which treatment is delivered, and adjusted to each individual's learning style, is critical to producing maximum benefits.

There have been other meta-analyses (M. A. Alexander, 1999; Gallagher, Wilson, Hirschfield, Coggeshall, & MacKenzie, 1999; Hall, 1995), but most reviewers consider these studies to have not been as discriminating as they should have been in selecting reports. Except for one of these other meta-analyses (Gallagher et al., 1999), the effect sizes for all reports (including Hanson et al., 2002, 2009; Lösel & Schmucker, 2005) fall within the small to medium range (ES = 0.1 to 0.28). For the most part, these reflect significant but modest effects. W. L. Marshall and McGuire (2003) showed that these effect sizes were equivalent to those generated by the treatment of nonsexual offenders and by medical treatments for several types of serious health problems. If we accept that the three meta-analyses we have described have produced satisfactory appraisals, then it is reasonable to conclude that overall sexual offender treatment is effective.

It is important to note that in each of these meta-analyses, there were studies (including some CBT reports) that failed to demonstrate effectiveness. One outstanding failure, which is often cited by those who want to claim that treatment is not effective, was the study reported by Marques, Weideranders, Day, Nelson, and van Ommeren (2005) of an RP program that was initially implemented in the mid-1980s. An examination of the details of this program (see W. L. Marshall & Marshall, 2007) revealed that few of the currently known criminogenic factors were targeted (which is to be expected given its startup date) and the restrictions of its RCT design constrained the therapist's abilities to adopt the flexibility necessary for effective therapy. Failures of this and other early programs (e.g., the report by Rice et al., 1991) seem to us to be expected in a field in which little evidence was available at the time of their implementation to guide the selection of treatment targets and to identify appropriate therapeutic approaches. Indeed, these failures provide some justification for the changes that have been evident in the treatment of sexual offenders over the past 20 years.

Correctional Service of Canada Studies

The Correctional Service of Canada (CSC) provides treatment for sexual offenders both in prison and in the community at postrelease. CSC triages sexual offenders to high intensity (for the high and very high risk/needs offenders), moderate intensity (for the moderate-high, moderate, and moderate-low risk/needs offenders), and low intensity treatment. Furthermore, CSC provides manuals to guide each of these programs and requires all treatment providers to undergo specialized therapy training for work with sexual offenders. It should be noted that RPS's programs are exempt from the requirement to follow CSC manuals, although all our staff have completed CSC training. Because CSC also insists on having all its rehabilitation programs based on sound research, it is expected that each program will report a long-term outcome study. Fortunately, Canada is one of the few countries in the world that has, since 1966, instituted a satisfactory national database of offenses, the Canadian Police Information Centre (CPIC). Police and prosecutors are required to enter into this database all charges (even if withdrawn) and convictions for all crimes, so it is a reasonably complete set of information. Researchers can get permission to access CPIC, and several CSC staff have done so to evaluate the long-term effects of various programs. We report some of these outcome studies relevant to sexual offender treatment.

The Regional Treatment Centre (Ontario, Canada), which is part of CSC, provides a sexual offender program for the very highest risk/needs offenders and has been in operation since 1973. Looman, Abracen, and Nicholaichuk (2000) evaluated this program by comparing treated subjects with a matched group of untreated offenders, although this was not an RCT study but rather an incidental assignment design. Over a period of 10 years at risk in the community, 23.6% of the treated clients and 51.7% of the untreated comparison group reoffended sexually. Also using an incidental design, Nicholaichuk, Gordon, Gu, and Wong (2000) reported the effects of the CSC program at the Regional Psychiatric Centre (Saskatoon), which primarily targets high-risk incarcerated sexual offenders. They found that treated offenders had a recidivism rate of 14.5%, whereas 33.2% of the untreated men reoffended sexually. Barbaree and his colleagues (Barbaree, Langton, & Peacock, 2003; Langton, Barbaree, Harkins, & Peacock, 2006) also found significant differences between treated and untreated sexual offenders in the CSC program operated at Warkworth Institution in Ontario, Canada. Although Barbaree et al. (2003) had fewer offenders in the lowest risk/needs category, the distribution of risk/needs in their study approximated the incidence apparent in all sexual offenders in CSC institutions across the country. The 468 treated offenders in Barbaree et al's study were found to have a sexual reoffense rate of 11.1% over a 5.9 year follow-up, compared with an expected rate (based on actuarial estimates) of 18%.

ROCKWOOD PSYCHOLOGICAL SERVICES STUDIES

As discussed in the introduction chapter, RPS provides treatment in two CSC prisons: Millhaven Institution (a maximum security prison), where we provide the RPS Preparatory Program; and Bath Institution (a medium security prison), where we provide both the RPS Primary Program and the RPS Deniers' Program. We describe the evaluations of these three programs separately. In each outcome evaluation, the research assistants relied not only on CPIC data (all charges and convictions) but also on the Offender Management System, which records all suspensions and revocations of parole and the reasons behind these decisions.

RPS Preparatory Program

The goals for the RPS Preparatory Program are to (a) increase the motivation of sexual offenders to address their problems, (b) enhance their optimism about their future, and (c) convince them that they can manage their lives effectively. The evaluation of the RPS Preparatory Program was conducted by CSC staff independently of any RPS staff. To determine whether the program achieved these goals, the following scales were administered at both the commencement of treatment and after treatment was complete: (a) the University of Rhode Island Change Assessment (McConnaughy, Prochaska, & Velicer, 1983), (b) the Adult State Hope Scale (Snyder et al., 1996), (c) the Adult Dispositional Hope Scale (Snyder et al., 1991), and (d) the Self-Efficacy Scale (Sherer et al., 1982). A group of 26 sexual offenders who completed the program were assessed on these scales.

In addition, the scores on the Treatment Readiness Scale (Serin & Kennedy, 1997) of a larger group ($N = 94$) who completed the program were compared with a matched group ($N = 94$) of sexual offenders who did not enter the Preparatory Program. These data were collected on the treated subjects once they had completed the program, whereas the comparison group was assessed at the same time in the same institution. The aim was to determine whether the Preparatory Program had achieved its goal of properly preparing clients for the subsequent full treatment program. All of the members of the comparison group subsequently received a full treatment program, as did the preparatory participants.

As an additional measure, the therapists in the subsequent programs were asked how quickly each client engaged in the treatment process. These therapists were blind to which of their group members had previously completed the Preparatory Program. Although these data were not collected in a fully systematic way, all the responses we were able to obtain from the therapists indicated that they quickly recognized which of their clients had done the Preparatory Program. They said these offenders were immediately engaged in treatment and from the outset were actively involved in all group discussions. The impression of these therapists was that offenders who had completed the Preparatory Program got more out of their full program because they were involved in addressing their issues from the first treatment session onward. Clients who had not done the Preparatory Program, these therapists said, took far longer to engage and some were never as fully involved as were the graduates of the Preparatory Program.

Finally, the two matched groups ($N = 94$ each), of which one completed both the Preparatory Program and a subsequent full program and the other completed only a full program, were followed up after release from prison.

Table 5.1 describes the motivational and outcome data for the RPS Preparatory Program. As can be seen, the data demonstrate the benefits on all issues, including particularly the motivational features. The fact that the difference in sexual reconviction rates is not statistically significant is to be expected, given the low base rate in the comparison group, but even this difference is clearly in the hoped-for direction. The positive reductions in both recidivism and returns to prison for other reasons, evident in the Preparatory Program participants compared with the other offenders, is presumably a result of the immediate and greater engagement in the full treatment program of the former clients.

TABLE 5.1
Outcome Data for the RPS Preparatory Program

Measure	Pretreatment ($N = 26$)	Posttreatment ($N = 26$)	Significance
	Motivational measures		
Self-efficacy	86.1 (12.89)	91.2 (8.82)	$p < .01$
Trait hope	23.3 (4.32)	25.0 (2.91)	$p < .05$
State hope	30.0 (6.60)	34.5 (4.63)	$p < .01$
URICA			
- Contemplation	88.5%	46.2%	
- Action	7.7%	53.8%	$p < .001$
- Maintenance	3.8%	0%	
	Preparatory group ($N = 94$)	Comparison group ($N = 94$)	Significance
Treatment readiness	38.17 (12.04)	28.5 (11.39)	$p < .05$
Variable	Preparatory group ($N = 94$)	Comparison group ($N = 94$)	Significance
	Comparative recidivism data		
Any return to custody	10.6%	22.1%	$p < .05$
Any reconviction	4.3%	12.8%	$p < .05$
Violent reconviction	1.0%	8.1%	$p < .05$
Sexual reconviction	1.0%	4.7%	ns

Note. All of the above data are derived from an appraisal reported by L. E. Marshall, Marshall, Fernandez, Malcolm, & Moulden (2008). RPS = Rockwood Psychological Services; URICA = University of Rhode Island Change Assessment.

RPS Primary Program

The RPS Primary Program has been in operation since 1991, and although still evolving, it was originally based on earlier RPS programs in four other CSC institutions in Ontario, Canada, and in 1991 was a match for the RPS community program (formerly The Kingston Sexual Behaviour Clinic; W. L. Marshall & Barbaree, 1988). Two research assistants, both of whom were naive about sexual offender treatment and had no expectations about the likely outcome, were hired to search and report the status (offense free or not) of all clients. The first research assistant determined the reoffense rates up to 2006, whereas second did so up to the year 2009. A comparison of the data extracted independently by these two research assistants, each of whom was unaware of the other's data, revealed exact matches in the clients who reoffended up to 2006.

The first study assessed the offenders' status at an average of 5.4 years postrelease, whereas the second study reported reoffense rates at an average of 8.4 years at risk in the community. The results of both studies are shown in Table 5.2. Note that the recidivism data included actual convictions plus any charges that were withdrawn, as well as revocations or suspensions of parole that reflected either a reoffense or a finding that the offender had placed himself at risk to reoffend. As can be seen from the table, at both 5.4-year and 8.4-year follow-up, treatment was effective in reducing recidivism for both sexual and nonsexual crimes; at the 8.4-year follow-up, it was also shown to be effective in reducing violent offending. Further analyses of both sets of these data (i.e., the 5.4- and 8.4-year follow-up data) revealed that the program had approximately equal effects for rapists and child molesters. We believe this observation is important because our strategy has always been to mix our treatment groups for offender types, a strategy that all CSC programs and most HMPS programs appear to follow. Some other treatment providers consider this unwise, although they have not been able to explain to us why.

Additional analyses were conducted on the 8.4-year data to identify factors that might predict reoffending. Seventy clients scored within the psycho-

TABLE 5.2
Outcome Data for the RPS Primary Program

	Treated	Expected[a]
5.4 year follow-up (N = 535)		
Sexual offenses	3.2%	16.8%
General offenses	13.6%	40.0%
8.4 year follow-up (N = 535)		
Sexual offenses	5.6%	23.8%
Violent offenses	8.4%	34.8%

Note. RPS = Rockwood Psychological Services.
[a]Based on the STATIC-99 and the Rapid Risk Assessment for Sexual Offence Recidivism.

pathic range (greater than or equal to 25) on Hare's (1991) Psychopathy Checklist–Revised (PCL-R). This indicates that approximately 13% of the sample scored within the psychopathic range, which is a percentage consistent with unpublished studies of CSC incarcerated sexual offenders (R. Serin, personal communication, May 1, 2009). Only one of these psychopathic sexual offenders reoffended. In further analyses, examining the predictive power of categorizing our clients as psychopaths or not, we identified those who scored either 25 and above or 30 and above on the PCL-R. The former criterion is used by the CSC and has been shown to identify the same level of psychopathy as is identified by a score of 30 for United States criminals (Cooke & Michie, 1999). Categorizing our offenders as psychopaths or nonpsychopaths using either one of these criteria failed to predict sexual recidivism (area under the curve [AUC] = .53, p = .77; AUC = .55, p = .64, respectively), nor did entering PCL-R scores as a continuous variable (AUC = .62, p = .16). However, entering the therapists' posttreatment ratings of progress did predict sexual reoffending (AUC = .64; p < .05). This latter observation supports the use of carefully constructed scales (see appendix for our Therapist Rating Scale–2) that provide a basis for the therapists to rate the benefits derived from treatment by sexual offenders.

Given our data on psychopaths, a few words of comment seem called for. There is considerable controversy regarding the amenability of psychopaths to treatment. Some studies have indicated that psychopaths' risk to reoffend is actually made worse by treatment (Hare, Clarke, Grann, & Thornton, 2000; Looman, Abracen, Serin, & Marquis, 2005; Rice, Harris, & Cormier, 1992), and as a result, some programs exclude psychopaths from sexual offender treatment (Beech et al., 2005). Harkins and Beech (2007a), however, pointed to problems with these studies and noted a study by Langton et al. (2006) showing that psychopathic sexual offenders who were rated as having done well in treatment had significantly lower reoffense rates than did psychopaths who were judged to have done poorly in treatment. Several authors have recently challenged the idea that psychopaths are intractable to treatment (D'Silva, Duggan, & McCarthy, 2004; Loving, 2002; Stalans, 2004; Wong, 2000), and in fact Salekin (2002) demonstrated, in a meta-analysis of 42 studies of psychopaths, a clear benefit for treatment.

The data reported previously for the RPS Primary Program add to this list of studies suggesting a more optimistic outlook for the treatment of psychopaths. Our view is that psychopathy is a responsivity factor. This view has led to the adoption by RPS programs of a strategy for treating psychopathic sexual offenders. Because it is typical that only approximately one in eight RPS clients meets criteria for psychopathy, we ensure that our treatment group of 10 includes no more than one psychopath. When a psychopath enters the RPS group (which is an open-ended or rolling group), he may try to be disruptive or to control the group; typically, this is vigorously resisted by the other nine group members with support from the therapist. Because the psychopath's efforts fail to get him what he wants, and because psychopaths are maximally responsive to short-term consequences, he typically soon gives up his disruptive behavior and becomes compliant with the group's operating style (cohesive, mutually supportive, and compassionately challenging). We believe it is the adoption of this strategy with psychopaths, along with the therapist adapting his or her style to the psychopath's response style, that results in the benefits these clients derive from our program.

RPS Deniers' Program

In the 7 years between 1998 and 2005, 56 categorical deniers (i.e., clients who claimed they never committed a sexual offense) completed the RPS Deniers' Program and have been released into the community for sufficient time to assess recidivism rates (L. E. Marshall & Marshall, 2008). Over half (52.5%) were released at two thirds of their sentence (i.e., statutory release, at which time parole is automatic unless the offender is judged to be at very high risk to reoffend), 40% were released on full parole prior to their automatic release date, and 7.5% were released on day parole (this involves release to a community halfway house prior to full parole). These data reflect something of a change in the National Parole Board's response to categorical deniers. Prior to the commencement of the RPS Deniers' Program, the majority of these men were held in prison until at least their statutory release date (i.e., two thirds of sentence), and many were not released until sentence completion. Apparently the National Parole Board takes a positive view of the benefits of the RPS Deniers' Program, a viewpoint apparently justified by the data.

As in the evaluations of the other RPS programs, follow-up analyses of recidivism among these men were based on an appraisal by a naive research assistant of the national database of offenses (CPIC) and the records of parole suspensions or revocations. It was found that 10% of the deniers who completed the program breached their parole conditions, but only 2.5% were identified as having reoffended sexually. Unfortunately, there are no available untreated deniers who could be used as a comparison group. However, the expected rate of recidivism among the treated group, although lower than the RPS admitting offenders, is still above 13%. The results of this study, although preliminary, are certainly promising. We are in the process of expanding our recidivism study as more data become available.

RPS Community Program

Finally, we describe the outcome for the RPS community-based program (formerly the Kingston Sexual Behaviour Clinic), which accepted sexual

TABLE 5.3
Outcome Data for the RPS Community Program

	Treated[a]	Untreated[a]	
Study 1			
Nonfamilial child molesters	13.3%	42.9%	
Incest offenders	8.0%	21.7%	

	Treatment A[b]	Treatment B[b]	Untreated[b]
Study 2			
Exhibitionists	23.5%	39.1%	57.1%

Note. Recidivism rates are the combined total of reoffenders identified in both official and unofficial records. All data are extracted from W. L. Marshall & Barbaree (1988) and W. L. Marshall, Eccles, & Barbaree (1991). RPS = Rockwood Psychological Services.
[a]These recidivism data reflect rates that are between 2.5 and 2.7 times higher than official records alone.
[b]These recidivism data reflect rates that are between 3.1 and 3.4 times higher than official records alone.

offenders referred from several sources: the National Parole Service referred sexual offenders released on parole from CSC institutions; the Provincial Probation Service referred offenders who were either released from prison or diverted by the courts for treatment; and Child Protection Services referred child molesters who were under their authority. W. L. Marshall and Barbaree (1988) compared 68 treated sexual offenders with 58 untreated offenders, where the latter attended the clinic for assessment only. Combining unofficial information of accusations of sexual offending held in police and child protection agencies files with official data from CPIC, Marshall and Babaree found that the treated offenders had significantly lower reoffense rates over a 45-month follow-up than did the untreated clients. Table 5.3 describes these data. It should be noted that these combined data reflect an almost three-fold greater rate of reoffending than do the official data only. W. L. Marshall, Eccles, and Barbaree (1991) similarly demonstrated effective RPS community treatment for exhibitionists by comparing a comprehensive program (i.e., one that targeted a range of problematic features) with a more restrictive program that focused primarily on deviant attitudes and interests.

CONCLUSION

As revealed by our review of the literature on evaluations of the effectiveness of sexual offender programs to achieve their stated goals of altering the criminogenic features of the offenders, there is limited but encouraging evidence that some sexual offender programs are effective in this respect. However, it is also clear that more careful and specific analyses are required.

We need to have a solid body of evidence showing that the application of specific procedures can indeed induce changes in all the specific treatment targets. When this has been demonstrated, and these procedures are applied in a program that embodies the effective process features outlined in Chapter 3, we can feel more optimistic about the likelihood that such a program will reduce recidivism.

In consideration of the overall data on the effects of treatment for sexual offenders, as well as in particular the demonstrated effectiveness of CSC programs and RPS programs, we believe that treatment can be, and has been shown to be, effective with sexual offenders. Treatment effectiveness, as we saw in the appraisal of the RPS Primary Program, appears to be equally effective for each type of sexual offender, and the RPS community program has demonstrated similar reductions across offender types.

This is not to say that all such programs, even all CBT programs, are or will be effective. There are many factors, over and above the adoption of a particular approach (e.g., CBT) or the deployment of specific procedures, that influence the effectiveness of treatment. As we showed in Chapter 3, therapeutic processes (i.e., therapist features, the therapeutic alliance, the group climate) account for a significant amount of the variance in change scores in the treatment of sexual offenders. Less than optimal application of these process features will clearly reduce treatment effectiveness. In the general clinical literature, it has been shown that specific procedures for modifying problematic features of clients accounts for approximately 15% of the variance in outcome (see Serran & Marshall, 2010, for a review). Combining the use of effective process features with the use of effective procedures will, therefore, account for such a significant amount of the variance in outcome that little will be left to explain in terms of the therapeutic orientation (i.e., CBT). We should be cautious, then, in overinterpreting the observation in Hanson et al.'s (2002) report that CBT programs were the only ones found to be effective. Perhaps they were the only ones found to be effective because, since the 1980s, they have been primarily the only ones subjected to careful evaluations.

No doubt, however, there are other features of treatment, some of which are as yet unidentified, that can facilitate or impede the achievement of therapeutic goals. Among those features that we now know are critical to an overall evaluation of treatment programs are refusal rates and dropouts from treatment. Both these rates vary considerably across programs and constitute a potential threat to the meaning of outcome studies. For instance, Mann and Webster (2002) reported that refusal rates for HMPS programs varied from 8% to 76%. In the RPS Primary Program, 96.2% of eligible offenders are persuaded to enter treatment; clearly, refusals are not a problem for RPS programs. Of course, if a program has a high refusal rate, then it will fail to treat many offenders and may be left with those clients least in need of treatment. It has been reported (K. D. Browne et al., 1998; Marques et al., 1994) that sexual offenders who drop out of treatment have higher reoffense rates than those who refuse to enter treatment, so it is essential to reduce dropouts. In the RPS Primary Program, 95.8% who enter treatment complete the program. Of the 4.2% dropouts, the majority were removed from the program for reasons beyond their or our control (e.g., death, deportation, or release at expiry of sentence). In both these respects (refusals and dropouts), RPS programs display a low threat to the integrity of their outcome evaluations.

Overall, we believe the available data offer at the very least encouraging support for the idea that sexual offender treatment can be effective in reducing reoffending and thereby save further innocent people from being the victims of sexual abuse. In Smallbone, Marshall, and Wortley's (2008) review of the possible strategies for preventing child sexual abuse, for example, the authors described treatment for the offenders as one of the most promising strategies. We encourage other treatment providers to evaluate their programs, and we (W. L. Marshall & Marshall, 2007) have suggested design alternatives to the use of the RCT, which, for at least practical reasons, can rarely be implemented. We are optimistic that the continuing and growing effectiveness of the treatment of sexual offenders will contribute in a significant way to making society safer.

The three chapters in Part II of this volume outline the application of the RPS treatment approach to three programs. First, we describe the RPS Preparatory Program that aims at familiarizing sexual offenders with the goals and processes of treatment, at instilling optimism in them about the benefits they will derive from treatment, and at motivating them to fully engage in subsequent treatment. Next, we describe the RPS Primary Program that addresses all obstacles to treatment engagement and all presently known criminogenic features in a positive motivational way. Finally, we outline the RPS novel approach to treating sexual offenders who categorically deny having committed an offense.

II

THE ROCKWOOD PSYCHOLOGICAL SERVICES PROGRAMS

6

ROCKWOOD PREPARATORY PROGRAM

We have found, as have so many other treatment providers, that when first offered treatment a significant number of sexual offenders either refuse to enter the program or have to be persuaded to enter and then do so with some reluctance or reserve. In addition, some who enter treatment later withdraw or are removed because of uncooperative behavior. Finally, among those who do complete treatment, some fail to satisfactorily attain the goals of the program, again because of a failure to fully engage. Although our positively based approach both to the invitation to enter treatment and during the course of treatment meant that the refusal rates for our program, the dropout rates, and the failures to attain the goals of treatment were lower than for most programs, all these rates were nevertheless higher than we wished. As a result, we designed a preparatory program aimed at overcoming these problems. In this chapter, we provide a description of that program, but first we briefly review the literature on the problems that prevent sexual offenders from entering and satisfactorily completing treatment.

Getting sexual offenders to fully engage in the process of change is key to reducing reoffending. This has become clear from research on the therapeutic process with sexual offenders (Beech & Fordham, 1997; Beech & Hamilton-Giachritsis, 2005; Burton & Cerar, 2005; Drapeau et al., 2004; W. L. Marshall, Serran, Fernandez, et al., 2003; W. L. Marshall, Serran, Moulden, et al., 2002; Pfäfflin et al., 2005; Simons et al., 2005), as well as from current theoretical approaches to treatment such as the good lives model (Ward & Marshall, 2004), in addition to motivational interviewing (W. R. Miller & Rollnick, 2002), research on dynamic risk factors (e.g., Hanson & Bussière, 1998; Hanson & Morton-Bourgon, 2005), and outcome evaluations (e.g., Marques, Weideranders, Day, Nelson, & van Ommeren, 2005). Some sexual offenders do not profit from treatment because they refuse to take part, drop out of treatment (either by personal choice or by removal by treatment staff), or simply go through the motions and fail to change. Marques et al. (2005) described this latter group of sexual offenders as those who did not "get it" (i.e., show the necessary changes), and they demonstrated that these offenders were at higher risk of reoffending than were those who effectively participated in treatment (i.e., "get it"). We consider the evidence on these obstacles to the effective entry into treatment.

Refusers

There are many issues related to successful completion of a sexual offender treatment program. Because treatment for sexual offenders can reduce recidivism (see Chapter 5, this volume), it is important to examine those sexual offenders who refuse to participate as they remain at whatever risk level they are assessed as having. Unfortunately, there are few empirical studies of treatment refusers and even fewer addressing sexual offender treatment refusers. Seager, Jellicoe, and Dhaliwal (2004) reported a refusal rate of 13% for their sexual offender program in a Canadian federal prison. Most important, they found refusers to have a higher recidivism rate (42%) as measured by any subsequent conviction for a sexual or violent offense than did those who completed treatment (4%). Other examinations of treatment refusal in sexual offenders have found similar rates. For example, in a study in the United States, Jones, Pelissier, and Klein-Saffran (2006) reported that of 404 treatment candidates, 16% were refused entry by treatment staff, and 22% refused an offer of treatment. Jones et al. found that it was only scores on a measure of motivation for treatment that predicted both those who were refused treatment by staff and those who refused to enter treatment.

In a study examining treatment refusal in Her Majesty's Prison Service (i.e., the prison system serving the United Kingdom), Mann and Webster (2002) reported rates of refusal in various institutions ranging from 8% to 76%, with an average of 52% across all institutions providing sexual offender treatment. Mann and Webster further examined these refusal rates by comparing three groups of sexual offenders who were offered a space in a treatment program: those who entered treatment, those who refused treatment because they claimed they were innocent, and those who acknowledged that they had committed an offense but still refused to enter a program. Qualitative analyses of interviews with this latter group, guided by research on refusal from the general psychotherapy and medical literature, revealed several reasons for refusing treatment. Some indicated a lack of trust in professionals. This lack of trust no doubt resulted from their experience with professionals during assessments for the court at the time of prosecution and may be reflected in their expectation that treatment staff would be punitive toward them (Stukenberg, 2001). Other offenders expressed fear that entering treatment would reveal to other inmates that they were sexual offenders and that, as a consequence, they would be exposed to harassment or violence. Some expressed concern that treatment would not be effective or that the process might cause them emotional distress. However, the most commonly expressed concern was that treatment would simply focus on details about their offense. Half of the offenders who indicated these concerns said they would enter treatment if it focused on broader goals that would give them a better life.

As a result of their findings, Mann and Webster (2002) suggested some simple strategies to overcome the refusal among sexual offenders to enter treatment, although many of the issues are most likely relevant to other types of offenders and to psychotherapy in general. These authors suggested informing nontreatment staff on the efficacy and methods of interventions for sexual offenders so that these staff may encourage sexual offenders to engage in the process of change. Suggestions for reducing refusal in sexual offenders included process issues reflective of motivational strategies, such as providing information about the efficacy, methods, and content of treatment and starting to build a therapeutic alliance prior to the offer of treatment by establishing rapport and building trust. Although the reasons for refusal are important to consider prior to treatment, they are also likely to be related to within-treatment resistance. The Rockwood Psychological Services (RPS) Preparatory Program seeks to overcome the reasons for refusal reported by Mann and Webster (2002) and to build motivation for treatment both prior to and within the program. The methods we use to do so are described in the following section.

Attrition

About one third to one half of medical and psychotherapy patients do not comply with the treatment that is prescribed or recommended (Melamed & Szor, 1999). Similarly, some sexual offenders who enter treatment drop out before successfully completing treatment. This group includes those who withdraw from the program as well as those who are removed from treatment by therapy staff. There are many reasons why sexual offenders drop out of treatment. Some incarcerated sexual offenders are unable to complete treatment because they delay entering a program until shortly before they are released, whereas some others quit because they are unsatisfied with the treatment methods or with the treatment environment. Some correctional services withhold treatment from offenders until immediately prior to release, believing that the shorter time period between treatment and reintegration into the community best prepares the offender for release. Unfortunately, this can also leave insufficient time to achieve the targets of treatment. Some offenders may drop out of treatment because of changes in their medical or psychiatric functioning, whereas others may be removed from the group by treatment staff as a result of their resistance to change or because of inappropriate or disruptive behaviors. Whatever the causes of dropout, it is a serious problem because the reoffense rate for treatment dropouts is reported to be higher than for those who do not enter treatment at all (Abel et al., 1988; K. D. Browne et al., 1998; Cook, Fox, Weaver, & Rooth, 1991; Hanson et al., 2002; Lee, Proeve, Lancaster, & Jackson, 1996; Marques et al., 1994; McGrath, Cumming, Livingston, & Hoke, 2003; Miner & Dwyer, 1995).

Attrition rates in sexual offender programs are often high. In an examination of all sexual offenders treated in Minnesota in 1992, McPherson, Chein, Van Maren, and Swenson (1994) reported that 383 (25%) out of 1,551 offenders dropped out before completing treatment. Forty percent of these dropouts were removed by staff for various reasons, such as failure to make progress, denial of having committed their offense, or rule violations. In a community program in Australia, Lee et al. (1996) found similarly high attrition rates. The overall dropout rate in this program was 36%. Of those dropouts, 67% stopped attending treatment, 28% were removed for program rule violations, and 5% were sent to prison. In his meta-analysis, Hall (1995) found that one third of sexual offenders dropped out before completing treatment. Shaw, Herkov, and Greer (1995) noted that 86% of sexual offenders failed to complete a prison-based program. Finally, Marques et al. (1994), in their report of California's Sex Offender Treatment and Evaluation Project, indicated that 18.9% of offenders who entered treatment dropped out before completion.

Although attrition rates as high as 80% have been reported (Proulx et al., 2004), there has been limited research aimed at discerning why sexual offenders drop out of, or are removed from, programs. Proulx et al. (2004) examined this issue and distinguished between pretreatment and within-treatment factors that influenced treatment withdrawal. Pretreatment factors included, among other things, low self-esteem, a lack of empathy, and poor coping. The within-treatment factors that influenced attrition rates were minimal commitment to treatment and a failure to engage effectively. Other researchers have found a variety of factors to be related to withdrawal from sexual offender treatment. For example, antisocial personality disorder (Moore, Bergman, & Knox, 1999), having adult victims (Beyko & Wong, 2005), and psychopathy (Olver & Wong, 2009) have been related to dropping out of treatment. Ware and Bright (2008) reported that withdrawal from treatment was related to significant levels of denial and minimization, an emotional coping style, and a greater external locus of control. Nunes and Cortoni (2007) used a measure of sexual offense recidivism to demonstrate that it was higher scores on general criminality items, but not on items reflecting sexual deviance, that were predictive of treatment attrition.

As noted previously, those sexual offenders who drop out of treatment typically have higher recidivism rates than do those who refuse treatment and, of course, higher rates than those who complete treatment. Thus, attrition is a serious problem that needs to be addressed as part of an overall treatment approach. Although various researchers (Abel et al., 1988; K. D. Browne et al., 1998; Chaffin, 1994; Cook et al., 1991; Geer, Becker, Gray, & Krauss, 2001; Marques et al., 1994; Miner & Dwyer, 1995; Shaw et al., 1995) have reported numerous client features that predict attrition, most of the features reported by these authors are unchangeable. Lee et al. (1996), on the other hand, suggested that lack of motivation may be the primary factor. In response to their idea, Lee et al. provided individual treatment initiated prior to involvement in group treatment that was aimed at enhancing motivation. As a result of this intervention, these researchers found significant reductions in attrition; a base rate of 42% went down to 29% among those offenders who had the pretreatment motivational intervention.

Proulx et al.'s (2004) problematic within-treatment factors (i.e., minimal commitment and a failure to engage) may be heightened in programs that consider it necessary to overcome denial and minimizations as a first step in treatment (Beech & Fisher, 2002; Mark, 1992; Prendergast, 1991). These therapists contended that an offender's failure to admit to all of the details of the offenses provided in official documents will prevent progress on all other treatment targets. Consequently, both Mark (1992) and Prendergast (1991) recommended a strongly confrontational approach to challenging denial, which they suggested should be maintained throughout treatment. These recommendations are consistent with those of Salter (1988) and Wyre (1989) that we mentioned in the Introduction. Confrontational approaches to treatment, however, have been demonstrated to be counterproductive to the goals of treatment for sexual offenders (W. L. Marshall, Serran, Fernandez, et al., 2003).

Research has shown that people with problem behaviors that have positive short-term effects but negative long-term effects typically progress through several stages of their commitment to change, each of which is characterized by greater or lesser motivation to change (Prochaska & DiClemente, 1982). DiClemente (1991) noted that a confrontational style is likely to be damaging to clients in one or another of the early stages of change, particularly the precontemplation and contemplation stages, but also possibly in the first steps of the action stage. He suggested that harsh challenges in these early stages are likely to generate resistance and noncompliance. Sexual offenders entering (or considering entering) treatment typically have low self-esteem (W. L. Marshall, Anderson, & Champagne, 1997), and studies have shown that a confrontational approach produces hostility in those high in self-esteem but withdrawal in those low in self-esteem (Baumeister, 1993). Challenging the sexual offender's remarks in a confrontational manner can be expected to lead to either disruptive behaviors, resulting in the client dropping out of or being removed from treatment, or a passive stance that results in a failure to achieve the goals of treatment. Neither of these reactions is conducive to a positive treatment outcome.

Attrition is clearly a problem in sexual offender treatment programs. Those sexual offenders who either withdraw from treatment or are removed by the therapist have higher reoffense rates than do those who refuse to enter treatment. Research has identified some important features that characterize dropouts and although some of these features (e.g., psychopathy, general criminality, having adult victims) are either unchangeable or difficult to change, other features (e.g., denial, poor coping, external locus of control) seem amenable to change. In particular, a lack of motivation to engage in change processes appears to be a modifiable predictor of attrition. One of the main targets in the RPS Preparatory Program is to enhance motivation for change, and in this respect the program appears to be successful (see Chapter 5).

In the RPS Primary Program described in Chapter 7, we have characteristically had low refusal and low attrition rates. This means that most of the sexual offenders who are offered treatment subsequently enter and complete the program. However, not all sexual offenders who enter this program are highly motivated for change; the majority are externally motivated. Some sexual offenders enter treatment because the parole board demands that they complete a sexual-offender-specific treatment program before being considered for early release. The same rules apply to transfers to a reduced security institution and even to earning visiting privileges, particularly conjugal visits. As a consequence, some sexual offenders may be motivated to complete the program but not necessarily to engage in the process of change. Engaging these offenders takes time away from addressing the treatment targets and presents therapists with difficult challenges. In fact, dealing with unmotivated, resistant, and difficult clients has been linked to therapist burnout (Ellerby, 1998). We believe that motivational strategies will not only reduce attrition rates but will also encourage resistant offenders to enter treatment. These effects should also reduce therapist burnout, although simply adopting a motivational approach is also likely to reduce burnout.

OTHER PRETREATMENT STRATEGIES

Various approaches to the pretreatment enhancement of motivation for change have been described in the general clinical literature. These have included posters, flyers, and information sessions designed to describe treatment and allay fears. In addition, there have been groups designed for various purposes, such as enhancing academic interest (Mayer, 2008), getting people ready for substance abuse treatment (Bell, 2008), improving responses to health-care recommendations (Huber & Gramer, 1991; McGlinn & Jackson, 1989), and preparing people for management-skills training (Friday, 1989). All of these methods have shown positive effects on a number of different measures of success, such as enhanced compliance and motivation for subsequent treatment or training. Research has demonstrated that programs designed to introduce and prepare participants for treatment increases the effectiveness for various psychological problems in both individual treatment (M. A. Davidson, 1998; Hoehn-Saric et al., 1964; D. L. Larsen, Nguyen, Green, & Attkisson, 1983) and in group programs (see Mayerson, 1984). For example, clients subsequently receiving treatment for depression and anxiety at a community mental health center were randomly assigned to receive either a pretreatment preparatory program or a no-pretreatment intervention. Individuals participating in the pretreatment program reported more realistic expectations for therapy and greater symptom reduction at 1-month follow-up compared with the group who received no such intervention (Zwick & Attkisson, 1985).

Additional studies have demonstrated that pretreatment interventions to prepare clients for group therapy produce positive effects on self-disclosure (Garrison, 1978; Whalen, 1969); more self-exploratory verbalizations (L. V. Annis & Perry, 1977, 1978; Garrison, 1978; Heitler, 1973); greater perceived personal value, investment, and participation (Conyne & Silver, 1980; Corder, Haizlip, Whiteside, & Vogel, 1980); and increased levels of motivation (Curran, 1978; Strupp & Bloxom, 1973). It seems likely that these positive effects of preparatory interventions will be transferable to treatment for sexual offenders and enhance their gains from subsequent full treatment programs.

There have been few pretreatment programs used in the sexual offender field. In one such program, Schlank and Shaw (1996, 1997; Shaw & Schlank, 1992, 1993) ran pretreatment groups aimed at overcoming denial in sexual offenders; they managed to get more than half of the deniers to move to admitting to their offenses. Following Shaw and Schlank's (1992, 1993) early reports, several other programs designed similar pretreatment interventions aimed at overcoming denial (Brake & Shannon, 1997; Burditt, 1995; J. J. Murphy & Berry, 1995; Norris, 1993); all of these studies reported encouraging data. Overall, the success rates of these programs in reducing denial varied from 30% to 60%, but they offered no evidence of increased motivation for treatment, of any facilitating effects on subsequent treatment involvement, nor of reductions in recidivism over and above that already achieved by their regular treatment program. However, it is now generally accepted in the field of sexual offender treatment that denial is not a relevant treatment target because of the fact that it does not predict reoffending (see Hanson & Bussière, 1998; Hanson & Morton-Bourgon, 2005).

Pithers (1994) implemented a pretreatment program aimed at increasing sexual offenders' awareness of the harm their abuse had caused; this was meant to enhance the offenders' empathy for their victims. Pithers thought that these increases in empathy would make the offenders more responsive to subsequent full treatment. He demonstrated enhanced empathy in the pretreatment program participants, but he did not produce evidence of greater motivation for treatment, nor did he comment on whether there was greater participation in the subsequent full treatment program.

As noted previously, Lee et al. (1996) implemented a preparatory program for sexual offenders with low motivation for treatment as a way to encourage engagement in the subsequent full treatment program. This preparatory program for sexual offenders with various paraphilias, combined with the subsequent full treatment program, produced changes in short-term variables such as reductions in the frequency and intensity of deviant sexual fantasies, increases in control over sexual problems, enhanced social skills, greater assertiveness, and improved sexual knowledge. Lee et al. also reported reductions in cognitive distortions associated with sexual deviance and long-term recidivism rates that were comparable to other treatment programs. However, the effects of the preparatory component of this program were not distinguished from the changes induced by the subsequent full treatment program, leaving the success, or lack thereof, of the preparatory program unclear.

THE ROCKWOOD PSYCHOLOGICAL
SERVICES PREPARATORY PROGRAM

The RPS Preparatory Program is offered to all available sexual offenders during the time they spend being oriented and assessed at a maximum security federal penitentiary that functions as the induction center for the Ontario Region of the Correctional Service of Canada's prisons. The program operates on a rolling (i.e., open-ended) basis, providing intervention to approximately eight clients at any given time. Each group member participates in the program for 6 to 8 weeks, although some are transferred earlier so they can complete a full treatment program before their release date. The primary goal of the RPS Preparatory Program is to begin addressing resistance to, and lack of motivation for, subsequent involvement in a full treatment program. The idea is not to provide treatment so much as it is to gain the client's cooperation; increase his motivation to engage in the process of treatment; and enhance his hope for, and optimism about, his future ability to function offense free.

Like each of the RPS programs, the Preparatory Program is grounded in the principles of positive psychology (Linley & Joseph, 2004b; Snyder & Lopez, 2005). Furthermore, the program builds on foundational theories, such as motivational interviewing (W. R. Miller & Rollnick, 2002), hope theory (Moulden & Marshall, 2005), self-efficacy theory (Bandura, 1977a), and self-determination theory (R. M. Ryan & Deci, 2000). Other positive approaches, such as an emphasis on collaborative work with the offenders (Shingler & Mann, 2006), the enhancement of self-esteem (W. L. Marshall, Anderson, & Champagne, 1997), and shifting the client's feelings from shame to guilt (Proeve & Howells, 2006), have been integrated into the style in which therapy is implemented in the RPS Preparatory Program. In attempting to achieve the goals of improved motivation and effective treatment engagement, these convergent theories and approaches all subscribe to the fundamental belief that by increasing the positive strengths of the client and enhancing his self-management skills, reductions in reoffending will be achieved.

The content and methods of the RPS Preparatory Program have been described in detail elsewhere (L. E. Marshall & Marshall, 2007; O'Brien, Marshall, & Marshall, 2009) and for brevity's sake are summarized here. The first step is the provision of information to address one of Mann and Webster's (2002) findings that sexual offenders lacked knowledge of the components and efficacy of treatment for sexual offending. For example, we describe the reasons for completing risk assessments, how these risk instruments were developed, and what purposes they serve. This is illustrated by having one client in the group complete his risk assessment himself. We inform the clients of the potential value to them of successfully completing their subsequent full treatment program—for example, a likely transfer to lower security; an increased chance of early parole; lowered supervision on release; less likelihood of a return to prison; and most important, enhanced chances of a better life.

Throughout the RPS Preparatory Program, we attend to those issues reported earlier that have been found to be related to refusal and attrition. We do, of course, also have specific targets that we address in the program, such as the enhancement of self-esteem and self-efficacy, a shift from shame to guilt, increased hope for the future, and improved emotion management. There are also other exercises that each offender is asked to complete. For example, they are all asked to identify background factors that preceded their offenses, they provide an autobiography, and they participate in other exercises that are based on the emerging case formulations made during the early stages of the Preparatory Program. However, the primary goal of all of the issues addressed and the exercises conducted in preparatory treatment is the enhancement of motivation.

The first target of the program is to acclimatize the offenders to the processes of therapy and to engage them fully in treatment. For example, we do not necessarily expect a full and honest disclosure of the events surrounding their offense, nor do we challenge the offender's disclosure as vigorously as might happen in their later full treatment program. We ask open-ended questions to clarify details of the offender's description, but these are meant to encourage the offender to become comfortable with self-challenging. When the client has given his disclosure, the therapist asks the other group members to comment only on the positive features of the disclosure—that is, what he did well in his exercise and how he met the aim of the exercise. The therapist also offers positive comments and deflects any criticisms or challenges by other group members. This is meant to convey to clients that therapy does not have to be threatening. This approach also facilitates the learning and motivation of other group members. When the other group members have to focus on what the target offender has done well, they learn as well as observe. Clients learn the targets of treatment and are encouraged by our approach to see that completing the relevant exercises is not punitive. Once they realize we will not attack them, the clients display signs of ease and are then typically more forthcoming and motivated to engage in treatment. As noted, the primary goal of the Preparatory Program is to engage the clients in the treatment process. It is the responsibility of their subsequent treatment program to challenge the clients and to explore issues in more detail.

Because the program is open-ended, and because offenders remain in the program only until they are transferred, we also have other topics that we cover if there is time and if they are relevant to the particular client. For example, we may begin to address relationship issues, coping skills, and healthy sexuality. We choose these targets because most sexual offenders have problems in these areas, and addressing these targets is likely to be seen by the clients as personally helpful and nonthreatening. Note that we simply begin the process of addressing these issues so that they will be better prepared to deal with them more completely in their later full treatment programs.

Just as we do in response to a client's disclosure, for all exercises in the Preparatory Program the therapist immediately praises the client for his effort and elicits praise from each of the other group members. No matter how poor the client's presentation is, the therapist searches for something to praise, and all other members of the group are required to comment favorably. The therapist should encourage positive and supportive participation by all group members and encourage the specific client's belief that he can succeed. For example, rather than have group members generate an acceptable disclosure, the therapist should make members feel comfortable revealing details that might otherwise be seen as threatening. The RPS Preparatory Program is not a full treatment program and does not, therefore, have the same aims of such a program. Its focus is on motivation and engagement.

The RPS Preparatory Program has been evaluated in terms of its ability to achieve its targets (see Chapter 5). Motivational targets include movement on the stages of change, increased hope for the future, greater treatment readiness, and improvements in self-efficacy. These changes will improve cooperation in later treatment and reduce the required intensity of subsequent treatment. Achievement of these goals should lead to earlier release and lower recidivism. These latter results, of course, are desired by the correctional system and by the public at large. As we saw in Chapter 5, the RPS Preparatory Program has been successful in achieving all these motivational and systems targets.

CONCLUSION

The RPS Preparatory Program was designed to overcome treatment resistance and to lead to full engagement in subsequent treatment programs. Unlike the Primary Program, the Preparatory Program does not target standard criminogenic factors; rather, it aims to motivate offenders and engage them in treatment. The program successfully achieves these goals.

7

ROCKWOOD PRIMARY PROGRAM

The fundamental principle of our approach to the treatment of sexual offenders, which has been an enduring guide over the past 40 years, is captured in the following sentiment: We believe that in every offender there is a good person waiting to throw off the burden of his dysfunctional past and that it is our job as therapists to facilitate the emergence of that good person.

Although this fundamental principle has remained the same, the Rockwood Psychological Services (RPS) Primary Program has evolved over the past 40 years (W. L. Marshall, 1971; W. L. Marshall, Anderson, & Fernandez, 1999; W. L. Marshall & Barbaree, 1988; W. L. Marshall et al., 1983; W. L. Marshall, Marshall, Serran, & Fernandez, 2006; W. L. Marshall & Williams, 1975) as a result of our clinical experience and our own research, as well as our careful attention to the research of others, to theoretical accounts, and in response to criticisms by other authors. As noted in the Introduction to this book, we have been strongly influenced by recent developments in the positive psychology movement (Linley & Joseph, 2004b; M. E. P. Seligman & Csikszentmihalyi, 2000; Snyder & Lopez, 2005) and by other notions, such as W. R. Miller and Rollnick's (2002) motivational interviewing. The present chapter describes in some detail the current iteration of the RPS Primary Program.

THE ROCKWOOD PSYCHOLOGICAL SERVICES PRIMARY PROGRAM

For the purposes of exposition, our primary program is conceptualized as a three-phase approach. Exhibit 7.1 describes these three phases and the intent and treatment targets of each phase.

It should be noted that although certain targets are initially addressed within each phase, many are carried on through each subsequent phase, and even those targeted in the final phase will already have been alluded to at early points in treatment. For example, the first step in Phase 1 (i.e., outline of treatment) involves an overall description of the program and the final aim of treatment, with the latter being explicitly addressed in detail in Phase 3.

Phase 1: Engagement

The goal of Phase 1 is to effectively engage the clients in the treatment process. Because the RPS Preparatory Program is only able to deal with a limited number of incoming sexual offenders (because of limited funding) and because many of its graduates are sent to other prisons, the majority of clients entering the RPS Primary Program have not had pretreatment motivational enhancement—hence the need for Phase 1 of the primary program. Although we address some treatment targets in this phase, it is not with the intention of achieving the goals of these targets; these targets are explicitly chosen to

EXHIBIT 7.1
Rockwood Psychological Services Primary Program Model

Phase 1 Goal: Engagement	Phase 2 Goal: Modifying criminogenic targets	Phase 3 Goal: Life-enhancement and self-management
Outline of treatment	Attitudes and cognitions	Modified good lives model
Confidentiality	Self-regulation issues	Limited set of avoidance
Background factors	Relationship problems	strategies
Enhancement of	Sexual issues	Generation of support
self-esteem/reduction		groups
of shame		Release/discharge plans
Improving coping and mood		
management		
Broaden empathy		

serve a motivational purpose. We hope to make this clear as we describe in detail the features of Phase 1.

Outline of Treatment

The first step involves a description of what treatment will encompass and a statement of the goals of treatment. Incoming clients are told the following:

> The aim of our program is to provide you with the skills necessary to have a happier, more fulfilling life than you have had to date. We do not aim specifically to reduce your risk to reoffend, although we will address issues that will achieve this purpose. Our belief is that you offended because you were unable to meet in appropriate ways the basic human needs that we all strive for. We will outline for you what these basic needs are and the skills necessary to achieve them. The program will equip you with these skills, including your attitudes toward yourself, and we will end by helping you plan the ways in which you will continue the processes involved in working toward achieving a better life.

Posted on the walls of the therapy group room are brief descriptions of not only each target addressed in treatment (e.g., self-esteem, empathy, relationships, sexual knowledge, sexual satisfaction, sexual interests) but also our adaptation of Ward and Mann's (2004) description of the good lives model (GLM), which is depicted in Exhibit 7.2. We direct our clients' attention to these postings and indicate that we will explain each of them in detail as we begin to address each issue. However, we provide a brief outline of the GLM and indicate that although this may seem overwhelming at this early stage, as treatment unfolds it will become clearer. It is important to note that we apply the GLM in a different way than does Ward. He uses the GLM to structure the assessment, treatment, and posttreatment planning and implementation, whereas we introduce it in detail only at the beginning of Phase 3 as a way to integrate all that the client has learned up to that point. We also make it clear, and we repeat this throughout treatment, that the aim of our program

EXHIBIT 7.2
A Modified Good Lives Model

1. Health—good diet and exercise
2. Mastery—in work and play
3. Autonomy—self-directiveness
4. Relatedness—intimate/sexual relationship, family, friends, kinship, and community
5. Inner peace—freedom from turmoil and stress, a sense of purpose and meaning in life
6. Knowledge and creativity—satisfaction from knowing and creating things—job- or hobby-related knowledge, playing music, writing

Note. Data from Ward and Mann (2004).

is to prepare clients sufficiently to continue the process after release of developing their own unique good life and generating the plans and actions necessary to this development. Treatment, we indicate, is just meant to start them on the road to greater fulfillment; it is up to them to continue this after discharge from our program. As we address each target in treatment (i.e., the other posted descriptions), we begin the process of equipping them with the skills necessary to continue their self-development when they are released from prison or discharged from treatment. We point out that happiness and fulfillment come from striving toward these goals. The GLM is essentially a condensed version of the various aspects or targets of positive psychology as outlined in the chapters of both Linley and Joseph's (2004b) and Snyder and Lopez's (2005) edited books. The interested reader is referred to these excellent summaries of the current state of positive psychology.

Confidentiality

The next step in Phase 1 involves outlining issues of confidentiality (i.e., both our responsibilities and those of each client), and we point out that we are obliged to share information of concern, as well as our final reports, with relevant correctional and parole/probation staff and possibly with police, although the latter rarely request our reports. This sharing of information, we point out, typically serves the clients' best interests, although this may not always be obvious to them. We indicate to the clients that we will always be honest with them as we hope they will be with us.

Once we have dealt with these essentially introductory issues, we begin the process of addressing the specific features described in Exhibit 7.1. Because the goal of Phase 1 is to motivate and fully engage the clients, the targets of this phase are selected for that purpose. Thus, some of these targets are not criminogenic features, but their attainment serves to enhance the client's belief that the therapist has his interests at heart and cares about him.

The way in which treatment, in this and the other two phases, is delivered follows the style outlined in Chapter 3 on processes of treatment and adopts the approach of positive psychology as detailed in the Introduction. We are consistently motivational throughout treatment and continue our focus on identifying and enhancing the clients' strengths.

Background Factors

This has two parts: (a) distal background factors and (b) proximal background factors. The *distal* factors are those that are evident in the life history of our clients from which the therapist and the clients can collaboratively infer difficulties that need to be addressed. These might include unresolved issues with their parents, unresolved losses, other emotional issues, educational deficits, relationship difficulties (e.g., intimacy, emotional loneliness, jealousy, limited or inappropriate friendships), or employment problems. These issues are best revealed by having the offender write an autobiography of no more than six to eight pages. If he has difficulties writing (e.g., if he is illiterate), this might imply a need for educational upgrading or literacy training, which is available in the prison settings where we work. However, in the interim this problem can be dealt with by collaboratively selecting another group member to act as a scribe. We have found that there are always volunteers within the group to act as scribes and that the scribe profits from the opportunity to be nurturing. In requesting lower functioning offenders to produce an autobiography, we follow Haaven's (Haaven et al., 1990) strategy of providing the client with a time line divided into childhood, adolescence, young adulthood, middle age, and older age. On this time line, the client enters, or reports at treatment sessions, the salient events and experiences of his life.

From the autobiography or time line, the client and therapist deduce the relevant strengths of the client as well as the problems that need to be addressed if he is to function effectively. After a client has presented his autobiography or time line information at a group session, each group member is invited to comment favorably on some aspect of the presentation. Although other group members, particularly those who are relatively new, will often want to point to what was lacking in the presentation, we immediately interrupt these comments and request a favorable comment. We want the client who is presenting his work, especially in the early stages of treatment, to be reinforced by all group members for his efforts. This is aimed at reducing clients' reluctance to freely express themselves and to make participation in treatment a rewarding experience. After each group member and the therapist have made favorable comments, we open the floor for questions to be addressed to the target person. The therapist intervenes when necessary to ensure that these questions are phrased in a supportive way rather than in an aggressively confrontational way. We want the group members to learn to be challenging but empathic, as well as supportive and rewarding, in their style of interacting with each other. This helps generate the group cohesiveness that is essential to effective treatment (Beech & Fordham, 1997; Beech & Hamilton-Giachritsis, 2005). The therapist diligently models the appropriate style of interaction. This is meant not only to encourage the target member but also to shape up in all participants a more prosocial way of interacting with others.

For the *proximal* factors, we have the client present a disclosure of the events that reasonably immediately preceded the offense. However, our requirements for a disclosure differ from that typically requested in most cognitive–behavioral therapy programs. Indeed, almost every program we have observed or read about requires each client to divulge in his disclosure every detail of the behaviors that occurred during the offense with the additional demand that these details match the official record (usually either the victim's report or the police report of the crime). Oddly enough, when we have asked each program director or the therapists who require this what purpose this disclosure serves, they struggle to answer and usually say something like, "It reveals how much responsibility they accept for their crime." There is, however, no evidence that accepting full responsibility for sexually offending is related to a reduction in risk. In fact, in his preliminary work with offenders released from prison, Maruna (2001) reported that those offenders who blithely acknowledge their guilt appear to be more likely to reoffend than are those who offer excuses or dodge responsibility. Consistent with this observation, large-scale meta-analyses involving thousands of sexual offenders have demonstrated that those offenders who deny having committed an offense are no more likely to reoffend than are those who fully admit (Hanson & Bussière, 1998; Hanson & Morton-Bourgon, 2005).

In any case, as we (W. L. Marshall, Marshall, & Ware, 2009) reported, the available evidence has indicated that victims' reports are unlikely to be accurate. Because there are no grounds for supposing that victims' accounts are accurate, there is no justification for pressuring sexual offenders to give an account of their offense that matches the official record. Indeed, there is every reason to not do this. If an offender decides, as he well might, that unless he provides an account matching the victim's statement, even if he believes it to be untrue, he will not be allowed to complete the treatment program, then we can expect him to provide a false story. This is definitely not what we want clients to do, and it will certainly alter their attitude toward the rest of treatment.

What we ask clients to do is to tell us in their disclosure what happened in their lives in the 3 to 6 months before their offense occurred and what events and experiences took place on the days immediately prior to the offense. We explicitly point out that we do not want them to tell us what they did during the offense and that we will not ask them for these details at any time during treatment. Most offenders are pleasantly surprised by this, and it clearly alleviates their anxiety and puts them in a positive frame of mind regarding treatment. From this account, in conjunction with their autobiography, we can collaboratively begin the process of inferring both stable dynamic risk factors and acute dynamic risk factors that are unique to the individual, thus providing a basis for the emergence of an individualized case formulation.

Self-Esteem/Reduction of Shame

In enhancing self-esteem, we ask the client to list positive features about himself: his good qualities and his strengths. An initial focus on their strengths surprises most of the clients and typically gives them a revised and positive vision of both the therapist and the therapy, a view that will encourage the client's engagement in treatment and increase his motivation to begin the difficult task of changing his way of life. Identifying strengths is the first and crucial step to enhancing the client's self-worth.

We have shown in a series of studies that sexual offenders typically score well below the normative mean on measures of self-esteem (Fernandez & Marshall, 2003; W. L. Marshall, 1997; W. L. Marshall, Champagne, Brown, & Miller, 1998; W. L. Marshall, Cripps, Anderson, & Cortoni, 1999; W. L. Marshall, Marshall, Sachdev, & Kruger, 2003; W. L. Marshall & Mazzucco, 1995; Sparks et al., 2003; Thornton et al., 2004) and that self-esteem among sexual offenders is linked to deficits in coping (W. L. Marshall, Cripps, et al., 1999); offense-facilitating attitudes (W. L. Marshall, Marshall, et al., 2003); problems in empathy, intimacy, and loneliness (W. L. Marshall, Champagne, Brown, et al., 1998); psychopathy (Fernandez & Marshall, 2003); shame (Sparks et al., 2003); and deviant sexual interests (W. L. Marshall, 1997). Thus enhancing self-esteem ought to facilitate the achievement of almost all other targets of treatment as well as to serve, on its own, to reduce recidivism. Some meta-analyses (e.g., Hanson & Bussière, 1998; Hanson & Morton-Bourgon, 2005) have reported that self-esteem did not predict recidivism, but the evidence of the relationship between self-esteem and several criminogenic treatment targets suggests that perhaps it has an indirect influence on the propensity to reoffend. In addition, Thornton et al. (2004) demonstrated that scores on their measure of self-esteem did, in fact, predict recidivism.

There are two further reasons to enhance self-esteem early in treatment. People low in self-esteem typically underestimate their ability to modify their behavior; they are afraid to try to change, they do not practice tasks that will help them learn new skills, and they give up trying to change when faced with minor obstacles (see Baumeister, 1993, for a summary of the evidence on the effects of low self-esteem). Thus, low self-esteem presents as an obstacle to engaging our clients in treatment. Second, we have shown that the effects of enhanced self-esteem are to increase hope for the future and move sexual offenders to a stage of change in which they are ready to engage in treatment (L. E. Marshall, Marshall, Fernandez, Malcolm, & Moulden, 2008). Fortunately, we have developed both a satisfactory (i.e., reliable, valid, and unifactorial) measure of self-esteem (Lawson, Marshall, & McGrath, 1979) as well as several procedures that demonstrably enhance self-esteem both in nonoffending populations (W. L. Marshall & Christie, 1982; W. L. Marshall, Christie, Lanthier, & Cruchley, 1982) and in sexual offenders (W. L. Marshall, Champagne, Sturgeon, & Bryce, 1997).

One of the procedures we use to enhance self-esteem involves assisting the client to identify activities that generate small degrees of pleasure (e.g., listening to favorite music, eating enjoyable foods, engaging in pleasing leisure activities). Once a range of these activities is identified, the client is instructed to increase the frequency of each of several of these activities over the following 4 to 6 weeks and attend to the pleasurable feelings induced by each instance of the chosen activities. Checks are made at each treatment session to ensure appropriate compliance. Another procedure we developed has the client similarly identify a range of social activities that he could engage in (e.g., meet a friend for coffee, have supper with friends, accept invitations to a party, join others in exercise, engage in opportunities for conversation, go to movies). He is then instructed to increase his engagement in these activities, ensuring as broad a range of social interchanges as possible, over the next 4 to 6 weeks. After each interaction he is to reflect on how enjoyable he found it. Again, clients report their progress at each treatment session.

We also work cooperatively with the client in identifying six to eight positive qualities about himself (e.g., he is generous, caring, loyal, compassionate, hard working, reliable, honest, skilled at sports). Although most people, including a good many therapists, may not regard sexual offenders as having good qualities, and in particular, given their offenses, may regard them as lacking in empathy and compassion, this view results from considering them only in terms of their offenses; they are all, as we have already pointed out, far more than just sexual offenders. Once the client has identified his positive qualities, he writes them on a pocket-sized card that he carries with him at all times. Three times per day he is to read each statement three times as emphatically as he can, over a period of 4 to 6 weeks. Again, checks are made at each session to ascertain compliance.

Finally, we assist each client to distinguish himself, as a person, from his offending behaviors. Again, we remind readers of John, the offender described in the Introduction who had 420 victims over 26 years but who spent only 8% of his recorded waking hours in pursuit of offending. All sexual offenders are far more than their offenses. They are someone's child, someone's intimate partner (or were), often someone's father; they hold a job, have friends, engage in various activities, and so on. We instruct them not to think, or speak, of themselves as offenders, but rather as people with many facets, most of which are prosocial. We actively discourage their use of self-labels such as *offenders* (much less *sexual offenders*), *deviants*, *child molesters*, *pedophiles*, or *rapists*, and we are quick to strongly discourage self-descriptions that reflect negative colloquial evaluations such as "rape hounds," "perverts," and "diddlers." If they feel a need to refer to their offending behaviors, we permit self-descriptors that are objective with no derogatory implications—for example, "I am a person who, in the past, committed a sexual offense."

Shame, like low self-esteem, with which it is highly correlated, is another important obstacle to effective engagement in treatment. Shame reflects an internal and stable attribution for problematic behavior (Tangney & Dearing, 2002). A person who responds with shame to having done something that does not fit with their ideals will internalize a statement something like, "I did a bad thing because I am a bad person." Someone who responds to the same behavior with guilt will say to himself something like, "I am a good person, but I did a bad thing." Thus, the attribution in the latter case is external and changeable. Not surprisingly, shame blocks attempts at change ("There is no point trying to change because I am inherently bad"), whereas guilt facilitates change ("I am a good person so I can stop doing bad things").

Fortunately, self-esteem and shame are highly correlated in both non-offenders (Tangney & Dearing, 2002) and in sexual offenders (Sparks et al., 2003). Therefore, if we enhance self-esteem, we should expect to see a reduction in the expression of shame. In an examination of a program similar to ours run in another local prison, we showed that addressing sexual offenders in a respectful way in treatment led to marked reductions in shame (L. E. Marshall et al., 2009).

Coping and Mood Management

Volatility of mood or emotional dysregulation is to a large extent a result of an inability to cope with life's problems and to properly manage stress (Gross, 2007). Effective coping is related to positive adjustment and to good health, whereas problematic coping, such as a passive aggressive response to stress or acting-out behaviors, predicts poor physical and mental health (Vaillant, 2004). People with poor coping styles, or who lack coping skills, experience high levels of emotional distress (Carver, Pozo, Harris, & Noriega, 1993), whereas those with good coping skills are less likely to feel uneasy or distressful (Larson, Allen, Imao, & Piersel, 1993) and less likely to be depressed (Bonner & Rich, 1987). Therefore, increasing a person's capacity to cope with life's problems should enhance emotional or mood management.

Several strategies have been suggested to enhance coping. Researchers have typically distinguished between coping styles and coping skills. Endler and Parker (1990), for example, identified three coping styles: problem focused, emotion focused, and avoidance focused. These are understood to be a person's prototypical response style to stress. Endler and Parker saw the problem-focused coping style as the only effective response. However, Stanton, Parsa, and Austenfeld (2005) made a compelling case for distinguishing effective emotional coping from ineffective emotional coping, in which the former involves an active acceptance of a stressful encounter and a positive emotional appraisal of it. In this case, Stanton et al. said, the person understands, accepts, and expresses his emotional responses to the stressful event. They pointed to evidence showing that this approach-oriented style is a very effective coping response (Tobin, Holroyd, Reynolds, & Wigal, 1989). An emotion-focused response that involves distressing reactions (e.g., depression, anxiety) that the person attempts to suppress leads to maladjustment (Stanton, Danoff-Burg, Cameron, & Ellis, 1994; Stanton, Kirk, Cameron, & Danoff-Burg, 2000). Effective emotional-focused coping, on the other hand, has been shown to result in marked increases in hope (Snyder et al., 2005) and optimism for the future (Carver & Scheier, 2005), both of which are associated with better long-term adjustment.

Humor has also been shown to be an effective coping response (Lefcourt, 2005). People who use humor when dealing with problems are less likely to experience stress and less likely to respond to stress with depression or anxiety (Nezu, Nezu, & Blissett, 1988). Of course, the use of problem-solving skills, just as Endler and Parker (1990) suggested, has been shown to be a very effective style in response to distressing events (Heppner & Lee, 2005). Actively seeking the benefits, however small they might be, of experiencing problems, and repeatedly reminding oneself of these benefits, is also a very effective coping response (Tennen & Affleck, 2005) that leads to healthy results (King & Miner, 2000).

In our approach to assisting sexual offenders to adopt a more effective coping style and to enhance their specific coping skills, we use an amalgam of the previous strategies. We encourage throughout our treatment program the expression of emotion as well as encouraging clients to recognize their current emotional states. S. M. Hudson et al. (1993) have shown that sexual offenders are less accurate than other people (including other offenders) at recognizing emotions in others, and this appears to result from their general inability to acknowledge and recognize their own emotions. We also encourage the use of humor, although we are careful to ensure that expressions of humor do not involve derogation of others. In addition, we teach problem-solving skills (D'Zurilla, 1986; D'Zurilla & Goldfried, 1971) and assertiveness (Gambrill, 2002). An earlier version of our coping skills training with sexual offenders was shown to be effective (Serran, Firestone, Marshall, & Moulden, 2007).

Empathy

On the basis of our earlier model (W. L. Marshall, Hudson, Jones, & Fernandez, 1995) that divided empathy into four successive stages (emotion recognition, perspective taking, a compassionate response, and reparative action), we developed a multicomponent training module (see W. L. Marshall, Anderson, & Fernandez, 1999, for a description). The specific ways we addressed empathy in this model derived from research showing that sexual offenders did not appear to have deficiencies in general empathy but rather simply did not apply these empathic responses to their own victims and to some extent to victims of sexual abuse in general (Farr, Brown, & Beckett,

2004; Fernandez & Marshall, 2003; Fernandez, Marshall, Lightbody, & O'Sullivan, 1999; D. D. Fisher, Beech, & Browne, 1999; W. L. Marshall, Champagne, Brown, & Miller, 1998; W. L. Marshall & Moulden, 2001; Webster & Beech, 2000).

Our more recent model of empathy (W. L. Marshall, Marshall, Serran, & O'Brien, 2009) proposes a link between empathy and low self-esteem, shame, and cognitive distortions. In this model, people who are low in self-esteem will experience shame for wrongdoing, which will lead them to adopt self-protective distorted beliefs and as a consequence inhibit any empathic responses they might otherwise display. Enhancing self-esteem and reducing shame, then, ought to remove the need for distorted thinking and release an empathic response. By this point in treatment, we will already have made progress in enhancing self-esteem and reducing shame, which typically results in a readiness in our clients to profit from empathy training.

However, Craig, Browne, and Stringer (2003) identified studies that revealed a lack of general empathy in sexual offenders, and their meta-analysis suggested that these deficits were criminogenic and thus needed to be addressed in treatment. Consistent with Craig et al.'s position, Farrington (1998) suggested that a lack of general empathy among offenders impairs their ability to understand how their behavior affects others. In his view, most people refrain from crime to avoid the emotional discomfort they would experience by distressing others. This is consistent with P. A. Miller and Eisenberg's (1988) observation that empathy inhibits aggression.

In an examination of Farrington's position, Jolliffe and Farrington (2004) conducted a meta-analysis of 35 relevant studies. As a result of this analysis, Jolliffe and Farrington concluded that empathy and offending were negatively related. In a detailed examination of their results, Jolliffe and Farrington reported that it was cognitive empathy that was most strongly related to offending in the way that Farrington had predicted. In the studies they examined, cognitive empathy was measured by Hogan's (1969) Empathy Scale. Unfortunately, an examination of the questions in Hogan's scale reveals a hodgepodge of unrelated questions reflected in the fact that its internal consistency is unacceptably low (Cross & Sharpley, 1982; J. A. Johnson, Cheek, & Struther, 1983). Hogan's measure is also unreliable over time (Serran, 2002). It does not, therefore, provide a sound basis for making inferences of any kind. Jolliffe and Farrington also found a relationship, although rather weak, between emotional empathy and offending. In this case, emotional empathy was assessed by a measure developed by Mehrabian and Epstein (1972), which, unfortunately, has serious psychometric problems similar to Hogan's scale (Dillard & Hunter, 1989; Langevin, Wright, & Handy, 1988). Again, this measure does not provide a sound basis for determining the relationship between empathy and offending.

It was just this problem with available measures of empathy, arising from a failure to agree on a definition of the concept (W. L. Marshall, 2002), that led us to first develop a conceptual model of empathy (W. L. Marshall et al., 1995), which we later refined (W. L. Marshall, Marshall, & Serran, 2009; W. L. Marshall, Marshall, Serran, & O'Brien, 2009), and then to generate measures derived from this conceptualization. What our subsequent research using these measures revealed was that sexual offenders did not appear to lack empathy toward people in general but were significantly unempathic toward their victims (Fernandez & Marshall, 2003; Fernandez, Marshall, Lightbody, & O'Sullivan, 1999; W. L. Marshall, Champagne, Brown, & Miller, 1998; W. L. Marshall & Moulden, 2001). These findings have been replicated by others (Farr et al., 2004; D. D. Fisher, 1997; D. D. Fisher, Beech, & Browne, 1999; Webster & Beech, 2000; Whittaker, Brown, Beckett, & Gerhold, 2006). Webster and Beech (2000), in a grounded theory analysis, found no relationship among sexual offenders between empathy toward people in general and victim-specific empathy.

As we can see, it is victim-specific empathy that consistently emerges as a problem for sexual offenders, not generalized empathy. A careful analysis of the apparent lack of victim empathy among sexual offenders reveals that it is simply yet another aspect of their tendency to distort in order to present themselves in a more favorable light (W. L. Marshall, Hamilton, & Fernandez, 2001). All people are readily capable of withholding empathy from others either because they have negative feelings toward the person (Hanson, 1997b) or because they wish to avoid emotional overload (Batson, 1991). Clearly all offenders are capable of the same responses. At present, we believe the research has yet to demonstrate that offenders commit crimes because they are unfettered by the same empathic capacities as the rest of us.

Of course, a lack of empathy toward people in general would have significant consequences for some of the Phase 2 criminogenic targets. For example, empathy is a feature of good-quality intimate relations and is important for all aspects of such relationships (Batson, Ahmad, Lishner, & Tsang, 2005; Harvey, Pauwels, & Zickmund, 2005). Similarly, without empathic concern for the other person, sexual satisfaction is unlikely to be attained. In particular, men who are sexually preoccupied have little concern for their sexual partners but are focused entirely on their own satisfaction, which, in the context of such driven behavior, is rarely more than minimally achieved (Carnes, 1989; L. E. Marshall & O'Brien, 2009). Thus, Craig et al.'s (2003) observation that general empathy deficits predict reoffending among sexual offenders may simply be because such a lack of empathy is inherently a component of other, more powerful predictors of sexual offending. In the context of addressing these other criminogenic targets, attention to empathic processes may be required.

In terms of techniques to enhance empathy, we have noted that the earlier elements in our RPS Primary Program (e.g., increasing self-esteem and reducing shame) should, according to our most recent model, make the task of overcoming empathy deficits easier. In terms of specific strategies, numerous authors (Carich & Calder, 2003; Garrett & Thomas-Peter, 2009; Hanson, 1997b; Pithers, 1994) have described a variety of approaches aimed at enhancing general empathy. Some of these suggested techniques are included in our approach.

As a result of the prior training in coping and mood management, we expect our clients to be reasonably able to identify emotions in others, which is the first step in our earlier staged model of empathy. The second stage in this model is perspective taking, and Hanson (1997b) outlined strategies for improving this skill, which is decidedly lacking in sexual offenders (Hanson & Scott, 1995). Role-plays in which the target offender and another group member participate can also be useful. In this scenario, the target offender first plays himself, and the other offender plays someone who is experiencing emotional difficulties. The other offender describes his problem as emotionally evocatively as he can, and then the target offender is asked to describe to the best of his ability the nature of the other person's problem and what emotions the other person was experiencing. He is then asked to describe his own emotional reactions to the other person's account. It is often useful to have the other offender role-play someone the target offender knows but for whom he has little compassion. Once the initial role-play and analysis is complete, the two actors then swap roles so the target offender can better experience the other person's situation. This training not only enhances empathic responses (W. L. Marshall, O'Sullivan, & Fernandez, 1996) but is also likely to increase the client's *theory of mind* (Keenan & Ward, 2000), which refers to his capacity to infer other people's thoughts, feelings, and intentions. People with a sophisticated theory of mind function better in all manner of ways than those with theory of mind deficits (Baron-Cohen, Tager-Flusberg, & Cohen, 1993). We do not use role-plays that involve someone enacting the victim, as many programs do, as it has been shown that at best this generates little change (Webster et al., 2005) and at worst can result in serious distress and legal complications (Pithers, 1997).

Other strategies that we commonly use to enhance empathy include group discussions concerning the consequences that might befall victims of sexual abuse or that might occur to a person who suffered something tragic (e.g., perhaps another group member who lost a loved one). These consequences are discussed and the target offender is asked how the victim might have felt and how he felt while thinking about the victim. Two final and related strategies can also be useful. For instance, the offender could write a hypothetical letter from one of his victims describing the victim's view of the impact of the offense. After the group reviews this letter and the client, if necessary, rewrites it, he is then asked to write another letter. In this second letter, the client responds to the first letter by writing back to the victim expressing responsibility for his actions. Alternatively, the offender could write a series of diary entries as if he was his victim, with these entries describing the emotional, behavioral, and cognitive disruptions common to victims of sexual abuse.

Phase 2: Criminogenic Targets

Before we focus on the specific targets of Phase 2, we need to note that those issues we addressed in Phase 1 are not seen as completed. Throughout treatment, we seize on naturally occurring opportunities to continue the enhancement of self-esteem, the reduction of shame, the increase in empathy, and the promotion of coping skills and mood management. We also frequently refer back to the client's autobiography and offense precursors when targeting other issues. Thus, our program is not modularized but is an ongoing comprehensive psychotherapeutic process that takes advantage of every opportunity for learning.

The targets specifically introduced in Phase 2 (see Exhibit 7.1) are those that have been shown to predict recidivism in sexual offenders. The identification of these criminogenic factors rests on a series of meta-analyses (e.g., Craig et al., 2003; Hanson & Bussière, 1998; Hanson & Morton-Bourgon, 2005) as well as other research reports (e.g., Hanson & Harris, 2000b; Thornton, 2002; Thornton & Beech, 2002). The results of these studies have been summarized by several authors (e.g., Cortoni, 2009; Craig et al., 2008, 2009; Hanson, 2006a), and the reader is referred to those sources for more detailed considerations. The detailed features of each criminogenic target are described in Exhibit 7.3, but before we address these we draw attention to what are often thought of as irrelevant issues.

We often address in treatment some specific aspects not listed in Exhibit 7.3, as well as some aspects that are not clearly criminogenic but are functionally related to features that are. These additional idiosyncratic targets emerge as we challenge each client in the context of dealing with a specific criminogenic feature, or as a consequence of a client bringing to the attention of the group an issue he is dealing with either within a prison setting or at his work if he is a community client. For example, an inmate client may describe a hostile interaction he had with a prison officer that upset him. As a result, he may feel powerless and lose self-respect. In several programs that we have been asked to evaluate, the therapists have dismissed problems like this as "outside issues" that they see as irrelevant to treatment. In our view, there are things to be learned from such situations that bear directly on criminogenic

EXHIBIT 7.3
Criminogenic Targets

---

1. Attitudes/cognitions
    Adversarial sexual beliefs
    – Men should dominate/control women
    – Women are deceitful
    – Hostile/distorted views of women
    – Some women deserve to be raped
    Child abuse supportive beliefs
    – see children as sexual beings
    Emotional identification with children
    Antisocial attitudes
    View themselves as low risk to reoffend
    Sense of entitlement
2. Self-regulation issues
    Poor behavioral regulation
    Poor coping/problem solving
    Emotional dysregulation
3. Relationship problems
    Intimacy deficits
    Lack of relationship skills
    Maladaptive attachment style
    Emotional loneliness
4. Sexual issues
    Poverty of sexual knowledge
    Any deviant or paraphilic sexual interest
    Sexual entitlement
    Sexual preoccupation

Note. Data from Cortoni (2009); Craig, Beech, and Harkins (2009); Craig, Browne, and Beech (2008); Hanson (2006a, 2006b); Hanson & Bussière (1998), Hanson and Harris (2000a2000b); and Hanson and Morton-Bourgon (2005).

factors (e.g., learning to see things from the perspective of the other person or acquiring assertiveness skills).

These seemingly irrelevant issues may provide the client with an opportunity to learn to deal with situations in which he views himself as having little or no power or by exploring ways he might adopt to resolve the issue. At the end of a sports season, when playoffs are underway, clients typically want to talk about the games. In other programs, this is often seen as irrelevant to treatment and the discussion is terminated. However, a discussion of a game can usefully lead to a discussion of the need for rules in all activities as well as the value of functioning as part of a team; both these notions can readily be made relevant to one or more of the clients in the group. Stopping an animated discussion of an exciting game and dismissing the discussion as irrelevant may not enhance the therapist's reputation among the clients. Allowing the conversation to continue, while raising treatment-relevant aspects of a game, is likely to make the clients warm to the therapist as well as develop prosocial views (e.g., value of rules). Nothing that a client brings to the group is, in fact, irrelevant to his treatment issues; it is the task of the therapist to seize every opportunity for learning and to translate these so-called outside issues into learning experiences that will better equip the client to deal with his world in a way that will minimize stress and maximize his satisfaction.

Attitudes and Cognitions

We have already discussed which of the so-called cognitive distortions that are so often mentioned in the literature are criminogenic and which are not (see Chapter 4). Those outlined in Exhibit 7.3 represent our distillation of the literature reporting which of these distortions predict reoffending among sexual offenders. They are the ones we specifically target, although we do challenge various other dysfunctional attitudes, perceptions, and beliefs because they may impair the achievement of a better life for our clients.

We do not address these criminogenic cognitions separately from the context within which they emerge. To have a separate "module" in which these cognitions are identified and challenged is artificial; attempts to elicit and challenge these distortions out of context is bound to have limited value. During discussions about coping and empathy, and particularly when relationships and sexual matters are the focus, an array of dysfunctional attitudes, thoughts, perceptions, and beliefs emerge. It is best to challenge distortions within these contexts because they provide an opportunity to have the client see how these views present obstacles to him acquiring the skills necessary to meet his needs in prosocial ways.

It is important, however, not to waste time addressing noncriminogenic cognitions. For example, most treatment programs insist on the client taking full responsibility for his offense, including fully admitting to having committed the offense; such programs attempt to eliminate offenders' tendencies to minimize various aspects of the offense. When these exculpatory attitudes (failure to take responsibility, denying or minimizing the offense) have been entered into meta-analyses, they have been found to not predict reoffending (Hanson & Bussière, 1998; Hanson & Morton-Bourgon, 2005). They are, therefore, noncriminogenic features that do not need to be addressed in treatment.

We use a variety of tactics to challenge distortions. A common approach is to use cognitive restructuring (W. D. Murphy, 1990), and this is useful for addressing many of the typical distortions sexual offenders display. This essentially involves asking the client why he believes what he has said and how useful this belief, attitude, or perception might be in achieving the goals he has set for himself, as well as offering him alternative views that are typically generated by other group members. Role-plays can be useful here. For example, if a client declares that women should be subservient to men, we might get him to generate a scenario from his past involving a woman he was attracted to. Then he will play himself, and another group member will play the woman. The client will be asked to present his view of a woman's role to the other actor, and this actor will be asked to respond as if he (i.e., she) disagrees. After completion of this role-play, the roles are reversed, with the client acting as the woman who is presented with the dysfunctional view. In this role-play the client is asked to submerge himself in the role of the woman and respond accordingly to the other actor. When both role-plays are completed, a discussion follows involving all group members. The target client is asked if he thinks the woman will still be interested in having a relationship with him, and if he fails to see the impact of his views, the other group members are encouraged to challenge him. Usually the client recognizes the dysfunctionality of his views during the role-plays or quickly catches on during the discussion.

Mann and Shingler (2006) correctly pointed out that the distortions characteristically held by sexual offenders are typically the product of schemas. Schemas, Mann and Shingler pointed out, are deep-seated structures that function as part of the client's information processing system. These structures have contents that influence and direct the perception and processing of information. Such schemas function as heuristics and are generated over years of experience. Some are functionally useful in that they facilitate the achievement of a person's goals, and some interfere with the attainment of these goals. Even those that facilitate immediate success may have detrimental long-term consequences. For example, a schema held by a child molester that children are sexual beings who are interested in sexual contact with adults will guide his behavior in antisocial and harmful directions. He will view a child's behavior as sexually inviting and interpret this as an invitation specifically directed at him. In this way he will achieve his short-term goal of being sexual with the child, but this will likely lead to his arrest with a long-term failure to remain free. Such a schema will also prevent the formation of a lasting and satisfying relationship with an adult.

Mann and Shingler (2006) recommended adapting Young's (1999) schema-focused therapy to the treatment of sexual offenders, and there is clear merit to this. In this approach, the recommendation is not to elicit schemas but to challenge distortions when they occur and use this opportunity to explain the nature of schemas, to consider their usefulness (i.e., their costs and benefits), to reflect on past experiences in which offenders have expressed some specific example of their distorted schema, and to generate evidence for and against the schema. This way of getting at the deeper structures behind the overt expressions of distortions seems more likely to produce generalization to circumstances outside the therapy group than simply challenging each distortion without helping the client make the correction to the schema that generates it. Presently, there is no evidence that either schema-focused therapy or cognitive restructuring produces the changes in sexual offenders that treatment is seeking, but both rest on a reasonably solid foundation and have been shown to be effective when used with other problems (Giesen-Bloo et al., 2006; Padesky, 1994; Salkovskis, 1996; Young, Klosko, & Weishaar, 2003).

Self-Regulation

Ward (1999; Ward & Hudson, 2000) has outlined an explanation of sexual offending that is based on self-regulatory deficits. He based his model on the extensive literature describing how it is that people engage in goal-directed actions (Baumeister & Vohs, 2004). To successfully achieve goals, a person must use internal and external processes that result in a regulation of their behavior. Those who fail to effectively self-regulate fail to achieve their goals. Ward (1999) suggested that self-regulatory failure might occur as a result of one of three types of problems: (a) The individual may fail to control his behavior or emotions, resulting in disinhibition; (b) he may use ineffective strategies to achieve his goals, which may be so upsetting as to produce a loss of control; or (c) he may select an inappropriate goal (e.g., to molest a child). In fact, only the first problem is a direct cause of behavioral and emotional dysregulation, although the second problem may lead to regulatory failure.

Basic research on self-regulation has always linked actions and affect (Carver, 2004), where affective self-control is seen as basic to the regulation of overt behavior. For some people, dysregulation of both behavior and emotions is a chronic feature of their life. Such people are described as impulsive and unable to delay gratification. Some sexual offenders appear to fit this description. Other people, including some sexual offenders, experience a loss of self-regulatory control only under particular circumstances. The typical trigger for a loss of self-regulation is a disturbance of some kind—for example, disruption in a romantic relationship, loss of a job, death of a loved one, financial stress, continued job pressure, or a blow to self-esteem. The problem in these circumstances is not chronic impulsivity, but rather an inability to cope with the disturbance. The disturbance triggers a response (e.g., excessive drinking), which might reduce inhibitions and result in acting out in a way that does not serve the client's long-term interests.

The model of dysregulation, as outlined previously, leads to interventions aimed at dealing with either the offender who is chronically impulsive or the person who is periodically dysregulated. For chronic impulsivity we use a variation on what has been referred to as either *cognitive-skills training* or *reasoning and rehabilitation* (R. R. Ross & Fabiano, 1985). The elements we use include problem-solving training (which our clients will have begun earlier in the program, but we remind them again of this); self-monitoring training; teaching clients to identify the chain of events leading to thoughts, leading to feelings, and leading to behaviors involved in effective regulation; and assisting clients in developing strategies to deal with interpersonal problems and helping them recognize the chains of behavior that have in the past led to problems. There is evidence available indicating the utility of cognitive-skills training (Robinson & Porporino, 2001). Coping strategies and mood management, which we described in Phase 1, are also reintroduced or reemphasized here to deal with aspects of mood management.

Emotional self-regulation involves the modulation of both excessive emotions (Bushman, 2002) and, in some instances, the enhancement of positive emotional states (Lucas, Diener, & Larsen, 2003). Mood management strategies (Parkinson, Totterdell, Briner, & Reynolds, 1996) and coping skills training (Lazarus & Folkman, 1984) are useful aspects of approaches to emotional self-regulation. However, a problem for many people concerns their inability to recognize their own emotions, as well as the emotions of others (Gross & Levenson, 1993, 1997), and sexual offenders appear to be particularly deficient in these skills (Gery, Miljkovitch, Berthoz, & Soussignan, 2009; S. M. Hudson et al., 1993; Suchy, Whittaker, Strassberg, & Eastvold, 2009). These deficits in the ability to recognize their own emotions appear to result from the offenders' attempts to suppress the expression of all emotions. Suppression of emotions produces damaging consequences (Pennebaker, 1997) and needs to be overcome.

L. S. Greenberg and Pavio (1997) developed emotion-focused therapy, and Kennedy-Moore and Watson (1999) used strategies to encourage emotional expressiveness in treatment. These two approaches offer strategies for developing emotional self-regulation. Additionally, in discussing affect regulation, R. J. Larsen and Prizmic (2004) offered useful insights that might be helpful to sexual offender therapists. Their crucial point is to encourage emotional expression because without such expression in therapy there would be no opportunity to provide feedback. Larsen and Prizmic also employ a discussion aimed at directing the appropriate control over, and the expression of, emotion. A failure to appropriately recognize and modulate emotions will, as we have seen, produce poor self-regulatory control over behavior. There is solid evidence for the efficacy of Greenberg's emotionally focused therapy (S. Johnson & Sims, 2000), but we have yet to evaluate our approach to enhancing self-regulatory skills.

Relationships

Early reports (Bancroft, 1978; Fagan & Wexler, 1988; Tingle, Barnard, Robbins, Newman, & Hutchinson, 1986) suggested that sexual offenders had difficulties in establishing and developing intimate relationships with adults, although no evidence was offered in support of this view. W. L. Marshall (1989) provided a detailed theoretical account of how intimacy deficits, and the corresponding emotional loneliness, might drive some men to sexually offend. He later (W. L. Marshall, 1993a) suggested that these presumed intimacy deficits resulted from insecure adult attachment styles. These proposed links between intimacy and attachment problems and sexual offending were further elaborated by W. L. Marshall and Marshall (2010b). The clear implications of these three papers were that sexual offenders should show intimacy deficits, experience emotional loneliness, and use inadequate attachment styles. Research has confirmed these expectations. Sexual offenders typically score low on measures of intimacy and high on measures of emotional loneliness (Bumby & Hansen, 1997; Cortoni & Marshall, 2001; Garlick, Marshall, & Thornton, 1996; W. L. Marshall, Champagne, Brown, & Miller, 1998; W. L. Marshall & Hambley, 1996; Seidman, Marshall, Hudson, & Robertson, 1994), and they also display dysfunctional attachment styles (Bumby & Hansen, 1997; S. M. Hudson & Ward, 1997; Jamieson & Marshall, 2000; Lyn & Burton, 2004; Marsa et al., 2004; Smallbone & Dadds, 1998; Ward, Hudson, & Marshall, 1996; Ward, Hudson, & McCormack, 1997).

Ward, Hudson, Marshall, and Siegert (1995) attempted to link the specific adult attachment styles of sexual offenders to the details of their abusive behavior. For example, they suggested that sexual offenders with a preoccupied style would be expected to target children. Furthermore, it was predicted that they would initiate these contacts by engaging in a drawn-out grooming process, much like the courting behavior seen in the prelude to adult romantic relationships. L. E. Marshall and Marshall (in press) examined these predictions and found that 66% of preoccupied offenders did in fact engage in protracted grooming before molesting a child. Ward et al.'s theory obviously lacks some precision but clearly has something to offer and has implications for treatment. Because a history of poor-quality relationships has been shown to predict sexual reoffending (Craig et al., 2003; Hanson & Bussière, 1998; Hanson & Morton-Bourgon, 2005), these features must be addressed in treatment.

We have developed strategies for addressing these problems. We present these to the clients as ways in which they can enhance their skills and thereby increase their chances of securing an enduring and satisfying relationship with an adult of their preferred gender. As a first step, we present clients with Bartholomew and Horowitz's (1991) two-dimensional, four-category model of attachment. Figure 7.1 describes our adaptation of this model.

This is a quite easy model to explain, and it captures the essence of the issues that our clients need to understand. We have found that sexual offenders respond positively to this presentation and spontaneously, or with very little prompting, identify themselves as having one or the other of the three

		Able to give love	Unable to give love
View of self	Lovable	SECURE	DISMISSIVE
	Unlovable	PREOCCUPIED (Anxious/ambivalent)	FEARFUL

Figure 7.1. Model of attachment styles. Data from Bartholomew and Horowitz (1991).

insecure attachment styles. From this it is easy to encourage the client to describe how he behaved in past relationships that would illustrate his insecure style. When the client is describing his past relationships, we encourage him to be as emotionally involved and as expressive as possible. S. Johnson and Sims's (2000) application of emotionally focused therapy to attachment difficulties stresses the importance of emotional expression. They (S. Johnson, Hunsley, Greenberg, & Schindler, 1999) showed that emotional expression during couples' therapy is essential to effective change. From our collaborative examination of clients' relationship history, there emerges an array of dysfunctional behaviors within the areas of communication, self-worth, lack of respect and empathy toward their partner, distrust of others, inappropriate emotional expressions, a coercive style, excessive jealousy, a failure to share mutually enjoyable leisure activities, distorted expectations about sex, and a poor basis for selecting partners.

Our treatment approach to the problem of lack of intimacy derives from this analysis of attachment styles and is tailored to each individual's unique constellation of intimacy-interfering behaviors. Relying on the extensive literature on relationship counseling (Christensen et al., 2004; Epstein & Baucom, 2002; Jacobson & Christensen, 1998) and on the evidence demonstrating its effectiveness (Dunn & Schwebel, 1995; Hahlweg & Klann, 1997; Shadish & Baldwin, 2005), we developed an intervention that we have applied to sexual offenders (Serran, Marshall, & Marshall, 2007). Previously we demonstrated the effectiveness of a slightly less comprehensive version of this intervention in increasing intimacy and in reducing loneliness among sexual offenders (W. L. Marshall, Bryce, Hudson, Ward, & Moth, 1996).

In this approach, we address each of the relationship issues we identified previously as typically problematic among sexual offenders. First, we identify the benefits of having an effective intimate relationship. These benefits include satisfaction in sex and in life, good physical health, and resistance to psychological problems (Dozier, Stovall, & Albus, 1999; Hazan & Zeifman, 1999; Hojat & Vogel, 1989). Next, using Bartholomew and Horowitz's (1991) attachment model (see Figure 7.1), we assist each client in identifying their typical attachment style. If they have difficulties doing this, we ask them to describe previous relationships and their behavior within those relationships. Most sexual offenders describe themselves as having insecure styles, although some characterize themselves as secure (W. L. Marshall & Marshall, 2010b). Once having identified the client's attachment style, we help him consider ways in which he can change. This leads to a discussion about the issues in relationships that make clients effective, such as selecting a compatible partner, good communication, empathy and respect, shared leisure activities, and dealing with issues in a mutually supportive and equitable way. We point out to clients that equitability in relationships generates maximal sexual satisfaction, which in turn leads to greater relationship satisfaction and more general life satisfaction. We also emphasize the importance of doing enjoyable things together with their partner, as this consolidates relationships.

We also discuss jealousy and note that persistent, unfounded jealousy derives from either a low sense of self-worth or the jealous person's own infidelity; in either case, the expression of unfounded jealousy often serves to control the jealous person's partner and markedly reduces relationship satisfaction. Some clients point out that their past expressions of jealousy were founded in fact. In these cases, a discussion is generated concerning what action should be taken. We try to encourage clients to consider whether any of their behaviors might have caused their partner to be unfaithful so that they can change these destructive behaviors. We emphasize the need to seek compatible partners. Too often our clients report rushing into relationships without considering whether they and their partner have interests in common, or they select a partner on the basis of physical appearance alone. A discussion focused on these issues follows. If a client is currently in a relationship, we discuss ways this relationship can be improved. Fortunately, the prisons we work in allow regular conjugal visits during which a client and his partner stay together for 24 to 48 hr in a small private house within the boundary fence of the prison. This allows clients to practice the relationship skills they have been learning and to provide the therapist with feedback about how effective they were.

Sexual Issues

Three issues are addressed in this section of treatment: (a) healthy sexuality, (b) sexual preoccupation, and (c) deviant sexual interests. We describe these three issues separately.

Healthy Sexuality. Although the absence of healthy sexuality itself has not been identified as a criminogenic factor, obviously sexually preoccupied offenders or clients with deviant sexual interests are not functioning in a healthful way. We view the presentation of a healthy sexuality component as an essential precursor to addressing sexual preoccupation and deviant sexual interests. As W. L. Marshall (1971) noted many years ago, it is not enough to remove deviant sexuality from the repertoire of sexual offenders; we must also provide them with the necessary knowledge and skills to function normatively. The previous target of enhancing relationship skills segues nicely into the issue of healthy sexuality, which in turn prepares clients to address a sexually preoccupied style and their deviant interests. Both O'Brien (2004) and Sinclair (2009) have described a healthy sexuality program specifically designed for sexual offenders. Both address almost identical issues, and our program integrates all features of these two approaches.

Our aim in sexual education is directed primarily at changing attitudes and beliefs about sex. An early unpublished study we conducted in the mid 1970s, and a more recent replication (L. E. Marshall, O'Brien, & Marshall, 2010), revealed excessively prudish attitudes among sexual offenders, and our clinical experience has confirmed these findings and expanded the range of dysfunctional attitudes among these men that need correction. We begin sexual education by asking the group to identify as many sexual behaviors as they can. We write these on a flip chart, and once the list is completed, we ask the group to indicate which are appropriate and which are not. The group is then asked to justify their decisions.

This process typically leads to the identification of three categories of sexual behaviors: appropriate, alternative/unusual, and deviant. This exercise typically reveals conservative attitudes among most sexual offenders. For example, oral sex is typically seen by many sexual offenders as unacceptable in their normative sexual relations. In our early study, sexual offenders rated oral sex as 4 out of 10 in terms of its social acceptability, but 9 out of 10 in terms of their personal desire for this act; obviously, there was a significant discrepancy between what they desired and what they thought was socially acceptable. We use this process of identifying beliefs about sexual acts as a way to illustrate beliefs that can interfere with sexual satisfaction. Oral sex, for example, is practiced by the majority of couples, better prepares females for intercourse, and increases the probability that the woman will have an orgasm as well as enhancing both partners' satisfaction with sex (McCarthy & McCarthy, 2002, 2003). Thus, adverse attitudes toward oral sex (or toward any other normative sexual practice) will interfere with the attainment of mutual sexual satisfaction between our clients and their partners.

Negative attitudes toward masturbation are also common. Most sexual offenders, and no doubt many other people, believe that masturbation reveals a weakness or is an indicator that the person is a "sex maniac." It is often seen by our clients as an activity that should only occur in teenagers or adults who are bereft of a partner, whereas the evidence indicates that it is commonly practiced across the age range and is functionally related to greater sexual satisfaction with a partner (McCarthy & McCarthy, 2003). Associated with these attitudes is the belief that older people (with the age cutoff being variable) should not be interested in sex; again, this is a view contradicted by the evidence (Kellett, 2000). We do point out that testosterone to some extent drives sexual desire, that it diminishes with age, and that this reduction is paralleled by a decreasing magnitude of maximal sexual arousal responses (Barbaree, Blanchard, & Langton, 2003). However, we make it clear that this does not mean that older men (including some of our clients) are not interested in, or should abstain from, sexual activities, including solitary sexual pleasures.

Because so many sexual offenders are guilt ridden about what are normal sexual activities, most particularly masturbation, we have developed a procedure for diminishing their guilt (W. L. Marshall, 1975). Because much of this guilt is driven by particular interpretations of their religious beliefs, we have successfully recruited clergy from various religions to assist us in convincing clients that masturbating, for example, is (at least for men in their circumstances) an acceptable behavior. This is necessary not only for them to develop more tolerant attitudes toward sex but also for the use of masturbatory procedures to attenuate deviant sexual interests (see later section). Also, there is often more widespread guilt about sex among some sexual offenders that needs to be modified. Our procedure for allaying sex guilt has been in use for over 30 years and has proved to be effective. It is essentially a simple reinforcement procedure involving the rehearsal of positive statements about masturbating (or any other appropriate sexual act) prior to, during, and particularly immediately after the sexual act. The association of these positive statements with the pleasurable experience of sexual arousal and satisfaction serves to change men's perspective of the act, and they need to be encouraged to overcome their inhibitions about expressing their gender interests with adults.

Other negative attitudes are elicited during broad-ranging discussions about sex. Many sexual offenders express the view that "good" women do not really desire or enjoy sex and that those women who do are described in pejorative terms. This odd bifurcation of females into good (but sexless) women or wicked (but sexually active) women does not help our clients develop effective sexual relationships but does serve to justify rape among some offenders. In addition, homophobic attitudes are common, and among those men who molest pubescent boys but who maintain they are heterosexual, these attitudes tend to be strongest. We (W. L. Marshall, Barbaree, & Butt, 1988) found that men who molested boys fell into two groups: those who selectively molested prepubescents and those who preferentially targeted postpubescents. In terms of their arousal to adult males or females, the former group displayed hetero-sexual preferences, whereas the latter group were clearly homosexual. In a related finding, Adams, Lohr, and Wright (1995) showed that nonoffending males who scored as homophobic (on a self-report measure) displayed greater erectile responses to adult males than did those who were not homophobic. Obviously, for sexual offenders who molest pubescent boys, the issue of shame about a possible homosexual orientation needs to be addressed.

Once we have established the range of sexual activities that are consid-ered normative, both in terms of the beliefs of sexually satisfied couples and in terms of their frequency in the population at large, we turn to discussions of attitudes associated with sex and the most effective strategies for maximizing both partners' sexual satisfaction. In generating group discussions about sex-ual attitudes, the following are commonly held as dysfunctional beliefs among sexual offenders. Many believe that having a small penis (however they define that) will lead to their partner being unable to achieve satisfaction and may very well lead to them being ridiculed. Evidence has indicated that sexual sat-isfaction is unrelated, in either partner, to the size of the man's penis (Masters & Johnson, 1966). When these issues arise, it gives us the opportunity to dis-cuss what attitudes and behaviors do, in fact, increase the likelihood of both partners being satisfied. Believing that women do not really desire sex, that men must lead in all things including sex, that women should be submissive to men, and that a focus on the physical aspects of sex to the exclusion of affec-tionate displays are all attitudes that are unhelpful in achieving the goal of mutual sexual enjoyment. Similar dysfunctional attitudes characterize some openly homosexual men who have committed sexual offenses.

A steady and calm presentation of the facts about human sexuality and the factors that inhibit or facilitate sexual satisfaction is necessary. The two books by McCarthy and McCarthy (2002, 2003) are particularly helpful for therapists attempting to guide sexual offenders toward a better understanding of healthful sexual relationships, and they can be usefully read by clients. How-ever, it is essential to get the group to do most of the work in these discussions. For some particularly intractable clients, we have them write an assignment defending their problematic beliefs and a second essay that challenges these beliefs. This is sometimes effective.

Sexual Preoccupation. Sexual preoccupation (sometimes called *sexual addiction*, *sexual compulsivity*, and *excessive sexual desire*) has been shown to be a significant criminogenic factor. In fact, in Hanson and Morton-Bourgon's (2005) study, sexual preoccupation was the strongest predictor of recidivism among sexual offenders. We (L. E. Marshall & Marshall, 2001, 2006; L. E. Marshall, Marshall, Moulden, & Serran, 2008) have shown that as many as 40% of sexual offenders meet criteria for sexual preoccupation; clearly this is a significant issue. Related to sexual preoccupation, and possibly driving it, is the tendency of some sexual offenders to use sex as a way of coping with life's problems (Cortoni & Marshall, 2001). In addition to Cortoni and Marshall's (2001) findings, other research has supported this claim. Looman (1999) and McKibben and his colleagues (McKibben, Proulx, & Lusignan, 1994; Proulx, McKibben, & Lusignan, 1996) found that when sexual offenders experienced stress, they displayed an increase in sexual activities, including fantasies and masturbation. During these stressful times, sexual offenders were more likely to engage in deviant sex than they were during stress-free periods.

For many sexual offenders, however, reports of being sexually preoccupied appear to have more to do with their attitudes toward their sexual behavior and their beliefs about the appropriate frequency of sexual desire than they do about actual rates of behavior. L. E. Marshall and Marshall (2001, 2006) found no differences in the frequency or diversity of sexual behaviors between those sexual offenders and nonoffenders who met criteria for sexual preoccupation and those who did not, despite significant differences in their attitudes toward their sexual behaviors. Compared with the nonoffenders, the sexual offenders tended to view the same rate of sexual activities as indicating sexual addiction. These differences seem to be a result of a lack of knowledge of, and prudishness about, normative sexual behaviors among the offenders. Thus, the first section of healthy sexuality serves to begin the processes of overcoming sexual preoccupation by reducing prudishness.

Recent years have shown a marked increase in convictions for the possession or distribution of images of child sexual abuse (Middleton, 2009; M. Taylor & Quayle, 2006). Many, if not most, of these offenders meet criteria for sexual preoccupation. Some men report being online for sexual purposes 11 hr or more per week (Cooper, Scherer, Boies, & Gordon, 1999), but information provided by our clients convicted on child pornography charges has indicated that many of them exceed these hours per week. Cooper, Griffin-Shelley, Delmonico, and Mathy (2001) found there were three types of people who display online sexual preoccupation: (a) The stress-reactive man uses Internet sex as a way of relieving stress, much like McKibben and his colleagues (McKibben et al., 1994; Proulx et al., 1996) found with preoccupied sexual offenders; (b) the depressive user seeks sex on the Internet as an escape from depression; and (c) the fiction and fantasy user escapes from a dull daily routine into a world that fulfills his fantasies. Thus providing these sexual offenders with effective coping strategies, mood regulation skills, and the capacity to find more enjoyable leisure activities (see Phase 3 for a description of this) should serve to reduce these sexually preoccupied tendencies. Providing all sexual offenders with more effective relationship skills and attitudes, as well as sexual education, also contributes to diminishing both sexual preoccupation and their excessive use of the Internet for sexual purposes (Goodman, 1998). There are also treatment approaches developed specifically for Internet pornography users that have been shown to be effective (Delmonico, Griffin, & Carnes, 2002; Goodman, 1998). We have adapted some aspects of these programs for the Internet users in our program. However, the problems that beset offenders who turn to images of child sexual abuse on the Internet will be best met by addressing their deviant interests in the same way we do for all sexual offenders.

Deviant Interests. There are several approaches to evaluating sexual interests. Phallometry, which involves measuring erectile responses to sexual stimuli, has a long history dating from the late 1950s (Freund, 1957). It has been used extensively in North America and has recently been implemented in prisons in the United Kingdom. Elsewhere, with the exception of New Zealand and the Czech Republic, it has been less popular. The evidence on the capacity of phallometric testing to reliably identify deviant sexual interests has been debated in the literature, with some authors unequivocally trumpeting its value in identifying deviance across all types of sexual offenders (Lalumière & Quinsey, 1994; Quinsey & Lalumière, 2001) and others expressing more conservative views. Our position is that phallometric testing has value in that it has been consistently shown to identify deviant interests in a reasonable number (some 40%) of nonfamilial child molesters but has a low hit rate in incest offenders and rapists (W. L. Marshall & Fernandez, 2003).

Abel and his colleagues (Abel, Huffman, Warberg, & Holland, 1998; Abel, Jordan, Hand, Holland, & Phipps, 2001; Abel, Jordan, Rouleau, et al., 2004) have offered an alternative procedure that involves measuring the viewing time offenders take to make assessments of images of clothed adults and children. Although there is some evidence supporting the value of Abel's approach (Letourneau, 2002), it is certainly not extensive. Others (Flak, Beech, & Fisher, 2007; Giotakis, 2005; Gress, 2005; Laws & Gress, 2004; Wright & Adams, 1994) have also developed procedures of this kind, and there is evidence supporting the use of their procedures (Gress & Laws, 2009).

Seto (Seto, Harris, Rice, & Barbaree, 2004; Seto & Lalumière, 2001) has designed a Screening Scale for Pedophilic Interests (SSPI) that is completed by a clinician on the basis of behavioral evidence. This scale produces an estimate of deviant sexual interests. Seto and colleagues have shown that the SSPI produces indices of deviance that essentially match those produced by phallometry. However, in independent studies the SSPI was not useful in predicting differential risk to reoffend between pedophilic and nonpedophilic child molesters (Kingston, Firestone, Moulden, & Bradford, 2007; Moulden, Firestone, Kingston, & Bradford, 2009).

When none of these technologies is available to them, clinicians typically rely on inferring deviance from the clients' offense histories. In fact, this may be as sound a basis for deducing deviance as phallometry. In our analyses of phallometric data, we (W. L. Marshall & Fernandez, 2003) showed that the only nonfamilial child molesters who displayed deviant arousal were those who both admitted to having offended and had at least three victims. It is interesting to note that Freund (1991) selected for the studies of the discriminant validity of phallometry only those child molesters who admitted offending and had three or more victims. Freund's data are the most often cited evidence indicating that phallometry identifies deviance in nonfamilial child molesters. It may be that it is simply those child molesters who are repeat offenders and who readily acknowledge their offenses who are shown to be deviant at phallometric assessments. Thus, offense histories may be the soundest basis for inferring deviance, and these histories provide the primary basis for Seto's SSPI measure.

Whatever way deviance is determined (in some cases by the client's report of persistent deviant fantasies or of masturbating exclusively to deviant images), when it is evident it should be addressed in treatment because it has been shown to be a criminogenic factor. Meta-analyses (Craig et al., 2003; Hanson & Bussière, 1998; Hanson & Morton-Bourgon, 2005) have consistently revealed that deviant sexual interests predict reoffending, although only a limited amount of the variance is accounted for by the index of deviance ($r = 0.32$ in Hanson & Bussière, 1998).

W. L. Marshall, O'Brien, and Marshall (2009) described in detail several behavioral procedures for modifying sexual interests that have some empirical support. As we pointed out in that article, the clients need to be encouraged to see that the application of these procedures is embedded in the treatment context of changing various related issues; relationship skills and healthy sexuality are particularly relevant, as are self-esteem, empathy, prosocial sexual attitudes, and coping skills. The therapist and client need to collaboratively identify individualized appropriate (i.e., nondeviant) sexual scripts that can serve as both templates for actual sexual relations and as images for masturbatory activities. These prosocial scripts need to identify the gender appropriate to each client's preference, the age of potential partners (approximately peer aged), and the activities involved. For some offenders, this may not be necessary because they may have adequately strong sexual interests in adult partners, but for some offenders, interest in adults may be minimal.

Typically, an important goal is to eliminate deviant interests or at least reduce them to a level where control is easily attained. In the latter case, where control over the expression (in imagination or overtly) of deviant interests is maintained over time and alternative appropriate expressions are persistently maintained, we can expect extinction of the deviant interests to occur. Unreinforced habitual behavior (in this case, deviant sexual interests) has been shown to extinguish such habits (Falls, 1998), particularly when associated with the repetitive reinforcement of a competing response (in this case appropriate sexual interests). Associated with the extinction phenomenon is a periodic recovery of the interest or habit. This is referred to as *spontaneous recovery* and so long as the replacement behavior is maintained, the magnitude of this recovery is not at the previous full-strength level. At each succeeding recovery, the magnitude of the old habit (i.e., deviant interest) is progressively diminished, resulting in an easier ability to control its expression. We point out to clients that the spontaneous recovery of deviant urges is to be expected and will most likely occur when they are under stress or when a vulnerable state is induced by some other means. The spontaneous recovery, we point out to clients, is not the problem; it is how they respond to it that determines whether or not they return to offending.

In as simple a language as is necessary, each client is apprised of the spontaneous recovery phenomenon so that he can be prepared for it and not respond with the *abstinence violation effect*. This latter effect describes the observed tendency among addicts (Marlatt & Gordon, 1985) to catastrophize whenever they experience a lapse (e.g., smoking one cigarette 3 months after quitting or simply feeling the urge to smoke). Pithers (1990) described the abstinence violation effect as it applies to sexual offenders, and Ward, Hudson, and Marshall (1994) provided evidence of its occurrence in sexual offenders. This catastrophizing occurs when the client sees the lapse (in the case of sexual offenders, the occurrence of a deviant thought or urge) as an indication that he has failed to benefit from treatment, and as a result, he gives up trying to maintain abstinence. For a sexual offender, this latter response would result in a return to offending.

Procedures for enhancing appropriate sexual interests typically involve masturbating to images selected collaboratively by the therapist and the client (see previous comments). Several variants on this approach have been described (see Laws & Marshall, 1991), but the strategy that seems most effective and acceptable to clients involves the following: At each occasion when he masturbates, the client is to generate arousal by whatever means necessary (including using deviant images); once he is aroused, the client is to switch to one of the preidentified appropriate images and continue to masturbate. If he loses arousal to the appropriate image, he is advised to switch to a deviant image until he is rearoused, at which point he is to switch to the appropriate image. This is continued until orgasm occurs. This procedure has been called *orgasmic reconditioning* (Marquis, 1970). It is important to note that it is not orgasm (despite Marquis's title) that reinforces the evocative power of the appropriate image, but rather the level of sexual arousal during masturbation that occurs prior to orgasm.

In an accompanying procedure, once orgasm has occurred, the client is to cease masturbating and begin rehearsing (aloud, if privacy is ensured, or subvocally if not) every variation he can generate on his deviant fantasies. He is to do this for a maximum of 10 min, and he is to ensure he completes this procedure every time he masturbates. Clients are not encouraged to increase their rate of masturbating but rather use these procedures whenever they naturally feel the urge. W. L. Marshall (1979; W. L. Marshall & Lippens, 1977) developed this procedure, which he called *satiation therapy* in the mid-1970s, and it quickly became popular with therapists working with sexual offenders. Masters and Johnson (1966) had shown that immediately after orgasm men enter what they called the *refractory period,* a period in which previously evocative sexual stimuli lose their capacity to generate sexual arousal. Marshall saw this natural phenomenon as an opportunity to extinguish the provocativeness of deviant images because evoking them during the refractory period would necessarily associate them with nonreinforcement (i.e., a nonarousal state). He also noted that quite early on in the history of behavior therapy, Edwin Guthrie (1935) had observed that the unreinforced repetition of an entrenched habit led to its elimination. Pairing these two observations, Marshall proposed satiation therapy as an effective way to eliminate deviant sexual interests. Subsequent research, using both controlled single-case designs (W. L. Marshall, 1979) and a series of group studies (Alford, Morin, Atkins, & Schoen, 1987; Hunter & Goodwin, 1992; Hunter & Santos, 1990; Johnston, Hudson, & Marshall, 1992), has demonstrated the effectiveness of satiation therapy in achieving the long-term cessation of deviant interests.

There are other procedures for reducing deviance, and, in keeping with our philosophy of offering clients a choice, we describe the several alternatives and allow the client to choose. Typically we do, however, encourage the use of satiation because it involves naturally occurring processes that we believe maximize its likely effectiveness. We do not offer electric aversion therapy despite some evidence indicating its effectiveness (Quinsey, Chaplin, & Carrigan, 1980), nor do we offer shame aversion (Serber, 1970), for which there is no solid supporting evidence despite its widespread use in the United States (see survey by McGrath, Cumming, & Burchard, 2003). These two procedures are experienced as stressful by the clients and can be disruptive to the therapeutic relationship. Similarly, we rarely offer olfactory aversion for these same reasons, although there are occasions (e.g., when the client indicates the importance of smell in his offending behaviors) when it seems to be the best choice, and we have had good results with its use (W. L. Marshall, 2006b; W. L. Marshall, Keltner, & Griffiths, 1974) as have others (Colson, 1972; Dougher, 1995a; W. A. Kennedy & Foreyt, 1968; Morganstern, 1974). Ammonia aversion can also be effective (Colson, 1972; Maletzky, 1991; Wolpe, 1969), and we have used it with exhibitionists (W. L. Marshall, 2006a) and with child molesters who report persistent and intrusive deviant thoughts throughout each day. Ammonia aversion involves the pairing of deviant thoughts or urges with the self-administration of an inhalation of the fumes from a small bottle of salts of ammonia (popularly known as smelling salts). The rapid inhalation of these fumes is relayed by the pain receptors to the brain and immediately removes any thought the client has. At this point the client is told to generate non-sexual thoughts.

Finally, covert sensitization (Cautela, 1967) involves having the client evoke the deviant image and follow this immediately with the evocation of an imaginal aversive consequence (e.g., getting caught in the act). We (W. L. Marshall, 2007a) have modified this procedure and renamed it *covert association*, primarily because the active ingredient appears not to be the aversiveness of the consequence but rather simply the paired association of the deviant image and the consequence. This procedure appeals to the majority of sexual offenders, and consequently it is frequently the first chosen option. Because it does not always bring relief (possibly as a result of noncompliance with the somewhat complex instructions), we offer the combination of orgasmic reconditioning and satiation as the alternative.

Whichever procedure, or combination of procedures, is chosen, the client reports his use at each group treatment session. Clients who are not complying with the instructions typically reveal this either directly or by their inability to answer questions put to them about their use of the specific procedure.

In addition to behavioral techniques, we also use pharmacological interventions with some clients. Other than the use of medications to assist in managing the various Axis I and Axis II disorders that some sexual offenders display (W. L. Marshall, 2007b), the institutional psychiatrist (on our referral) offers other pharmacological treatments to our clients (see W. L. Marshall, Booth, Bradford, & Marshall, 2009). For sexually preoccupied offenders who appear unresponsive to our psychological treatment, we use one of the selective serotonin reuptake inhibitors (SSRIs). These SSRIs have been shown to decrease libido (Rothschild, 2000) and may therefore give sexual addicts greater control over the expression of their sexual desires. What limited evidence there is on the use of SSRIs with either sexually preoccupied men or sexual offenders has indicated positive results (Bradford, Greenberg, Gojer, Martindale, & Goldberg, 1995; D. M. Greenberg & Bradford, 1997; Kafka, 1994; Kafka & Prentky, 1992). We wait, where possible, to see the effects of our psychological interventions before we recommend the use of an SSRI, but some clients are, quite early in treatment, clearly distracted by sexual thoughts, and some behave sexually inappropriately with staff. For these clients, we suggest to them that placing them on an SSRI will facilitate their engagement in psychological treatment by removing distractions and thereby enhance the gains they will derive from treatment. As clients make progress in psychological treatment, we gradually reduce the dosage of the SSRI.

For treatment-resistant but nonpreoccupied clients, we suggest that one or another of the antiandrogens or hormonal treatments may be worth a trial.

For sexual offenders who clearly meet criteria for sexual sadism, we suggest they take one of these agents at least partly because the Canadian National Parole Board, not unreasonably, considers this to be an essential strategy for these offenders before release to the community; the parole board believes this makes the community safer. Evidence on the value of medroxprogesterone acetate (Provera), cyproterone acetate (Androcur), and gonadotropin-releasing hormone analogues (e.g., Leuprolide) in reducing the danger sexual offenders present is consistently supportive (see Bradford, 2000; W. Glaser, 2003; Saleh, 2009; for reviews), although most studies are not well-controlled trials. Except for the sexual sadists, we again only recommend these pharmacological agents when psychological treatment is failing, and again once effects are apparent, we gradually withdraw drug treatment.

Phase 3: Self-Management

This final phase of the program aims at integrating what has been learned so far into plans for release and for the continued development of a more fulfilling life. The first step involves identifying the goals, and plans to achieve these goals, within the framework of our version of the GLM.

The Good Lives Model

The GLM was developed and introduced to the field of sexual offender treatment by Ward (2002) and subsequently elaborated by Ward and various colleagues (see Ward, Collie, & Bourke, 2009, and P. M. Yates & Ward, 2008, for the latest versions of the model and a summary of the relevant publications). As depicted in Exhibit 7.2, our version of the GLM has collapsed some of Ward's statements of the goods involved to a more manageable list for our clients, and we describe these goods in accessible language. This list is posted on the wall of the group room, and from the beginning and throughout treatment all clients are instructed to read and reread it as they work at generating their own plans for a more fulfilling life. At the beginning of Phase 3, we work collaboratively with each client to assist him in generating both a set of goals derived from the GLM as well as the plans he has to achieve, or work toward, these goals. We point out to our clients that they have, by this point in treatment, acquired many skills and attitudes that will facilitate their efforts at achieving a better life. They are, we point out, far better equipped to develop effective relationships, they have acquired coping skills that will ensure greater inner peace, and they have developed greater self-directive skills and self-confidence. For the clients, this aspect of treatment is characteristically experienced as enjoyable but only when the goals are reasonably circumscribed and not overwhelming.

Although many sexual offenders have as a goal better health as well as a purpose in life (typically within a religious affiliation), for most of them their primary goal is the enhancement of their work skills, which may be associated with the pursuit of further education. These two goals (mastery in work and increased knowledge) appear in all versions of the GLM and are fundamental to increasing the client's sense of security on release. We also strongly encourage them to generate a list of leisure activities or to enhance the range and frequency of current leisure interests. Idle time and its associated boredom can put sexual offenders at risk to reoffend, so we take the generation of a list of leisure pursuits, and their active engagement, as critical factors.

Once goals are specified, we ask the client to indicate his plans for working toward his goals. We point out that most of the GLM goals are not completely achieved in anyone's lifetime, so that each client needs to see the striving toward his goals as a lifelong, enjoyable process. However, working toward the goals and achieving small steps (i.e., each subplan) along the way can be very satisfying. In particular, achieving improvements in health, upgrading education, and training for a better job are all attainable within a limited time span, and achievement of the subgoals can serve to motivate the client's continued devotion to the overall goals. We encourage clients not to take on too many overall goals (we usually try to limit them to two or at most three goals) and to set clear subgoals and outline plans to achieve each of these subgoals.

By this point in treatment, the client should have developed a sufficient level of self-efficacy (i.e., a belief that he can attain his goals and a belief that the achievement of them will enhance his life) such that as long as his goals and subgoals are a reasonable match for his talents, he should be strongly motivated to achieve the beginnings of his good life. These individual plans and goals are presented by the client to the group and all group members are invited to give feedback. Feedback, we remind group members, should begin with complimenting the presenter on what he has done well before any suggestions for improvement are offered. We expect clients to have begun the processes necessary to implement their plans (e.g., identifying courses to upgrade job skills or education and contacting appropriate training programs) before discharge from treatment.

Avoidance Strategies

As we noted earlier (see Introduction), we reject those relapse-prevention approaches that require the clients to generate an elaborate list of situations, people, and thoughts that might put them at risk and that then require them to identify ways in which they will avoid these so-called risk factors. In these RP approaches, the clients are typically required to either carry these lists with them at all times or to reread them on a regular basis. In most cases, the lists are too long for any person to be able to abide by these instructions. As a result, we guess that many sexual offenders who have completed one of these RP-based programs will discard their avoidance lists and soon forget them. Insofar as this happens, it would appear to increase their risk to reoffend because they have been convinced during treatment that these plans and strategies are crucial. It is, in our view, far better to limit avoidance plans to no more than one or two strategies partly for the reasons outlined previously but also because, as we saw earlier, avoidance plans are rarely maintained (Gollwitzer & Bargh, 1996). Having some approach plans as an alternative, as embodied in the GLM, is far more likely to lead to success (Emmons, 1996; Gollwitzer & Bargh, 1996). As we noted earlier, Mann et al. (2004) showed that sexual offender programs that emphasized avoidance plans failed to properly engage clients who, as a consequence, did not complete between-sessions practice, were reluctant to disclose issues, and were not committed to remain offense free; sexual offenders in programs that emphasized approach plans were, on the other hand, engaged, motivated, eager to disclose important information, and determined to complete all their between-sessions tasks.

For most child molesters, the simple avoidance plan we encourage them to adopt involves never being alone with a child. We point out to them that even if they are confident they will not molest a child, being observed alone with a child could readily generate suspicion in others and might invite a false accusation. For rapists, we suggest that they avoid engaging in behaviors they previously used to contact a victim (e.g., cruising lonely roads with the aim of finding an isolated woman or picking up single women at late-night bars). For many sexual offenders, abstinence from intoxicants is an essential avoidance plan.

Support Groups

Most programs for sexual offenders include a requirement that each offender identify people who can assist him in readjusting after release from prison or discharge from a community treatment facility (see the survey by McGrath et al., 2003). Specific strategies for enlisting family, friends, and others as supports for released or discharged sexual offenders have been described by Cumming and her colleagues (Cumming & Buell, 1996; Cumming & McGrath, 2000). The most detailed and demonstrably effective type of support program has been described in a series of publications (Mennonite Central Committee of Ontario, 1996; Quaker Peace and Social Justice, 2005; R. J. Wilson, 2007). Now called the Circles of Support and Accountability (COSA), this program involves two teams: volunteers and professionals. The volunteers include four to six community members who have agreed to provide 24-hr access to the client, whereas the professionals (who also volunteer

their time) provide advice and support for the volunteers. COSA was originally developed in Ontario, Canada, but has been implemented in the United
Kingdom. In both settings the evidence indicates that COSA is effective in
reducing reoffending (see summary by R. J. Wilson, 2007). More recently,
R. J. Wilson, Cortoni, and McWhinnie (2009) reported an evaluation of
COSA showing that only 2.3% of high-risk sexual offenders involved in this
program reoffended over a 3-year follow-up despite being released at expiry
of their sentence and therefore with no parole supervision. A matched group
of high-risk sexual offenders released under the same conditions, but without
the assistance of COSA, had a recidivism rate for sexual offenses of 13.7%.
These are impressive data.

As for the more common strategy, and one that we follow, of having the
offender identify a personally defined support group of friends and family, there
is evidence demonstrating its value. Data on the specific provision of support
groups have indicated that they add to the effectiveness of other strategies
including treatment (Grubin, 1997; Gutiérrez-Lobos et al., 2001; Willis, 2008).
With nonsexual offenders, Dowden, Antonowicz, and Andrews (2003) showed
in a meta-analysis that when significant others are trained to assist an offender
adjust to an offense-free life after release from prison, powerful and positive
reductions in reoffense rates are apparent.

We ask clients to identify family, friends, or workmates who might serve
as supports, and we require them to specify what each of these supports will
do to assist them. Clients are also asked to identify professionals who might
also assist them. This latter group might include their parole or probation officer or a sexual offender treatment provider in their community, but it should
also include professionals who can assist them in various other ways. For
example, they might need financial advice, they might need help preparing a
résumé, they might have to have help in repairing damaged relationships, or
they may have an Axis I disorder or a health problem that will require treatment. Generally clients recognize the value of having supports, and most
work diligently on forming these groups.

Release Plans

The primary targets here are to have the client identify where he is
going to live, how he will generate an income, and what he will do with his
spare time. Each release plan, when successful, can serve as a protective factor. However, we are careful to ensure that accommodations, jobs, and leisure
activities do not put the client at risk and do not give him ready access to victims. If he is to return to live with a previous partner, or one he has established contact with while in treatment, it must be clear that this living
arrangement does not provide him with access to victims. Some jobs and
some leisure pursuits can similarly place him at risk.

FINAL REPORT

Once all these plans (i.e., the individualized GLM, limited avoidance strategies, the identification of support groups, and the generation of sensible release plans) are in place, the offender is evaluated to determine how ready he is for release and whether he needs further treatment. A report is generated reflecting these concerns, as well as describing his involvement in treatment, his commitment to staying offense free, and the degree to which treatment has lowered his risk.

We base our report on the therapist's observations and information provided by case management officers, correctional staff, and staff involved in the jobs the client has participated in. We assimilate these sources of information, and on the basis of this and observations made during treatment, the therapist completes the current version of our Therapist Rating Scale (TRS-2). The original version (TRS-1) of this was described in a previous book (W. L. Marshall, Marshall, Serran, & Fernandez, 2006). It identified 17 topics on which the therapists had to rate the client in terms of (a) the degree to which he could articulate the critical features of each topic and (b) the degree to which he had demonstrated the appropriate behaviors, thoughts, and emotions associated with each topic. We also reported in that earlier book evidence on the satisfactory interrater reliability of the scale. As a result of feedback from clinicians using the TRS-1 at different sites in different countries, we modified it. Initially it was too complex and had too many topics, which discouraged its diligent completion. We have responded to this feedback by reducing the topics to 10 and by simplifying the instructions. Clinicians have responded positively to this latest version. We have attached as an appendix the revised version (TRS-2).

CONCLUSION

In this chapter, we have provided the details of our therapeutic approach, the targets (both engagement facilitating and criminogenic) we address, and the procedures we use to address those targets in the RPS Primary Program. Although we hope to have made a persuasive case for the value of our approach, we have also been able to evaluate the long-term effectiveness of this program. As we saw in Chapter 5, the long-term outcome evaluation of the program revealed positive results. Reoffenses were tracked in the official records of charges and convictions over a long-term follow-up (M = 8.4 years, range = 5–18 years) of 535 treated sexual offenders. This study showed that the program effectively reduced reoffending. Other results from this study showed that the therapist's rating of the benefits (or otherwise) that each client derived from treatment was the only factor that predicted recidivism or not; neither scores on risk assessment instruments (i.e., Rapid Risk Assessment for Sex Offence Recidivism, Hanson, 1997a; STATIC-99, Hanson & Thornton, 1999) nor scores on the Psychopathy Checklist–Revised (Hare, 1991) predicted recidivism. Other researchers (e.g., Hogue, 1994, 2009; Stirpe, Wilson, & Long, 2001) have shown that similar therapist rating measures completed by therapists accurately predict success or failure after discharge from treatment.

In the next chapter, we describe how we have adapted the RPS Primary Program to treat those men who not only claim they were wrongly convicted (i.e., they declare they have never committed a sexual offense) but also refuse to enter any program that is aimed at challenging their denial.

8

ROCKWOOD DENIERS' PROGRAM

The majority of sexual offender treatment providers have excluded deniers from their programs (Happel & Auffrey, 1995; Schwartz, 1995). Cohen (1995) pointed out that this is neither therapeutically sensible nor legally appropriate. We share Cohen's view that every effort should be made to involve all offenders in treatment because they all pose a potential future threat to others. As Maletzky (1996) put it, "To deny a crime is natural; to deny treatment to those who deny is a crime itself" (p. 4). To date, a number of different approaches have been taken to treating those men who categorically deny having committed a sexual offense. Most of these approaches, as Schneider and Wright (2004) noted, have been developed on the assumption that denial of offending is a significant barrier to effective treatment that must be overcome. These programs are, therefore, designed to move convicted sexual offenders who are in categorical denial to accept responsibility for their sexual offending so that they can then enter a program designed for those who admit to their offenses. The assumption involved in this approach is that admitting to the offense is a necessary prerequisite for successful treatment engagement (Barbaree, 1991; Lombardo, & DiGiorgio-Miller, 1988). Yet, as demonstrated earlier in this book, denial is not a criminogenic factor.

However, it is clear that men convicted of a sexual offense who categorically deny ever having committed the crime present a problem. Most refuse to enter a treatment program and, as a result, will eventually be released from custody without their problems being addressed. If in fact they did commit a sexual offense, as seems almost certain in most cases, then they will be at risk to abuse or assault another innocent victim. This seems to us to be too high a price to allow the continued neglect of these men's treatment. As a result of our concerns and those of the Correctional Service of Canada and the Canadian National Parole Board, both of which have expressed worries about releasing untreated sexual offenders, we designed a program aimed at reducing the risk posed by these categorical deniers. This chapter describes the Rockwood Psychological Services (RPS) Deniers' Program. First, however, we review earlier approaches to treating deniers.

EARLIER APPROACHES

One of the earliest reports of the treatment of deniers was the intervention described by O'Donohue and Letourneau (1993), which aimed at overcoming denial. They reported that 65% of the deniers became admitters after their seven-session program, which included cognitive restructuring and educational components. Schlank and Shaw (1996) described an account of the procedures they used involving 16 sessions focusing on providing face-saving ways in which deniers could change their position. In their study, five of the 10 clients admitted to their offenses postintervention. A similar reduction was reported by Brake and Shannon (1997), whose 21-session, one-on-one program included face-saving tactics, motivational strategies, explanations of the purpose of denial, reframing, and tactics aimed at enhancing victim empathy.

In the RPS Primary Program in the early 1990s, we (W. L. Marshall, 1994) emphasized, as we still do, focusing on acceptance of the client but not of the offense. At that time, we made an effort to have a mix of admitters and deniers in the same program. The senior members of the program were seen as pivotal in helping the newer clients to give a disclosure that was at least somewhat inculpatory. Using this approach, only two of the 25 group members who entered the program as deniers remained in denial after completing the program. Other strategies referred to in the literature, which unfortunately have not been accompanied by research data, include Jenkins's (1990) description of his *invitations to responsibility* approach, which involves 3 years of individual and group psychotherapy, and Winn's (1996) approach, which involves metaconfrontation, which he described as "a strategic process of challenging the offender to challenge himself" (p. 30). Other apparently successful approaches have focused on individual motivational interviewing (Mann, Ginsburg, &

Weekes, 2002) and individual assessment feedback procedures, including feedback of the results of phallometry (Bradford & Greenberg, 1998). All these approaches, however, were aimed at overcoming denial and were deemed to be successful if, and only if, the barriers to admitting were breached.

These approaches appear to have generated some success. Some, however, were rather long and somewhat confrontational, which might disrupt the therapeutic process in the remaining parts of a comprehensive treatment program. Given that denial is not a criminogenic factor (Hanson & Bussière, 1998; Hanson & Morton-Bourgon, 2005), the goal of these programs appears unsound and, as Maletzky (1998) showed, overcoming denial is not a necessary precondition for engaging sexual offenders in treatment. Maletzky (1998) found no differences in the long-term outcome of treated admitters versus treated deniers, although it must be said that his report was not originally designed to evaluate the relative effectiveness of treating deniers. Beckett et al. (1994) and H. G. Kennedy and Grubin (1992) found that reducing denial and minimization (i.e., taking responsibility for offending) did not necessarily produce changes in other treatment targets.

As noted, Hanson and his colleagues (Hanson & Bussière, 1998; Hanson & Morton-Bourgon, 2005) found no relationship between denial of the sexual offense and sexual recidivism in either treated or untreated offenders. Oddly enough, two studies (Kahn & Chambers, 1991; Langström & Grann, 2000) found that denial of an offense among adolescent sexual offenders actually predicted a lower propensity to subsequently reoffend sexually, a finding consistent with Maruna's (2001) observations. A possible reason for these perhaps counterintuitive findings was suggested by Hanson (2003), who reasoned that "excusing one's own behavior is less problematic than believing that it is okay for others to do the same thing" (p. 9). Other researchers (Beech & Fisher, 2002; D. D. Fisher, Beech, & Browne, 1998; Simourd & Malcolm, 1998) have suggested that equating denial with risk is a logical fallacy. These commentators have pointed out that many high-risk offenders can be quite open about their offending in contrast to low-risk offenders, among whom a significant number are in denial.

DEVELOPMENT OF THE RPS DENIERS' PROGRAM

The evidence reviewed previously suggests that there may be no need to work to overcome denial. Coupling this with the need to provide these offenders with effective treatment led W. L. Marshall, Thornton, Marshall, Fernandez, and Mann (2001) to formulate an alternative approach to treating sexual offenders in categorical denial. This approach was developed in direct response to the fact that many deniers refuse to enter a treatment program in which the aim is to overcome their exculpatory account. In the institutional setting in which we work, refusals to enter treatment resulted in these deniers occupying beds for extended periods as they were being held until the expiry of their sentence. This meant that these beds could not be used to house sexual offenders who were eager to enter treatment. We therefore decided to design a program aimed exclusively at deniers that would set aside the issue of their denial and focus on the criminogenic needs identified in the literature. In other words, the RPS Primary Program we described in Chapter 7 is applied to deniers, except that we do not challenge their position on their responsibility for their offense.

We have now operated this program since the late 1990s and have had almost no refusals of our offer of treatment to the deniers. We present the program to these men as an opportunity for them to learn the skills and attitudes necessary to avoid placing themselves in the future in a position in which they could be falsely accused again. We tell them that, for the purposes of treatment, we will not challenge their view that they were falsely accused and convicted in the past. Laws (2002), in commenting on this approach, suggested that it adopted an ingenious tactic in dealing with denial:

> By making a simple promise and keeping to it, the therapists engage the clients in a programme they say they do not need, for a problem they say they do not have, to prevent another offence that they say they did not commit in the first place. (p. 187)

As outlined in greater detail in Chapter 7, our general approach to treating men who have sexually offended is grounded in positive psychology and adopts a motivational approach. The foundation of our treatment model is based on group processes and emphasizes the importance of therapist characteristics. Our approach is flexible and individualized for each client, and we emphasize the development of a trusting client–therapist relationship.

The RPS Deniers' Program was first implemented in 1998 at a medium security prison in Ontario, Canada. As noted, a significant number of clients incarcerated at this institution were refusing treatment because they were categorically denying their offenses. One of the most immediately pressing issues was that these clients could not be moved to lower security or get parole because of their untreated status. Often, these men were seen as resistant and treated as such by other staff and by the National Parole Board. However, some of them indicated that they would be willing to participate in programming but would not agree to join a group in which they would be forced to admit to their offenses. We run approximately one Deniers' Program each year, consisting of eight to 10 participants. The program is run on a closed basis because of the lack of continuing numbers that would be necessary for it to be run as a rolling format.

PROGRAM DESCRIPTION

Although most of what we do in the RPS Deniers' Program is a match for the RPS Primary Program, we provide details here (albeit somewhat truncated) so that readers who are interested in implementing a deniers' program do not have to continually refer back to the Primary Program. We tell the clients that the treatment goal is to help them identify problems in their lives that led them to be falsely accused of sexual offending. This stated goal is aimed at motivating these men to fully participate in treatment. Consistent with the RPS Primary Program, we address all dynamic risk factors that are relevant to sexual offending. The following represents an overview of the components.

Preparatory Sessions

At the outset, most deniers present as suspicious and distrustful of the intentions of the program. They tend to be focused on attempting to "retry" their case with every professional they meet, including the therapists. These clients frequently appear disinterested (e.g., sitting slumped over, falling asleep), engage in problematic group behavior (e.g., making inappropriate comments, whispering, giggling), or fail to engage meaningfully in session discussions. Because of the demonstrated value of the RPS Preparatory Program for readying offenders for treatment (see Chapter 6), we begin with two preparatory sessions for the deniers.

These sessions are motivational in nature and provide information about the behavior that will best contribute to the clients achieving their goals (i.e., early release). Group rules (confidentiality, participation, attendance, respect) are discussed, and group members are encouraged to contribute to building group rules. Participants are also provided information about treatment content, the nature of our final treatment reports, and the results and meanings of their risk assessments. We follow this with a group exercise addressing clients' self-esteem, which, as we showed in Chapter 7, facilitates the attainment of various other treatment targets. The other domains in which self-esteem deficits are evident include relationship functioning, physical appearance, academic and occupational performance, and social and sexual functioning. Clients are required to identify several strengths in each of these areas of functioning and share those with the group during discussion. This exercise allows the therapist to develop insight into each client's view of himself and provides an opportunity to emphasize the client's strengths. Group members are encouraged to identify strategies to improve their confidence (see Chapter 7), such as expanding their social activities, attending to and increasing pleasurable experiences, and repeatedly articulating positive self-statements.

The following sections address issues described in detail in the RPS Primary Program (Chapter 7). Here we briefly outline our strategies for addressing the various topics with deniers, but we essentially address each issue in the same detail as in the RPS Primary Program.

Background Factors

The first assignment the group members complete is their version of the circumstances surrounding the "accusation." When they present this, we make no effort to challenge their version of events, which gives us the opportunity to demonstrate that we are not trying to coerce them into admitting to the offense. Instead, we focus on the themes we described in the RPS Primary Program as background factors. These include use of intoxicants, relationship problems, other ongoing stressors, and being in a situation in which their behavior could be misconstrued. These are among the relevant proximal factors preceding the event that prompted the allegation.

As part of our attempt to identify more distal factors, we have the clients complete an autobiography between sessions that they then present to the group. For this exercise, we follow the same processes as outlined in Chapter 7. Problem areas identified collaboratively in this process allow us to determine the specific issues to concentrate on during treatment. One particularly problematic and reasonably common autobiography given by deniers involves a presentation that reflects a "perfect" life. This type of client is one of the most challenging to work with as he is not willing, at least initially, to acknowledge any problematic aspects of his life. In these cases, we provide direct feedback emphasizing that it is important to identify problem areas so that we can offer help, and we point out that no one (including the therapist) has a life history free of any problems. Other group members are not initially very helpful in providing challenges at this stage of treatment, but fortunately there is usually one who responds appropriately. We reinforce successive approximations to a full account of background factors by initially encouraging any semblance of the responses we want and by subsequently reinforcing more elaborate accounts. If the client continues to insist he has no problems, we explain the consequences to him of continuing to present in this way; most important, we explain that this will limit our ability to provide a final report that will be favorably considered by the National Parole Board.

Clients are required to examine the circumstances and their actions around the time of the accusation. The goal is to help them identify proximal factors that occurred at the time of the alleged event (e.g., anger, intoxication, perceived failures, problems in relationships). These, plus the distal factors (e.g., ongoing relationship difficulties, sexual preoccupation, poor self-regulation), are the criminogenic features we address during treatment. Clients are then asked to consider those factors that might place them at risk of being falsely accused again in the future (i.e., risk factors and awareness exercise). These factors differ for each group member, although there are often similarities. These factors typically include feeling depressed, lonely, isolated, or rejected; having casual sexual relationships, particularly when alcohol is involved; using a computer to access pornography; and having unsupervised contact with minors. We assist clients in developing strategies for avoiding these issues or escaping from circumstances that might pose a threat or provide someone with the opportunity to falsely accuse them. Although we do not emphasize these relapse prevention issues in the RPS Primary Program, we find that this exercise with the deniers helps clarify for them situations that might place them at risk in the future for being suspected or accused of offending.

Relationships

To initiate a discussion of past relationships and their problems, we begin by presenting a discussion of adult attachment, including a presentation of Bartholomew's (Bartholomew & Horowitz, 1991) four adult styles of attachment (see Chapter 7). Clients are assisted in identifying their prototypical attachment style and its associated costs and benefits. This analysis typically encourages the participants to recognize the need to develop the skills and knowledge necessary to achieve a more secure approach to relationships. We discuss characteristics of a healthy relationship, including trust, communication, the value of equitability, and healthy sexual behaviors, and also issues such as jealousy, loneliness, and coping with rejection. Group members describe their previous relationships and are encouraged to consider any unhealthy patterns (e.g., tendency to avoid conflict, failure to communicate, having extramarital affairs). The clients identify and practice positive relationship skills, including communication and feedback, the ability to compromise, the development of trust, and choice of an appropriate partner. The practice of these behaviors occurs by in-group role-playing and between sessions in interactions with staff and other inmates. Healthy sexuality, in the context of a healthy intimate relationship, is also discussed. Group members are advised that effective communication and a satisfactory degree of intimacy are factors related to increased sexual satisfaction, which in turn is related to relationship satisfaction and life enhancement.

Coping and Mood Management

As we saw in Chapter 7, research has demonstrated that sexual offenders have dysfunctional coping strategies. Inadequate coping strategies generate stress and distress, both of which increase the likelihood of coping through sex and fantasy. Clients are required to identify problems from their past and describe how they attempted to cope with them. The discussion of their presentations centers on generating various alternative strategies, along with the benefits and costs of adopting those strategies. We also discuss the different coping styles (emotion focused, task focused, and avoidance focused), and we encourage group members to identify their prototypic style. Skill building (e.g., appropriate assertiveness) is offered by way of role-plays, and clients are encouraged to put their newly acquired skills into practice between treatment sessions at every opportunity. Additionally, we encourage clients to identify and appropriately express their emotions to develop better emotional regulation.

Victim Harm

The National Parole Board insists that deniers in particular show that they understand the harm that befalls victims of sexual abuse, even if not for their own presumed victim. As a result, we address this in some detail while at the same time encouraging the expression of empathy toward various other people.

In discussing victim harm (the recognition of which is a prerequisite to victim empathy), we are careful to ensure that our clients do not think we are trying to trick them into admitting they committed the offense. To this end, the discussion focuses on the potential effects on the victims of other perpetrators. If any client does become defensive about engaging in these discussions, we inform him that this topic is one of particular concern to the National Parole Board. Each client is required to identify the effects of sexual abuse on the victims, both in the short and long term. The participants are informed that by understanding the effects of sexual abuse, they will be more sensitive to signs that it is happening and this will help them avoid or withdraw from situations in which abuse might be occurring so that no one can accuse them of offending.

Self-Management

In the final step, group members construct a self-management plan in which they design strategies and learn the behaviors necessary to enhance their life. We focus on helping them build a positive and satisfying lifestyle (based on the good lives model; Ward, 2002), pointing out that this will decrease the likelihood of their being "falsely accused" again. Clients are required to set realistic and positive goals for themselves in two or three domains (particularly around education, work, leisure pursuits, and relationships). They are also asked to develop a support network consisting of family, friends, organizations (e.g., John Howard Society, Salvation Army), and professionals (e.g., counselors). We encourage the development of approach rather than avoidance goals, as these are more motivating and easier to achieve. By emphasizing the development of skills, attitudes, and beliefs that are supportive of a positive and prosocial lifestyle, it is assumed that clients will be less likely to reoffend (or, in their view, less likely to be falsely accused). In a collaborative and constructive manner, we work with each client to help him identify an individualized set of goals consistent with his interests and abilities. Finally, we help our clients identify, develop, and practice the skills required to achieve their goals.

CONCLUSION

Typically, categorical deniers have posed a problem for most treatment providers. In other programs, deniers have either refused treatment or been barred from entering treatment. If they enter treatment, all too often programs remove these clients for failing to admit to their recorded offense. We have developed a motivational approach that addresses the key issues leading to the accusation without directly dealing with the issue of their denial. This approach has effectively served to engage clients and allowed us to address issues relevant to risk. The program accepts clients who are in categorical denial but who express some interest in working toward a more favorable parole outcome or who express some interest in dealing with problems they have encountered in their life.

Clearly, sexual offenders who are in denial can be motivated to engage in effective treatment aimed at identifying and overcoming the problems in their lives that led them to offend or, as they view it, led them to place themselves in a position in which they could be successfully accused and convicted of a sexual offense they did not commit. We have conducted a tentative evaluation of the RPS Deniers' Program that is described in Chapter 5. This evaluation suggests that the program is effective in reducing long-term recidivism. The results indicate that the program is as effective as is the RPS Primary Program, which targets clients who admit to having sexually offended.

AFTERWORD: SUMMARY AND IMPLICATIONS FOR FUTURE TREATMENT AND RESEARCH

In this volume, we have outlined the influences that guide the present state of Rockwood Psychological Services' (RPS) treatment programs. Although the nature of these programs has been influenced by our clinical experience over the past 40 years and by the available literature on sexual offenders, we have also been persuaded that the current approaches to a broad range of psychological problems, embodied primarily within the framework of positive psychology (Linley & Joseph, 2004b; Snyder & Lopez, 2005), are applicable to the treatment of sexual offenders. Similarly, like many others in the sexual offender field, Miller and Rollnick's (2002) motivational interviewing approach has significantly influenced our work. In the Introduction to the present book, we outlined these various influences.

In the first main section of the book, Research and Theory on Sexual Offender Treatment, we reviewed the literature on a variety of issues. As a result of these reviews, we have summarized what we believe to be the most useful adaptations of the relevant literature. For instance, in Chapter 1 we described various approaches to assessment and case formulation. From this we suggested that although risk/needs assessments can usefully guide allocation to appropriate levels of treatment, a battery of other tests administered during pretreatment provide little in the way of value for the task of producing a case formulation. Our conclusion is that case formulation is best served by a treatment framework based on known criminogenic features (i.e., a nomothetic-based identification of generic treatment targets) that is adapted by information derived from each client once he enters the treatment process (i.e., an idiographic-based specific case formulation).

We then provided an overview (see Chapter 2) of the decisions that must be made about treatment design and procedures, such as whether to use manuals, group versus individual therapy, rolling versus closed groups, and the influence of various operating features (e.g., length and number of sessions per week, total time in treatment, and whether there should be one or more therapists per group). Although there is little in the way of evidence to guide us on any of the important decisions noted in Chapter 2, we offered suggestions, based on our experience and what little has been written, for the resolution of these necessary decisions.

A consideration of the general clinical literature, as well as a consideration of the limited but helpful research with sexual offenders, provided us in Chapter 3 with a basis on which to identify the essential personal and interpersonal factors for effective therapeutic treatment. Our review of the evidence led us to conclude that the essential characteristics of an effective sexual offender therapist were warmth, empathy, rewardingness, and directiveness, whereas the important group climate features involved cohesion and expressiveness. We also noted that emotional expressiveness on the part of the clients appears to be essential to the achievement of the goals of sexual offender treatment.

Most sexual offender programs seem to us to approach treatment from an excessively cognitive perspective. In Chapter 4, we critically appraised treatment programs in terms of this focus, and we suggested that although most programs are described as cognitive–behavioral therapy (CBT), they in fact use little in the way of behavioral strategies and often neglect the importance of between-sessions practice. Most important, we suggested that most CBT programs for sexual offenders are all but devoid of the encouragement of emotional expressiveness by the clients; indeed, we suggested that most CBT programs actively discourage such expressions, whether intentionally or not. Our suggestion is that—given that humans inescapably function in a unified cognitive, behavioral, and emotional way—it is best to conduct therapy in such a way that these three arbitrarily distinguished processes are actively encouraged. Human learning, we suggested, is maximally achieved when concepts (i.e., cognitions) are actively practiced (i.e., behavioral enactments) and attached to an emotional commitment (i.e., acquired while the client is emotionally expressive).

In the final chapter (Chapter 5) of Part I, we reviewed the evidence on the effectiveness of sexual offender treatment. First, we pointed to the often neglected need to determine whether programs actually achieve their goals of producing appropriate improvements in the targets of treatment (i.e., the enhancement of skills and attitudes related to criminogenic targets and other issues addressed treatment). Next, we considered the value of different research designs used to evaluate the long-term outcome of sexual offender treatment (i.e., no reoffense). We then offered our appraisal of what the various evaluations of treatment tell us about the general effectiveness of sexual offender programs. We concluded that the evidence offers encouragement for the idea that treating sexual offenders can reduce subsequent recidivism, although we are aware that some published evaluations report ineffectiveness. We pointed out that most of these failures represent evaluations of programs that are now considered outdated and as such provide a basis for the development of a different, perhaps more comprehensive and positive approach to treating sexual offenders. We ended this section of the book by describing the appraisals of our own RPS programs, each of which showed clear benefits in reducing subsequent recidivism.

Part II of the book described in some detail the three RPS programs: the Preparatory Program, the Primary Program, and the Deniers' Program. Each of these programs derives its approach from our distillation of the various issues discussed in the Introduction of this book; most particularly, the issues raised by a positive psychology framework that emphasizes a strength-based approach to treatment and by motivational interviewing. The issues focused on in each of these programs result from our understanding of problems that may limit the effective engagement of our clients (e.g., resistance, lack of trust, low self-esteem, shame), as well as what the evidence has identified as criminogenic features of sexual offenders (e.g., inadequate coping skills; poor emotional, sexual, and general behavioral regulation; dysfunctional attachment styles and related inadequacies in relationship skills; deviant sexual interests). Although these latter criminogenic targets are framed in the literature as deficits, we construe them as indications of the need to assist our clients in building their strengths in these areas, which is facilitated by pointing out to them that they do have some strengths already in each of these areas of functioning.

The RPS Preparatory Program is meant to increase our clients' motivation to engage in treatment and to help them understand that treatment will lead to an enhancement of their lives and increase the likelihood that they will live offense-free lives. The RPS Primary Program has three phases. The first phase is simply aimed at engaging the clients by building their confidence in themselves and in the therapist by using motivational strategies, by pointing to their strengths, and by raising their hopes for their future. The second phase is focused on addressing their criminogenic features, and the final phase integrates what they have learned into a self-management approach partly derived from

Ward's (2002) good lives model (GLM). Our goal in the RPS Primary Program is to take the clients far enough along a path of self-development, such that when they are discharged from treatment they are in a position to continue this process of self-enhancement throughout the rest of their lives. Like Ward's view of his GLM, we believe that if our clients continue the process of improving their lives, this will reciprocally inhibit their prior tendencies to offend. Of course, in developing skills in each of the criminogenic targets of treatment, our program also succeeds in meeting Andrews and Bonta's (1994) sensible demand that treatment must address known criminogenic features if it is to be effective.

We hope what we have outlined in the present book will encourage readers to see the value in our suggested change to the approach to treating sexual offenders to a more positively, motivationally oriented way of dealing with our clients' problematic behaviors. We hope we have provided a convincing case indicating not only that such a positive approach serves to overcome the clients' criminogenic difficulties, but also that it provides them with the skills necessary to meet their needs in prosocial ways that will lead them to both abstain from future offending and to develop a more satisfying life. The emerging literature describing what is called *positive psychology* we believe offers endless suggestions for modifying sexual offender treatment in a way that will enhance its effectiveness and thereby further reduce reoffending. The reduction in reoffending not only achieves the very important aim of saving future innocent victims from suffering at the hands of our clients but also saves taxpayers considerable money (W. L. Marshall, 1992; Prentky & Burgess, 1990).

Of course, what we have outlined in this book is only our adaption of the various relevant bodies of literature. We encourage all providers of sexual offender treatment to read for themselves the body of literature on positive psychology, motivational interviewing, and strength-based approaches to human problems. We have cited references that will provide readers with an entry into this fascinating and newly developing literature. It is our belief that as more people in our field access this literature, developments will occur that will make the approach we have described outdated in the near future. The continued evolution of sexual offender treatment programs along these lines, we believe, will increase the effectiveness of such treatment, but this evolution will happen only when other clinicians take up our challenge to change the focus of treatment approaches.

Such progress will also, of course, depend on expanding the research agenda to examine hypotheses derived from positive psychology as it might be applied to sexual offenders. Examining the strengths of sexual offenders in various areas of functioning, rather than the present focus on searching for their deficits, would be invaluable and should be the prime targets of research. It is a rare sexual offender, in our experience, who is totally devoid of skills in any of the criminogenic features that have so far been identified. Indeed, if there were such an offender, it would be all but impossible to effectively treat him.

In addition, all sexual offenders appear to have strengths in other areas of functioning in which the identification of these strengths could provide information to therapists that they could use to motivate clients. It has been our observation that child molesters, for example, have had numerous opportunities to offend in their past that they chose not to seize; indeed, it seems almost certain that child molesters have had far more opportunities to offend that they ignored than that they took the chance to act on. Research to date has focused entirely on seeking to understand why child molesters offended on the occasions when they did. We suggest that an exclusive focus of this kind derives from an essentially deficit model. A more strength-based research agenda would search for the reasons why child molesters resist the temptations so frequently offered by their environments.

No doubt a period of reflection by our readers will suggest to them an array of other issues that a strength-focused research agenda could identify. Changing our focus in treatment is not enough; we need to also change the issues we seek to examine in research if we are to build a soundly based positive approach to treating these clients. We, therefore, encourage researchers to take a new look at the issues they might address so that our treatment programs can continue to become more effective.

APPENDIX: THERAPIST RATING SCALE-2

TRS-2 RATING FORM

Topics	Categories	
	Intellectual Understanding	Acceptance/ Demonstration
1 SENSE OF AGENCY		
• Believes in and demonstrates ability to control own life		
• Takes responsibility for making life changes		
• Can identify and take steps to achieve goals		
2 GENERAL EMPATHY		
• Can perceive the emotions of others		
• Is able to put self in other's shoes		
• Responds with appropriate emotion to other's emotions		
• Attempts to comfort others when possible and appropriate		
3 PROSOCIAL ATTITUDES		
• Espouses, and behaves in accordance with, prosocial attitudes		
• Challenges antisocial attitudes expressed by other group members		
• Cooperates with supervisor/supervision or case management staff		
4 ADEQUATE COPING SKILLS/STYLES		
• Responds to stressors with appropriate emotionality		
• Understands how emotions can impact ability to cope		
• Faces problematic issues		
• Is able to problem solve		
5 ADEQUATE INTIMACY SKILLS		
• Values others		
• Appropriately self-discloses		
• Able to make friends, establish relationships, with others		
• Has realistic beliefs about relationships		
6 POSITIVE SELF-ESTEEM		
• Has a realistic belief in own abilities		
• Sees value and engages in positive self-talk		
• Does not use either self-deprecating or derogatory humor		

(continues)

Topics	Categories	
	Intellectual Understanding	Acceptance/ Demonstration
7 GOOD GENERAL SELF-REGULATION		

7   GOOD GENERAL SELF-REGULATION
- Can adapt to changing circumstances
- Not impulsive or overly negative
- Is neither overly emotional nor suppresses emotions
- Sees value of, and has the capacity, for some degree of stability in life

8   GOOD SEXUAL SELF-REGULATION
- Doesn't use sex to cope
- Is not preoccupied with sex
- Has normative sexual interests
- Has a healthy approach to sexuality

9   UNDERSTANDS RISK FACTORS
- Has an awareness of actual and possible risk factors and situations
- Able to take feedback from others

10   QUALITY OF FUTURE PLANS
- Has realistic plans and goals for the future
- Has adequate community supports
- Engages in and recognizes the value of leisure activities
- Has employable skills or is financially independent

RATINGS

Note: Average is compared to nonoffenders, "normal, average, non-offending, everyday" people on the street.

- Level 4 = Optimal functioning
  - Significantly better than average
- Level 3 = Normative
  - Average functioning
  - Mostly achieves target of treatment
- Level 2 = Approaching normative
  - Approaching average functioning
  - May achieve level 3 posttreatment
- Level 1 = Unsatisfactory
  - Needs to redo treatment component

Information on Ratings

- Levels should vary across topics.
- Levels should vary between categories.

- Avoid "halo" and opposite effect.
- When learning to use, have therapists complete separately and independently and then discuss differences— aiming for inter-rater agreement 8–9 times out of 10 (i.e., does not have to be perfect agreement on all items).

DATA COLLECTION

At the moment, we are collecting data on interrater reliability. If you have more than one therapist in a treatment group and are willing to be part of our data collection, please have therapists complete the forms separately and independently and identify which forms belong to which therapists and which group member (there are many ways to do this, such as by a number or alphabet system), then therapists are encouraged to compare answers and complete a final combined Therapist Rating Scale form, which can be kept for your records and reports. Please send the interrater data to any one of the following:

- E-mail to TRS@rockwoodpsyc.com
- Fax to 011-613-530-2895
- Mail to TRS Data Collection
  c/o Rockwood Psychological Services
  303 Bagot Street, Suite 304
  Kingston, Ontario, Canada
  K7K 5W7

If you require any assistance, please do not hesitate to contact us. We will also keep those participating in data collection informed of our results as soon as they are known.

HOW TO DO IT

- Using the descriptors (e.g., "Believes in own ability to control life") below each topic heading (e.g., SENSE OF AGENCY), rate your impressions of where the offender is at this moment in terms of his Intellectual Understanding of the issue and how much he has taken it on board (i.e., Acceptance/Demonstration), using the described 4-point rating scale.
- Intellectual Understanding is often reflected by the offender being able to say the right things and this usually, but not always, occurs prior to Acceptance/Demonstration. For example, an offender may espouse appropriate attitudes in the program, but may still be saying inappropriate things outside the group.

- Acceptance/Demonstration is when an offender is not just saying the right things, but also putting them into practice. For example, being empathic toward others, espousing appropriate attitudes toward people outside the group, contacting supports in the community, and establishing relationships with prosocial peers.
- As an example of QUALITY OF FUTURE PLANS, an offender might report seeing the importance of establishing good community supports and thus receive a 3 or 4 on his intellectual understanding of the topic, but not have actually contacted, or established, any good community supports yet and therefore receive a 1 or 2 on acceptance/demonstration of the issue.
- When struggling with a particular topic, it may be useful, until comfortable with that topic, to rate the offender on each of the descriptors of the topic and average them out.

WHEN TO DO IT

- It is suggested to use the TRS-2 approximately halfway through an offender's time in treatment and then again at the end of treatment. Using the TRS-2 halfway through treatment helps therapists to have a sense of where the offender is, well before the end of the program, in order to direct the remaining time in treatment to the most pressing issues. Using the TRS-2 at the end of treatment will give a sense of how close the offender is to "normal functioning" and inform report writing. Reports based on the TRS-2 can inform on whether subsequent treatment is necessary and what the focus of subsequent treatment should be. We recommend using the topics of the TRS-2 as headings in treatment reports and including the ratings within the body of reports and attaching a copy of the complete TRS-2 to the report; parole boards and supervisors report this to be helpful.

INTERPRETATION

- Although the TRS-2 has not yet been empirically validated, it is based on the original TRS-1 (17-item version), which has received some examination (e.g., good interrater reliability) and what is known about dynamic risk in sexual offenders. At the moment, the TRS-2 is intended as a guide for therapists.

- Offenders are considered to have reached the target of treatment when they achieve a score of 3 on an item. Ideally, group members will achieve a 3 on both intellectual understanding and acceptance/demonstration for each of the 10 topics. However, this is unlikely to occur and consequently therapists will have to use good judgement about the overall impact of treatment. A total score of somewhere near 60 (possible range of the TRS-2 is 20–80) is a possible indicator of success in treatment, with lower scores (below 50) likely indicating a need for further treatment.

WHO CAN I APPLY THE TRS-2 TO?

- The TRS-2 was developed for use with sexual offenders; however, the issues in the TRS-2 apply to many forms of group treatment for offending behavior.

WHO CAN USE THE TRS-2?

- Using the TRS-2 does not require any particular educational level (e.g., bachelor, masters, PhD degrees) in any particular discipline (e.g., psychology, psychiatry, social work). However, knowledge of dynamic risk factors in offenders is recommended, and training programs designed to enhance knowledge of these issues in offenders are available.

The following is a case example of the use of the TRS-2 with a sexual offender who participated in one of our treatment programs.

CASE EXAMPLE

Background/Assessment Information
Independent Assessment Results
    Medium-low static risk
    Moderate dynamic treatment needs

Offender and Offense Information

- 28-year-old recidivist offender
- 2-year sentence for Sexual Interference and Sexual Exploitation

- Victim was his 5-year-old stepson
- Pled guilty and admitted to offences at assessment
- Entered the victim's bedroom while he was asleep
- Fondled the victim's penis, waking him up, and then directed victim to fondle himself
- Living with the victim's mother for 5 years
- Extensive criminal history, including sexually motivated Assault With a Weapon
- Previously received a short sentence (less than 2 years)
- Previously attended treatment but did not complete
- Disclosed own sexual abuse at assessment
- Involved in fire setting
- Prostitute from ages 15 to 18 years (hundreds of clients)
- Many consensual partners (most one-night stands)
- Participated in group sex with various combinations of both genders on many occasions
- Masturbated a lot to adult pornography magazines
- "Experimental sexual relationship" with his partner involving sadomasochistic activities (and had affairs)
- Phallometric assessment —sexual interest in adult males and passive prepubescent children

First TRS-2 Scoring

- TRS-2 completed after 12 sessions (including disclosure and autobiography)
- Initially anxious to share his offence details
- Later discussed his offending in reasonable detail, omitting a prior conviction
- Reported that disclosing felt like a "big weight lifting"
- Did well to focus on certain issues, including his "possible" sexual preoccupation
- Was more accepting of his sexual interests (homosexuality with adults)
- Group helped him acknowledge stress as a risk factor
- Reported that as a result of stress he was masturbating five or six times a day
- Acknowledged substituting coping using drugs with coping using sex
- He said that doing this provided him with a sense of escape and release

- Indicated that he now wanted to focus on celibacy and a lifetime of bible study
- Talked of getting a dog as a primary companion
- Became more open in general group discussions
- Disclosed increasing personal information
- Reported asking for a longer sentence in order to get treatment but had been getting "cold feet"
- Increasingly able to develop key "realizations" about himself and his past
- Increasingly enthusiastic about treatment
- "Now I would happily pay money from my 'inmate account' to come to this group!!!!"

INITIAL TRS-2

Topics	Categories	
	Intellectual Understanding	Acceptance/ Demonstration
1 SENSE OF AGENCY	2	1
• Believes in and demonstrates ability to control own life		
• Takes responsibility for making life changes		
• Can identify and take steps to achieve goals		
2 GENERAL EMPATHY	3	2
• Can perceive the emotions of others		
• Is able to put self in other's shoes		
• Responds with appropriate emotion to other's emotions		
• Attempts to comfort others when possible and appropriate		
3 PROSOCIAL ATTITUDES	3	3
• Espouses, and behaves in accordance with, prosocial attitudes		
• Challenges antisocial attitudes expressed by other group members		
• Cooperates with supervisor/supervision or case management staff		
4 ADEQUATE COPING SKILLS/STYLES	2	2
• Responds to stressors with appropriate emotionality		
• Understands how emotions can impact ability to cope		
• Faces problematic issues		
• Is able to problem solve		

(continues)

	Categories	
Topics	Intellectual Understanding	Acceptance/ Demonstration

5   ADEQUATE INTIMACY SKILLS
    • Values others
    • Appropriately self-discloses
    • Able to make friends, establish relationships, with others
    • Has realistic beliefs about relationships
	2	1

6   POSITIVE SELF-ESTEEM
    • Has a realistic belief in own abilities
    • Sees value and engages in positive self-talk
    • Does not use either self-deprecating or derogatory humor
	1	2

7   GOOD GENERAL SELF-REGULATION
    • Can adapt to changing circumstances
    • Not impulsive or overly negative
    • Is neither overly emotional nor suppresses emotions
    • Sees value of, and has the capacity for, some degree of stability in life
	2	2

8   GOOD SEXUAL SELF-REGULATION
    • Doesn't use sex to cope
    • Is not preoccupied with sex
    • Has normative sexual interests
    • Has a healthy approach to sexuality
	1	1

9   UNDERSTANDS RISK FACTORS
    • Has an awareness of actual and possible risk factors and situations
    • Able to take feedback from others
	2	2

10   QUALITY OF FUTURE PLANS
    • Has realistic plans and goals for the future
    • Has adequate community supports
    • Engages in and recognizes the value of leisure activities
    • Has employable skills or is financially independent
	1	1

POSTTREATMENT

Treatment Gains

- Improved self-esteem
- Reduced shame
- Increased coping ability
- Improved knowledge about relationships
- Greater focus on achieving intimacy
- Learning about healthy sexuality

- Improved goal setting
- Better able to deal with loneliness
- Improved problem-solving ability
- Improved emotion management strategies

RECOMMENDATIONS

- Posttreatment risk considered to be LOW
- HOWEVER, IF . . .
    - Resumes sexually-centered lifestyle
    - Uses sex to cope
    - Had access to potential victims
- RISK WOULD INCREASE
- Avoid unsupervised contact with children
- Further community treatment to focus on healthy relationships and sexuality

POSTTREATMENT TRS-2

	Categories	
Topics	Intellectual Understanding	Acceptance/ Demonstration
1 SENSE OF AGENCY • Believes in and demonstrates ability to control own life • Takes responsibility for making life changes • Can identify and take steps to achieve goals	4	3
2 GENERAL EMPATHY • Can perceive the emotions of others • Is able to put self in other's shoes • Responds with appropriate emotion to other's emotions • Attempts to comfort others when possible and appropriate	3	3
3 PROSOCIAL ATTITUDES • Espouses, and behaves in accordance with, prosocial attitudes • Challenges antisocial attitudes expressed by other group members • Cooperates with supervisor/supervision or case management staff	3	3

(continues)

| | Categories | |
Topics	Intellectual Understanding	Acceptance/ Demonstration
4 ADEQUATE COPING SKILLS/STYLES • Responds to stressors with appropriate emotionality • Understands how emotions can impact ability to cope • Faces problematic issues • Is able to problem solve	3	3
5 ADEQUATE INTIMACY SKILLS • Values others • Appropriately self-discloses • Able to make friends, establish relationships, with others • Has realistic beliefs about relationships	3	2
6 POSITIVE SELF-ESTEEM • Has a realistic belief in own abilities • Sees value and engages in positive self-talk • Does not use either self-deprecating or derogatory humor	3	3
7 GOOD GENERAL SELF-REGULATION • Can adapt to changing circumstances • Not impulsive or overly negative • Is neither overly emotional nor suppresses emotions • Sees value of, and has the capacity for, some degree of stability in life	3	3
8 GOOD SEXUAL SELF-REGULATION • Doesn't use sex to cope • Is not preoccupied with sex • Has normative sexual interests • Has a healthy approach to sexuality	3	2
9 UNDERSTANDS RISK FACTORS • Has an awareness of actual and possible risk factors and situations • Able to take feedback from others	3	3
10 QUALITY OF FUTURE PLANS • Has realistic plans and goals for the future • Has adequate community supports • Engages in and recognizes the value of leisure activities • Has employable skills or is financially independent	3	3

REFERENCES

Abel, G. G. (1995). *New technology: The Abel Assessment for Interest in Paraphilias*. Atlanta, GA: Abel Screening.

Abel, G. G., Becker, J. V., & Cunningham-Rathner, J. (1984). Complications, consent and cognitions in sex between children and adults. *International Journal of Law and Psychiatry, 7*, 89–103. doi:10.1016/0160-2527(84)90008-6

Abel, G. G., & Blanchard, E. B. (1974). The role of fantasy in the treatment of sexual deviation. *Archives of General Psychiatry, 30*, 467–475.

Abel, G. G., Blanchard, E. B., & Becker, J. V. (1978). An integrated treatment program for rapists. In R. Rada (Ed.), *Clinical aspects of the rapist* (pp. 161–214). New York, NY: Grune & Stratton.

Abel, G. G., Gore, D. K., Holland, C. L., Camp, N., Becker, J. V., & Rathner, J. (1989). The measurement of the cognitive distortions of child molesters. *Annals of Sex Research, 2*, 135–152. doi:10.1007/BF00851319

Abel, G. G., Huffman, J., Warberg, B., & Holland, C. L. (1998). Visual reaction time and plethysmography as measures of sexual interest in child molesters. *Sexual Abuse, 10*, 81–95. doi:10.1177/107906329801000202

Abel, G. G., Jordan, A., Hand, C. G., Holland, L. A., & Phipps, A. (2001). Classification models of child molesters utilizing the Abel Assessment for Sexual Interest. *Child Abuse & Neglect, 25*, 703–718. doi:10.1016/S0145-2134(01)00227-7

Abel, G. G., Jordan, A., Rouleau, J. L., Emerick, R., Barboza-Whitehead, S., & Osborn, C. (2004). Use of visual reaction time to assess male adolescents who molest children. *Sexual Abuse, 16*, 255–265. doi:10.1177/107906320401600306

Abel, G. G., Mittelman, M., Becker, J. V., Rathner, J., & Rouleau, J. L. (1988). Predicting child molesters' response to treatment. *Annals of the New York Academy of Sciences, 528*, 223–234. doi:10.1111/j.1749-6632.1988.tb42076.x

Abracen, J., & Looman, J. (2004). Issues in the treatment of sexual offenders. *Aggression and Violent Behavior, 9*, 229–246. doi:10.1016/S1359-1789(01)00074-X

Abracen, J., Looman, J., Mailloux, D., Serin, R., & Malcolm, B. (2005). Clarification regarding Marshall and Yates's critique of "Dosage of treatment to sexual offenders: Are we overprescribing?" *International Journal of Offender Therapy and Comparative Criminology, 49*, 225–230. doi:10.1177/0306624X05275238

Abramson, L. Y., Seligman, M. E., & Teasdale, J. D. (1978). Learned helplessness in humans: Critique and reformulation. *Journal of Abnormal Psychology, 87*, 49–74. doi:10.1037/0021-843X.87.1.49

Adams, H. E., Lohr, B. A., & Wright, L. W. (1995, March). *Is homophobia associated with homosexual arousal?* Paper presented at the Southeastern Psychological Association Conference, Savannah, GA.

Alexander, J. F., Barton, C., Schiavo, S., & Parsons, B. V. (1976). Systems-behavioral intervention with families of delinquents: Therapist characteristics, family behavior and outcome. *Journal of Consulting and Clinical Psychology, 44*, 656–664. doi:10.1037/0022-006X.44.4.656

Alexander, M. A. (1999). Sexual offender treatment efficacy revisited. *Sexual Abuse, 11*, 101–116. doi:10.1007/BF02658841

Alford, G. S., Morin, C., Atkins, M., & Schoen, L. (1987). Masturbatory extinction of deviant sexual arousal. *Journal of Behavior Therapy and Experimental Psychiatry, 18*, 265–271.

Allam, J., Middleton, D., & Browne, K. D. (1997). Different clients, different needs? Practice issues in community-based treatment for sex offenders. *Criminal Behaviour and Mental Health, 7*, 69–84. doi:10.1002/cbm.145

American Academy of Child and Adolescent Psychiatry. (2004, October). *Child sexual abuse* (Facts for families). Retrieved from http://www.aacap.org/

American Psychiatric Association. (2000). *Diagnostic and statistical manual of mental disorders* (4th ed., text rev.). Washington, DC: Author.

Anderson, J. R. (1995). *Cognitive psychology and its implications* (4th ed.). New York, NY: W. H. Freeman.

Anderson, R. D., Gibeau, D., & D'Amora, D. A. (1995). The sex offender treatment rating scale: Initial reliability data. *Sexual Abuse, 7*, 221–227.

Andrews, D. A. (2001). Principles of effective correctional programs. In L. L. Motiuk & R. C. Serin (Eds.), *Compendium 2000 on effective correctional programming* (pp. 9–17). Ottawa, Ontario, Canada: Correctional Service of Canada.

Andrews, D. A., & Bonta, J. (1994). *The psychology of criminal conduct*. Cincinnati, OH: Anderson.

Andrews, D. A., & Bonta, J. (1995). *LSI-R: The Level of Supervision Inventory*. Toronto, Ontario, Canada: Multi-Health Systems.

Andrews, D. A., Bonta, J., & Hoge, R. D. (1990). Classification for effective rehabilitation: Rediscovering psychology. *Criminal Justice and Behavior, 17*, 19–52. doi:10.1177/0093854890017001004

Andrews, D. A., Dowden, C., & Gendreau, P. (1999). *Clinically relevant and psychologically informed approaches to reduced reoffending: A meta-analytic study of human service, risk, need, responsivity, and other concerns in justice contexts* (Unpublished manuscript). Department of Psychology, University of Carleton, Ottawa, Ontario, Canada.

Andrews, D. A., Zinger, I., Hoge, R. D., Bonta, J., Gendreau, P., & Cullen, F. T. (1990). Does correctional treatment work? A clinically relevant and psychologically informed meta-analysis. *Criminology, 28*, 369–404. doi:10.1111/j.1745-9125.1990.tb01330.x

Annis, H. M., & Chan, D. (1983). The differential treatment model: Empirical evidence from a personality typology of adult offenders. *Criminal Justice and Behavior, 10*, 159–173. doi:10.1177/0093854883010002002

Annis, L. V., & Perry, D. F. (1977). Self-disclosure modeling in same-sex and mixed-sex unsupervised groups. *Journal of Counseling Psychology, 24*, 370–372. doi:10.1037/0022-0167.24.4.370

Annis, L. V., & Perry, D. F. (1978). Self-disclosure in unsupervised groups: Effects of videotaped models. *Small Group Behavior, 9,* 102–108.

Ashby, J. D., Ford, D. H., Guerney, B. G., & Guerney, L. F. (1957). Effects on clients of a reflective and leading type of psychotherapy. *Psychological Monographs, 453,* 71.

Ashton, J., & Stepney, R. (1982). *Smoking: Psychology and pharmacology.* London, England: Tavistock.

Austin, J. T., & Vancouver, J. B. (1996). Goal constructs in psychology: Structure, process, and content. *Psychological Bulletin, 120,* 338–375. doi:10.1037/0033-2909.120.3.338

Babcock, J. C., Green, C. E., & Robie, C. (2004). Does batterers' treatment work? A meta-analytic review of domestic violence treatment. *Clinical Psychology Review, 23,* 1023–1053. doi:10.1016/j.cpr.2002.07.001

Bach, G. R. (1966). The marathon group: Intensive practice of intimate interaction. *Psychological Reports, 18,* 995–1002.

Bachelor, A. (1995). Clients' perception of the therapeutic alliance: A qualitative analysis. *Journal of Counseling Psychology, 42,* 323–337. doi:10.1037/0022-0167.42.3.323

Baddeley, A. D., & Longman, D. J. A. (1978). The influence of length and frequency of training session on the rate of learning to type. *Ergonomics, 21,* 627–635. doi:10.1080/00140137808931764

Bagley, C. (1991). The long-term psychological effects of child sexual abuse: A review of some British and Canadian studies of victims and their families. *Annals of Sex Research, 4,* 23–48. doi:10.1007/BF00850138

Bagley, C., & McDonald, M. (1984). Adult mental health sequels of child sexual abuse, physical abuse, and neglect in maternally separated children. *Canadian Journal of Community Mental Health, 3,* 15–26.

Bagley, C., & Pritchard, C. (2000). Criminality and violence in intra- and extra-familial child abusers in a 2-year cohort of convicted perpetrators. *Child Abuse Review, 9,* 264–274. doi:10.1002/1099-0852(200007/08)9:4<264::AID-CAR635>3.0.CO;2-6

Bancroft, J. (1978). The prevention of sexual offenses. In C. B. Qualls, J. P. Wincze, & D. H. Barlow (Eds.), *The prevention of sexual disorders: Issues and approaches* (pp. 42–66). New York, NY: Plenum Press.

Bandura, A. (1973). *Aggression: A social learning analysis.* Englewood Cliffs, NJ: Prentice-Hall.

Bandura, A. (1977a). Self-efficacy: Toward a unifying theory of behavior change. *Psychological Review, 84,* 191–215. doi:10.1037/0033-295X.84.2.191

Bandura, A. (1977b). *Social learning theory.* Englewood Cliffs, NJ: Prentice-Hall.

Bandura, A. (1978). On paradigms and recycled ideologies. *Cognitive Therapy and Research, 2,* 79–103. doi:10.1007/BF01172518

Bandura, A. (1998, August). *Swimming against the mainstream: Accenting the positive aspects of humanity*. Invited address presented at the annual meeting of the American Psychological Association, San Francisco.

Bandura, A., Lipsher, D. H., & Miller, P. E. (1960). Psychotherapists' approach-avoidance reactions to patients' expressions of hostility. *Journal of Consulting Psychology, 24*, 1–8. doi:10.1037/h0043403

Barbaree, H. E. (1991). Denial and minimization among sex offenders: Assessment and treatment outcome. *Forum on Corrections Research, 3*, 30–33.

Barbaree, H. E. (1997). Evaluating treatment efficacy with sexual offenders: The insensitivity of recidivism studies to treatment effects. *Sexual Abuse, 9*, 111–128.

Barbaree, H. E., Blanchard, R., & Langton, C. M. (2003). The development of sexual aggression through life span: The effect of age on sexual arousal and recidivism among sex offenders. *Annals of the New York Academy of Sciences, 989*, 59–71. doi:10.1111/j.1749-6632.2003.tb07293.x

Barbaree, H. E., Langton, C., & Peacock, E. J. (2003, October). *The evaluation of sex offender treatment efficacy using samples stratified by levels of actuarial risk*. Paper presented at the 22nd Annual Research and Treatment Conference of the Association for the Treatment of Sexual Abusers, St. Louis, MO.

Barbaree, H. E., Seto, M. C., Langton, C. M., & Peacock, E. J. (2001, November). *Psychopathy, treatment behavior and sexual offender recidivism: An extended follow-up*. Paper presented at the 20th Annual Research and Treatment Conference of the Association for the Treatment of Sexual Abusers, San Antonio, TX.

Barkham, M., & Shapiro, D. A. (1986). Counselor verbal response modes and experienced empathy. *Journal of Counseling Psychology, 33*, 3–10. doi:10.1037/0022-0167.33.1.3

Barlow, D. H., & Agras, W. S. (1973). Fading to increase heterosexual responses in homosexuals. *Journal of Applied Behavior Analysis, 6*, 355–366. doi:10.1901/jaba.1973.6-355

Baron-Cohen, S., Tager-Flusberg, H., & Cohen, D. J. (Eds.). (1993). *Understanding other minds*. Oxford, England: Oxford University Press.

Bartholomew, K., & Horowitz, L. (1991). Attachment styles among young adults: A test of a four-category model. *Journal of Personality and Social Psychology, 61*, 226–244. doi:10.1037/0022-3514.61.2.226

Bastien, C. H., Morin, C. M., Ouellet, M. C., Blais, F. C., & Bouchard, S. (2004). Cognitive-behavioral therapy for insomnia: Comparison of individual therapy, group therapy, and telephone consultations. *Journal of Consulting and Clinical Psychology, 72*, 653–659. doi:10.1037/0022-006X.72.4.653

Batson, C. D. (1991). *The altruism question: Toward a social-psychological answer*. Hillsdale, NJ: Erlbaum.

Batson, C. D., Ahmad, N., Lishner, D. A., & Tsang, J. (2005). Empathy and altruism. In C. R. Snyder & S. J. Lopez (Eds.), *Handbook of positive psychology* (pp. 485–498). New York, NY: Oxford University Press.

Baumeister, R. F. (Ed.). (1993). *Self-esteem: The puzzle of low self-regard*. New York, NY: Plenum Press.

Baumeister, R. F., Bushman, B. J., & Campbell, W. K. (2000). Self-esteem, narcissism, and aggression: Does violence result from low self-esteem or from threatened egotism? *Current Directions in Psychological Science, 9*, 26–29. doi:10.1111/1467-8721.00053

Baumeister, R. F., & Heatherton, T. F. (1996). Self-regulation failure: An overview. *Psychological Inquiry, 7*, 1–5. doi:10.1207/s15327965pli0701_1

Baumeister, R. F., & Vohs, K. D. (Eds.). (2004). *Handbook of self-regulation: Research, theory, and applications*. New York, NY: Guilford Press.

Baumeister, R. F., Zell, A. L., & Tice, D. M. (2007). How emotions facilitate and impair self-regulation. In J. J. Gross (Ed.), *Handbook of emotion regulation* (pp. 408–426). New York, NY: Guilford Press.

Becker, J. V., Abel, G. G., Blanchard, E. B., Murphy, W. D., & Coleman, E. (1978). Evaluating social skills of sexual aggressive. *Criminal Justice and Behavior, 5*, 357–368. doi:10.1177/009385487800500407

Beckett, R., Beech, A. R., Fisher, D. D., & Fordham, A. S. (1994). *Community-based treatment of sex offenders: An evaluation of seven treatment programs* (Home Office Occasional Report). London, England: Home Office Publications Unit.

Beckham, E. E. (1992). Predicting drop-out in psychotherapy. *Psychotherapy: Theory, Research, & Practice, 29*, 177–182. doi:10.1037/0033-3204.29.2.177

Bednar, R., & Kaul, T. (1994). Experiential group research: Can the canon fire? In A. E. Bergen & S. L. Garfield (Eds.), *Handbook of psychotherapy and behavior change* (pp. 631–663). New York, NY: Wiley.

Beech, A. R., & Fisher, D. D. (2002). The rehabilitation of child sex offenders. *Australian Psychologist, 37*, 206–214. doi:10.1080/00050060210001706886

Beech, A. R., & Fisher, D. D. (2004). Treatment of sex offenders in the UK in prison and probation settings. In H. Kemshall & G. McIvor (Eds.), *Managing sex offender risk* (pp. 137–163). London, England: Jessica Kingsley.

Beech, A. R., Fisher, D. D., & Beckett, R. C. (1999). *STEP 3: An evaluation of the prison sex offender treatment programme* (Home Office Occasional Report). London, England: Home Office Publications Unit. Available electronically from www.homeoffice.gov.uk/rds/pdfs/occ-step3.pdf

Beech, A. R., Fisher, D. D., Beckett, R. C., & Fordham, A. S. (1996). Treating sex offenders in the community. *Home Office Research and Statistics Directorate Research Bulletin, 38*, 21–25.

Beech, A. R., Fisher, D. D., & Thornton, D. (2003). Risk assessment of sex offenders. *Professional Psychology, Research and Practice, 34*, 339–352. doi:10.1037/0735-7028.34.4.339

Beech, A. R., & Fordham, A. S. (1997). Therapeutic climate of sexual offender treatment programs. *Sexual Abuse, 9*, 219–237.

Beech, A. R., & Hamilton-Giachritsis, C. E. (2005). Relationship between therapeutic climate and treatment outcome in group-based sexual offender treatment programs. *Sexual Abuse, 17,* 127–140. doi:10.1177/107906320501700204

Beech, A. R., & Mann, R. E. (2002). Recent developments in the assessment and treatment of sexual offenders. In J. McGuire (Ed.), *Offender rehabilitation and treatment: Effective programmes and policies to reduce re-offending* (pp. 259–288). Chichester, England: Wiley.

Beech, A. R., Oliver, C., Fisher, D. D., & Beckett, R. C. (2005). *STEP 4: The Sex Offender Treatment Programme in prison: Addressing the needs of rapists and sexual murderers.* Retrieved from http://www.homeoffice.gov.uk/rds

Beech, A. R., Oliver, C., Fisher, D. D., & Beckett, R. C. (2006). *STEP 4: The Sex Offender Treatment Programme in prison: Addressing the needs of rapists and sexual murderers.* Birmingham, England: University of Birmingham. Retrieved from www.hmprisonservice.gov.uk/assets/documents/100013DBStep_4_SOTP_report_2005.pdf

Belanger, N., & Earls, C. (1996). Sex offender recidivism prediction. *Forum on Corrections Research, 8,* 22–24.

Bell, J. B. (2008). Volitional control, self-regulation, and motivational interviewing in veterans with alcohol problems. *Dissertation Abstracts International, 67*(7-B), 4810.

Bernard, M. E. (2006). It's time we teach social-emotional competence as well as we teach academic confidence. *Reading and Writing Quarterly: Overcoming Learning Difficulties, 22,* 103–119.

Beutler, L. E., Dunbar, P. W., & Baer, P. E. (1980). Individual variation among therapists' perceptions of patients, therapy process and outcome. *Psychiatry: Journal for the Study of Interpersonal Processes, 43,* 205–210.

Beutler, L. E., Malik, M., Alimohamed, S., Harwood, T. M., Talebi, H., Nobel, S., & Wong, E. (2004). Therapist variables. In M. J. Lambert (Ed.), *Handbook of psychotherapy and behaviour change* (5th ed., pp. 227–306). New York, NY: Wiley.

Beutler, L. E., Pollack, S., & Jobe, A. M. (1978). "Acceptance," values and therapeutic change. *Journal of Consulting and Clinical Psychology, 46,* 198–199. doi:10.1037/0022-006X.46.1.198

Beyko, M. J., & Wong, S. C. P. (2005). Predictors of treatment attrition as indicators for program improvement not offender shortcomings: A study of sex offender treatment attrition. *Sexual Abuse, 17,* 375–389. doi:10.1177/107906320501700403

Birgden, A., Owen, K., & Raymond, B. (2003). Enhancing relapse prevention through the effective management of offenders in the community. In T. Ward, D. R. Laws, & S. M. Hudson (Eds.), *Sexual deviance: Issues and controversies* (pp. 317–337). Thousand Oaks, CA: Sage.

Blackburn, I. M., James, I. A., & Flitcroft, A. (2006). Case formulation in depression. In N. Tarrier (Ed.), *Case formulation in cognitive behavior therapy: The treatment of challenging and complex cases* (pp. 113–141). New York, NY: Routledge.

Blackburn, R. (2009). Subtypes of psychopath. In M. McMurran & R. C. Howard (Eds.), *Personality, personality disorder and violence* (pp. 113–132). Chichester, England: Wiley.

Bless, H., & Forgas, J. P. (2000). *The message within: The role of subjective experience in social cognition and behavior*. Philadelphia, PA: Psychology Press.

Bloom, K. C., & Shuell, T. J. (1981). Effects of massed and distributed practice on the learning and retention of second-language vocabulary. *The Journal of Educational Research, 74*, 245–248.

Bohart, A. C., & Tolman, K. (1998). The person as active agent in experiential therapy. In L. S. Greenberg, J. C. Watson, & G. Lietaer (Eds.), *Handbook of experiential psychotherapy* (pp. 178–200). New York, NY: Guilford Press.

Bok, S. (1978). *Lying: Moral choice in public and private life*. Hassocks, Sussex, England: John Spiers.

Bolen, R. M., & Lamb, J. L. (2004). Ambivalence of non-offending guardians after child sexual abuse disclosure. *Journal of Interpersonal Violence, 19*, 185–211. doi:10.1177/0886260503260324

Bond, I. K., & Evans, D. R. (1967). Avoidance therapy: Its use in two cases of underwear fetishism. *Canadian Medical Association Journal, 96*, 1160–1162.

Bonner, R. L., & Rich, A. R. (1987). Toward a predictive model of suicide ideation and behavior: Some preliminary data in college students. *Suicide & Life-Threatening Behavior, 17*, 50–63.

Braaten, E. B., Otto, S., & Handelsman, M. (1993). What do people want to know about psychotherapy? *Psychotherapy: Theory, Research, & Practice, 30*, 565–570. doi:10.1037/0033-3204.30.4.565

Bradford, J. M. W. (2000). The treatment of sexual deviation using a pharmacological approach. *Journal of Sex Research, 37*, 248–257. doi:10.1080/00224490009552045

Bradford, J. M. W., & Greenberg, D. M. (1998). Treatment of adult male sexual offenders in a psychiatric setting. In W. L. Marshall, Y. M. Fernandez, S. M. Hudson, & T. Ward (Eds.), *Sourcebook of treatment programs for sexual offenders* (pp. 247–256). New York, NY: Plenum Press.

Bradford, J. M. W., Greenberg, D., Gojer, J., Martindale, J. J., & Goldberg, M. (1995, May). *Sertraline in the treatment of pedophilia: An open label study* (New Research Program Abstracts NR 441). Paper presented at the American Psychiatric Association Meeting, Miami, FL.

Braithwaite, J., & Braithwaite, V. (2001). Shame, shame management and regulation. In E. Ahmed, N. Harris, J. Braithwaite, & V. Braithwaite (Eds.), *Shame management through reintegration* (pp. 3–18). Cambridge, England: University of Cambridge.

Brake, S. C., & Shannon, D. (1997). Using pre-treatment to increase admission in sex offenders. In B. K. Schwartz & H. R. Cellini (Eds.), *The sex offender: New insights, treatment innovations and legal developments* (pp. 5.1–5.16). Kingston, NJ: Civic Research Institute.

Breiling, J. (2005, November). *Lessons from bio-medical arena for determining how well treatment works.* Paper presented at the 24th Annual Research and Treatment Conference of the Association for the Treatment of Sexual Abusers, Salt Lake City, UT.

Briere, J., & Elliott, D. M. (2003). Prevalence and psychological sequelae of self-reported childhood physical and sexual abuse in a general population sample of men and women. *Child Abuse & Neglect: The International Journal, 27,* 1205–1222. doi:10.1016/j.chiabu.2003.09.008

Brown, S. (2005). *Treating sex offenders: An introduction to sex offender treatment programmes.* Devon, England: Willan.

Browne, A., & Finkelhor, D. (1986). Impact of child sexual abuse: A review of the research. *Psychological Bulletin, 99,* 66–77. doi:10.1037/0033-2909.99.1.66

Browne, K. D., Foreman, L., & Middleton, D. (1998). Predicting treatment dropout in sex offenders. *Child Abuse Review, 7,* 402–419. doi:10.1002/(SICI)1099-0852(199811/12)7:6<402::AID-CAR530>3.0.CO;2-9

Brownell, K. D. (1980). Multifaceted behavior therapy. In D. J. Cox & R. J. Daitzman (Eds.), *Exhibitionism: Description, assessment, and treatment* (pp. 151–186). New York, NY: Garland STPM Press.

Brownell, K. D., Marlatt, G. A., Lichtenstein, E., & Wilson, G. T. (1986). Understanding and preventing relapse. *American Psychologist, 41,* 765–782. doi:10.1037/0003-066X.41.7.765

Bruch, M., & Bond, F. W. (Eds.). (1998). *Beyond diagnosis: Case formulation approaches to CBT.* Chichester, England: Wiley.

Budman, S. H., Soldz, S., Demby, A., Davis, M., & Merry, J. (1993). What is cohesiveness? An empirical examination. *Small Group Research, 24,* 199–216. doi:10.1177/1046496493242003

Bumby, K. M. (1996). Assessing the cognitive distortions of child molesters and rapists: Development and validation of the MOLEST and RAPE scales. *Sexual Abuse, 8,* 37–54.

Bumby, K. M., & Hansen, D. J. (1997). Intimacy deficits, fear of intimacy, and loneliness among sex offenders. *Criminal Justice and Behavior, 24,* 315–331. doi:10.1177/0093854897024003001

Burditt, T. (1995, October). *Treating sex offenders who deny their guilt: The application of motivational interviewing to the denier's pilot study.* Paper presented at the 14th Annual Research and Treatment Conference of the Association for the Treatment of Sexual Abusers, New Orleans, LA.

Burgess, A. W., & Holstrom, L. (1974). *Rape: Victims of crisis.* Bowie, MD: Robert J. Brady.

Burns, D. D., & Auerbach, A. (1996). Therapeutic empathy in cognitive-behavioural therapy: Does it really make a difference? In P. Salkovskis (Ed.), *Frontiers of cognitive therapy* (pp. 135–164). New York, NY: Guilford Press.

Burton, D., & Cerar, K. (2005, November). *Therapeutic alliance*. Paper presented at the 24th Annual Research and Treatment Conference of the Association for the Treatment of Sexual Abusers, Salt Lake City, NV.

Bushman, B. J. (2002). Does venting anger feed or extinguish the flame? Catharsis, rumination, distraction, anger, and aggressive responding. *Personality and Social Psychology Bulletin, 28,* 724–731. doi:10.1177/0146167202289002

Buss, A. H., & Durkee, A. (1957). An inventory for assessing different kinds of hostility. *Journal of Consulting Psychology, 21,* 343–349. doi:10.1037/h0046900

Calhoun, K. S., McCauley, J., & Crawford, M. E. (2006). Sexual assault. In R. D. McAnulty & M. M. Burnette (Eds.), *Sex and sexuality: Sexual deviation and sexual offenses* (Vol. 3, pp. 97–130). Westport, CT: Praeger.

Calhoun, K. S., & Wilson, A. E. (2000). Rape and sexual aggression. In L. T. Szuchman & F. Muscarella (Eds.), *Psychological perspectives on human sexuality* (pp. 573–602). New York, NY: Wiley.

Canadian Centre for Justice Statistics. (1999). *Criminal victimization in Canada* (Statistics Canada, Vol. 20, No. 10).

Carich, M. S., & Calder, M. C. (2003). *Contemporary treatment of adult male sex offenders*. Lime Regis, England: Russell House.

Carich, M. S., Dobkowski, G., & Delehanty, N. (2009). No, the spirit of RP is important: A response to Yates & Ward (2009) on abandoning RP. *ATSA Forum, 21,* 1–8.

Carich, M. S., Michael, D. M., & Stone, M. (1992). Categories of disowning behaviors. *Inmas Newsletter, 5,* 1–13.

Carnes, P. (1989). *Contrary to love: Helping the sexual addict*. Minneapolis, MN: CompCare.

Carroll, K. M. (2001). Constrained, confounded, and confused: Why we really know so little about therapists in treatment outcome research. *Addiction, 96,* 203–206. doi:10.1046/j.1360-0443.2001.9622032.x

Carver, C. S. (2004). Self-regulation of action and affect. In R. F. Baumeister & K. D. Vohs (Eds.), *Handbook of self-regulation: Research, theory, and applications* (pp. 13–39). New York, NY: Guilford Press.

Carver, C. S., Pozo, C., Harris, S. D., & Noriega, V. (1993). How coping mediates the effect of optimism on distress: A study of women with early stage breast cancer. *Journal of Personality and Social Psychology, 65,* 375–390. doi:10.1037/0022-3514.65.2.375

Carver, C. S., & Scheier, M. F. (1990). Principles of self-regulation: Action and emotion. In E. T. Higgins & R. M. Sorrentino (Eds.), *Handbook of motivation and social behavior* (pp. 3–52). New York, NY: Guilford Press.

Carver, C. S., & Scheier, M. F. (2005). Optimism. In C. R. Snyder & S. J. Lopez (Eds.), *Handbook of positive psychology* (pp. 231–243). New York, NY: Oxford University Press.

Castelli, P., Goodman, G. S., Edelstein, R. S., Mitchell, E. B., Paz Alonso, P. M., Lyons, K. E., & Newton, J. W. (2006). Evaluating eyewitness testimony in adults and children. In I. B. Weiner & A. K. Hess (Eds.), *The handbook of forensic psychology* (3rd ed., pp. 243–304). Hoboken, NJ: Wiley.

Cautela, J. R. (1967). Covert sensitization. *Psychological Reports, 20,* 459–468.

Ceci, S. J., Ross, D. R., & Toglia, M. P. (1987). Suggestibility of children's memory: Psycholegal implications. *Journal of Experimental Psychology: General, 116,* 38–49. doi:10.1037/0096-3445.116.1.38

Chaffin, M. (1994). Research in action: Assessment and treatment of child abusers. *Journal of Interpersonal Violence, 9,* 224–237. doi:10.1177/088626094009002006

Chambers, W. M., & Ficek, D. E. (1970). An evaluation of marathon counselling. *International Journal of Group Psychotherapy, 20,* 372–379.

Charcot, J. M., & Magnan, V. (1882). Inversion du sens genital. *Archives of Neurology, 3,* 53–60.

Christensen, A., Atkins, D. C., Berns, S., Wheeler, J., Baucom, D. H., & Simpson, L. E. (2004). Traditional versus integrative behavioral couple therapy for significantly and chronically distressed married couples. *Journal of Consulting and Clinical Psychology, 72,* 176–191. doi:10.1037/0022-006X.72.2.176

Cohen, F. (1995). Right to treatment. In B. K. Schwartz & H. R. Cellini (Eds.), *The sexual offender: Corrections, treatment, and legal practice* (pp. 24.1–24.18). Kingston, NJ: Civic Research Institute.

Collie, R. M., Ward, T., & Vess, J. (2008). Assessment and case conceptualization in sex offender treatment. *Journal of Behavior Analysis of Offender and Victim—Treatment and Prevention, 1,* 64–81.

Colson, C. E. (1972). Olfactory aversion therapy for homosexual behavior. *Journal of Behavior Therapy and Experimental Psychiatry, 3,* 185–187. doi:10.1016/0005-7916(72)90071-7

Conte, J. R., & Schuerman, J. R. (1987). The effects of sexual abuse on children: A multi-dimensional view. *Journal of Interpersonal Violence, 2,* 380–390. doi:10.1177/088626058700200404

Conyne, R. K., & Silver, R. J. (1980). Direct, vicarious, and vicarious-process experiences: Effects on increasing therapeutic attraction. *Small Group Behavior, 11,* 419–429. doi:10.1177/104649648001100407

Cook, D. A. G., Fox, C. A., Weaver, C. M., & Rooth, F. G. (1991). The Berkeley Group: Ten years' experience of a group for non-violent sex offenders. *The British Journal of Psychiatry, 158,* 238–243. doi:10.1192/bjp.158.2.238

Cooke, D. J., & Michie, C. (1999). Psychopathy across cultures: North America and Scotland compared. *Journal of Abnormal Psychology, 108,* 58–68. doi:10.1037/0021-843X.108.1.58

Cooke, D. J., & Philip, L. (2001). To treat or not to treat: An empirical perspective. In C. Hollin (Ed.), *Handbook of offender assessment and treatment* (pp. 17–34). Chichester, England: Wiley.

Cooley, E. J., & LaJoy, R. (1980). Therapeutic relationship and improvements as perceived by clients and therapists. *Journal of Clinical Psychology, 36,* 562–570.

Cooper, A., Griffin-Shelley, E., Delmonico, D. L., & Mathy, R. M. (2001). Online sexual problems: Assessment and predictive variables [Special issue: Preparing for DSM-V]. *Sexual Addiction & Compulsivity: The Journal of Treatment and Prevention. 8*, 267–285.

Cooper, A., Scherer, C., Boies, S. C., & Gordon, B. (1999). Sexuality on the internet: From sexual exploration to pathological expression. *Professional Psychology, Research and Practice, 30*, 154–164. doi:10.1037/0735-7028.30.2.154

Corder, B. F., Haizlip, T., Whiteside, R., & Vogel, M. (1980). Pre-therapy training for adolescents in group psychotherapy: Contract, guidelines, and pre-therapy preparation. *Adolescence, 15*, 699–706.

Cordess, C. (2002). Building and nurturing a therapeutic alliance with offenders. In M. McMurran (Ed.), *Motivating offenders to change: A guide to enhancing engagement in therapy* (pp. 75–86). Chichester, England: Wiley. doi:10.1002/9780470713471.ch5

Cormier, W. H., & Cormier, L. S. (1991). *Interviewing strategies for helpers.* Pacific Grove, CA: Brooks/Cole.

Correctional Service of Canada. (2000). *Standards for the provision of assessment and treatment services to sex offenders.* Ottawa, Ontario, Canada: Author.

Cortoni, F. (2009). Factors associated with sexual recidivism. In A. R. Beech, L. A. Craig, & K. D. Browne (Eds.), *Assessment and treatment of sex offenders* (pp. 39–52). Chichester, England: Wiley.

Cortoni, F. A., & Marshall, W. L. (2001). Sex as a coping strategy and its relationship to juvenile sexual history and intimacy in sexual offenders. *Sexual Abuse, 13*, 27–43. doi:10.1177/107906320101300104

Cox, D. J., & Daitzman, R. J. (Eds.). (1980). *Exhibitionism: Description, assessment, and treatment.* New York, NY: Garland STPM Press.

Craig, L. A., Beech, A. R., & Harkins, L. (2009). The predictive accuracy of risk factors and frameworks. In A. R. Beech, L. A. Craig, & K. D. Browne (Eds.), *Assessment and treatment of sex offenders: A handbook* (pp. 53–74). Chichester, England: Wiley.

Craig, L. A., Browne, K. D., & Beech, A. R. (2008). *Assessing risk in sex offenders: A practitioner's guide.* Chichester, England: Wiley. doi:10.1002/9780470773208

Craig, L. A., Browne, K. D., & Stringer, I. (2003). Risk scales and factors predictive of sexual offence recidivism. *Trauma, Violence, and Abuse: A Review Journal, 4*, 45–68.

Cross, D. G., & Sharpley, C. F. (1982). Measurement of empathy with the Hogan Empathy Scale. *Psychological Reports, 50*, 62.

Crowne, D. P., & Marlowe, D. (1960). A new scale of social desirability independent of psychopathology. *Journal of Consulting Psychology, 24*, 349–354. doi:10.1037/h0047358

Cull, D. M., & Wehner, D. M. (1998). Australian aborigines: Cultural factors pertaining to the assessment and treatment of Australian aboriginal sexual offenders. In

W. L. Marshall, Y. M. Fernandez, S. M. Hudson, & T. Ward (Eds.), *Sourcebook of treatment programs for sexual offenders* (pp. 431–444). New York, NY: Plenum Press.

Cullari, S. (1996). *Treatment resistance: A guide for practitioners.* Boston, MA: Allyn and Bacon.

Cumming, G. F., & Buell, M. M. (1996). Relapse prevention as a supervision strategy for sex offenders. *Sexual Abuse, 8,* 231–241.

Cumming, G. F., & McGrath, R. J. (2000). External supervision: How can it increase the effectiveness of relapse prevention? In D. R. Laws, S. M. Hudson, & T. Ward (Eds.), *Remaking relapse prevention with sex offenders: A sourcebook* (pp. 236–253). Thousand Oaks, CA: Sage.

Curran, T. (1978). Increasing motivation to change in group treatment. *Small Group Behavior, 9,* 337–348. doi:10.1177/009055267893005

Curtis, J. M. (1982). The effect of therapist self-disclosure on patient's perceptions of empathy, competence, and trust in an analogue psychotherapeutic interaction. *Psychotherapy: Theory, Research, & Practice, 19,* 54–62. doi:10.1037/h0088417

Dahle, K. P. (1997). Therapy motivation in prisons: Towards a specific construct for the motivation to enter psychotherapy for prison inmates. In S. Redondo, V. Garrido, J. Perez, & R. Barberet (Eds.), *Advances in psychology and law: International contributions* (pp. 431–441). Berlin, Germany: Walter de Gruyter.

Davidson, K. M. (2006). Cognitive formulation in personality disorder. In N. Tarrier (Ed.), *Case formulation in cognitive behavior therapy: The treatment of challenging and complex cases* (pp. 216–237). New York, NY: Routledge.

Davidson, M. A. (1998). The effects of pre-therapy information audiotape on client satisfaction, anxiety level, expectations, and symptom reduction. *Dissertation Abstracts International, 58,* 4441.

Davis, A. J., Marshall, L. E., Bradford, J. M. W., & Marshall, W. L. (2008, October). *Group climate in a program for seriously mentally ill sexual offenders.* Paper presented at the 27th Annual Research and Treatment Conference of the Association for the Treatment of Sexual Abusers, Atlanta, GA.

Davis, M. H. (1983). Measuring individual differences in empathy: Evidence for a multidimensional approach. *Journal of Personality and Social Psychology, 44,* 113–126. doi:10.1037/0022-3514.44.1.113

Deci, E. L., & Ryan, R. M. (2000). The "what" and "why" of goal pursuits: Human needs and the self-determination of behavior. *Psychological Inquiry, 11,* 227–268. doi:10.1207/S15327965PLI1104_01

Dellarosa, D., & Bourne, L. E. (1985). Surface form and the spacing effect. *Memory & Cognition, 13,* 529–537.

Delmonico, D. L., Griffin, E., & Carnes, P. J. (2002). Treating online compulsive sexual behavior: When cybersex is the drug of choice. In A. Cooper (Ed.), *Sex and the internet: A guidebook for clinicians* (pp. 147–167). New York, NY: Brunner-Routledge.

Dempster, F. M. (1988). A case study in the failure to apply the results of psychological research. *American Psychologist, 43*, 627–634. doi:10.1037/0003-066X. 43.8.627

DiClemente, C. C. (1991). Motivational interviewing and the stages of change. In W. R. Miller & S. Rollnick (Eds.), *Motivational interviewing: Preparing people to change addictive behavior* (pp. 191–202). New York, NY: Guilford Press.

Diener, E., & Diener, M. (1995). Cross-cultural correlates of life satisfaction and self-esteem. *Journal of Personality and Social Psychology, 68*, 653–663. doi:10.1037/0022-3514.68.4.653

Diener, E., Lucas, R. E., & Oishi, S. (2005). Subjective well-being: The science of happiness and life satisfaction. In C. R. Snyder & S. J. Lopez (Eds.), *Handbook of positive psychology* (pp. 63–73). New York, NY: Oxford University Press.

Di Fazio, R., Abracen, J., & Looman, J. (2001). Group versus individual treatment of sex offenders: A comparison. *Forum on Corrections Research, 13*, 56–59.

Dillard, J. P., & Hunter, J. E. (1989). On the use and interpretation of the Emotional Empathy Scale, the Self-Consciousness Scale, and the Self-Monitoring Scale. *Communication Research, 16*, 104–129. doi:10.1177/009365089016001005

Dinges, N. G., & Weigel, R. G. (1971). The marathon group: A review of practice and research. *Small Group Research, 2*, 439–458. doi:10.1177/1046496471 00200401

Dodge, K. A. (1993). Social-cognitive mechanisms in the development of conduct disorder and depression. *Annual Review of Psychology, 44*, 559–584. doi:10.1146/annurev.ps.44.020193.003015

Doren, D. M. (2002). *Evaluating sex offenders: A manual for civil commitments and beyond.* Thousand Oaks, CA: Sage.

Dougher, M. J. (1995a). Behavioral techniques to alter sexual arousal. In B. K. Schwartz & H. R. Cellini (Eds.), *The sex offender: Corrections, treatment and legal practice* (Vol. 1, pp. 15.1–15.8). Kingston, NJ: Civic Research Institute.

Dougher, M. J. (1995b). Clinical assessment of sex offenders. In B. K. Schwartz & H. R. Cellini (Eds.), *The sex offender: Corrections, treatment and legal practice* (Vol. 1, pp. 11.1–11.13). Kingston, NJ: Civic Research Institute.

Dowden, C., & Andrews, D. A. (2004). The importance of staff practice in delivering effective correctional treatment: A meta-analytic review of core correctional practice. *International Journal of Offender Therapy and Comparative Criminology, 48*, 203–214. doi:10.1177/0306624X03257765

Dowden, C., Antonowicz, D., & Andrews, D. A. (2003). The effectiveness of relapse prevention with offenders: A meta-analysis. *International Journal of Offender Therapy and Comparative Criminology, 47*, 516–528. doi:10.1177/0306624X03253018

Dozier, M., Stovall, K. C., & Albus, K. E. (1999). Attachment and psychopathology in adulthood. In J. Cassidy & P. R. Shaver (Eds.), *Handbook of attachment: Theory, research, and clinical applications* (pp. 497–519). New York, NY: Guilford Press.

Drake, C. R., & Ward, T. (2003). Treatment models for sex offenders: A move toward a formulation-based approach. In T. Ward, D. R. Laws, & S. M. Hudson (Eds.), *Sexual deviance: Issues and controversies* (pp. 226–243). Thousand Oaks, CA: Sage.

Drake, C. R., Ward, T., Nathan, P., & Lee, J. K. P. (2001). Challenging the cognitive distortions of child molesters: An implicit theory approach. *Journal of Sexual Aggression, 7,* 25–40. doi:10.1080/13552600108416165

Drapeau, M. (2005). Research on the processes involved in treating sexual offenders. *Sexual Abuse, 17,* 117–125. doi:10.1177/107906320501700203

Drapeau, M., Korner, C. A., Brunet, L., & Granger, L. (2004). Treatment at La Macaza Clinic: A qualitative study of the sexual offenders' perspective. *Canadian Journal of Criminology and Criminal Justice, 46,* 27–44.

D'Silva, K., Duggan, C., & McCarthy, L. (2004). Does treatment really make psychopaths worse? A review of the evidence. *Journal of Personality Disorders, 18,* 163–177. doi:10.1521/pedi.18.2.163.32775

Duncan, B. L., Miller, S. D., & Sparks, J. A. (2004). *The heroic client: A revolutionary way to improve effectiveness.* San Francisco, CA: Jossey-Bass.

Dunn, R. L., & Schwebel, A. I. (1995). Meta-analytic review of marital therapy outcome research. *Journal of Family Psychology, 9,* 58–68. doi:10.1037/0893-3200.9.1.58

Dush, D. M., Hirt, M. L., & Schroeder, H. E. (1983). Self-statement modification with adults: A meta-analysis. *Psychological Bulletin, 94,* 408–422. doi:10.1037/0033-2909.94.3.408

D'Zurilla, T. J. (1986). *Problem-solving therapy: A social competence approach to clinical intervention.* New York, NY: Springer.

D'Zurilla, T. J., & Goldfried, M. R. (1971). Problem solving and behavior modification. *Journal of Abnormal Psychology, 78,* 107–126. doi:10.1037/h0031360

Eells, T. D. (1997). *Handbook of psychotherapy case formulation.* New York, NY: Guilford Press.

Egan, G. (1998). *The skilled helper: A problem-management approach to helping.* Pacific Grove, CA: Brooks/Cole.

Eid, M., & Larsen, R. J. (Eds.). (2008). *The science of subjective well-being.* New York, NY: Guilford Press.

Eisen, M. L., Quas, J. A., & Goodman, G. S. (2002). *Memory and suggestibility in the interview: Personality and clinical psychology series.* Mahwah, NJ: Erlbaum.

Eisenthal, S., Emery, R., Lazare, A., & Udin, H. (1979). "Adherence" and the negotiated approach to patienthood. *Archives of General Psychiatry, 36,* 393–398.

Ellerby, L. A. (1998). *Providing clinical services to sex offenders: Burnout, compassion fatigue, and moderating variables* (Unpublished doctoral dissertation). University of Manitoba, Winnipeg, Canada.

Elliott, R., Barker, C. B., Caskey, N., & Pistrang, N. (1982). Differential helpfulness of counselor verbal response modes. *Journal of Counseling Psychology, 29,* 354–361. doi:10.1037/0022-0167.29.4.354

Ellis, H. (1915). *Studies in the psychology of sex: Vol. 2. Sexual inversion.* Philadelphia: Davis.

Emmons, R. A. (1996). Striving and feeling: Personal goals and subjective well-being. In P. M. Gollwitzer & J. A. Bargh (Eds.), *The psychology of action: Linking cognition and motivation to behavior* (pp. 313–337). New York, NY: Guilford Press.

Emmons, R. A. (1999). *The psychology of ultimate concerns.* New York, NY: Guilford Press.

Endler, N. S., & Parker, J. D. A. (1990). Multidimensional assessment of coping: A critical evaluation. *Journal of Personality and Social Psychology, 58,* 844–854. doi:10.1037/0022-3514.58.5.844

Endler, N. S., & Parker, J. D. A. (1999). *The coping inventory for stressful situations: Manual* (2nd ed.). Toronto, Ontario, Canada: Multi-Health Systems.

Epperson, D. L., Kaul, J. D., & Hesselton, D. (1998, October). *Final report on the development of the Minnesota Sex Offender Screening Tool<em Revised (MinSOST-R).* Paper presented at the 17th Annual Conference of the Association for the Treatment of Sexual Abusers, Vancouver, British Columbia, Canada.

Epstein, M. B., & Baucom, D. H. (2002). *Enhanced cognitive-behavioral therapy for couples: A contextual approach.* Washington, DC: American Psychological Association. doi:10.1037/10481-000

Ertz, D. J. (1997). The American Indian sexual offender. In B. K. Schwartz & H. R. Cellini (Eds.), *The sex offender: New insights, treatment innovations and legal developments* (pp. 14.1–14.12). Kingston, NJ: Civic Research Institute.

Eysenck, H. J. (1959). Learning theory and behaviour therapy. *The Journal of Mental Science, 105,* 61–75.

Fagan, J., & Wexler, S. (1988). Explanations of sexual assault among violent delinquents. *Journal of Adolescent Research, 3,* 363–385. doi:10.1177/074355488833010

Falk, D. R., & Hill, C. E. (1992). Counselor interventions preceding client laughter in brief therapy. *Journal of Counseling Psychology, 39,* 39–45. doi:10.1037/0022-0167.39.1.39

Falls, W. A. (1998). Extinction: A review of theory and evidence suggesting that memories are not erased with nonreinforcement. In W. O'Donohue (Ed.), *Learning and behavior therapy* (pp. 205–229). Boston, MA: Allyn & Bacon.

Farr, C., Brown, J., & Beckett, R. (2004). Ability to empathise and masculinity levels: Comparing male adolescent sex offenders with a normative sample of non-offending adolescents. *Psychology, Crime & Law, 10,* 155–167. doi:10.1080/10683160310001597153

Farrington, D. P. (1998). Individual differences and offending. In M. Tonry (Ed.), *The handbook of crime and punishment* (pp. 241–268). New York, NY: Oxford University Press.

Fava, G. A., Rafanelli, C., Cazzaro, M., Conti, S., & Grandi, S. (1998). Well-being therapy: A novel psychotherapeutic approach for residual symptoms of affective disorders. *Psychological Medicine, 28*, 475–480. doi:10.1017/S0033291797006363

Fava, G. A., Rafanelli, C., Grandi, S., Conti, S., & Belluardo, P. (1998). Prevention of recurrent depression with cognitive behavioral therapy. *Archives of General Psychiatry, 55*, 816–820. doi:10.1001/archpsyc.55.9.816

Fava, G. A., Rafanelli, C., Ottolini, F., Ruini, C., Cazzaro, M., & Grandi, S. (2001). Psychological well-being and residual symptoms in remitted patients with panic disorder and agoraphobia. *Journal of Affective Disorders, 65*, 185–190.

Feelgood, S., Cortoni, F., & Thompson, A. (2005). Sexual coping, general coping, and cognitive distortions in incarcerated rapists and child molesters. *Journal of Sexual Aggression, 11*, 157–170. doi:10.1080/13552600500073657

Feelgood, S., Golias, P., Shaw, S., & Bright, D. A. (2000). *Treatment changes in the dynamic risk factors of coping style in sexual offenders: A preliminary analysis*. New South Wales, Australia: N.S.W. Department of Corrective Services Sex Offender Programmes Custody-Based Intensive Treatment.

Fernandez, Y. M., & Marshall, W. L. (2003). Victim empathy, social self-esteem and psychopathy in rapists. *Sexual Abuse, 15*, 11–26. doi:10.1177/107906320301500102

Fernandez, Y. M., Marshall, W. L., Lightbody, S., & O'Sullivan, C. (1999). The Child Molester Empathy Measure: Description and an examination of its reliability and validity. *Sexual Abuse, 11*, 17–32. doi:10.1177/107906329901100103

Fernandez, Y. M., Shingler, J., & Marshall, W. L. (2006). Putting "behavior" back into the cognitive-behavioral treatment of sexual offenders. In W. L. Marshall, Y. M. Fernandez, L. E. Marshall, & G. A. Serran (Eds.), *Sexual offender treatment: Controversial issues* (pp. 211–224). Chichester, England: Wiley.

Finkelhor, D. (1984). *Child sexual abuse: New theory and research*. New York, NY: Free Press.

Finkelhor, D. (1994). The international epidemiology of child sexual abuse. *Child Abuse & Neglect, 18*, 409–417. doi:10.1016/0145-2134(94)90026-4

Fisher, A. (2008, March). *Revisioning male violence: Men of courage*. Paper presented at the First Provincial Conference on Male Sexual Victimization, Toronto, Ontario, Canada.

Fisher, D. D. (1997). *Assessing sexual offenders' victim empathy* (Unpublished doctoral thesis). University of Birmingham, Birmingham, England.

Fisher, D. D., Beech, A. R., & Browne, K. D. (1998). Locus of control and its relationship to treatment change and abuse history in child sexual abusers. *Legal and Criminological Psychology, 3*, 1–12.

Fisher, D. D., Beech, A. R., & Browne, K. D. (1999). Comparison of sex offenders to non-offenders on selected psychological measures. *International Journal of Offender Therapy and Comparative Criminology, 43*, 473–491. doi:10.1177/0306624X99434006

Flak, V., Beech, A. R., & Fisher, D. D. (2007). Forensic assessment of sexual interests: The current position. *Issues in Forensic Psychology, 6*, 70–83.

Ford, J. (1978). Therapeutic relationship in behavior therapy: An empirical analysis. *Journal of Consulting and Clinical Psychology, 46*, 1302–1314. doi:10.1037/0022-006X.46.6.1302

Frank, J. D. (1971). Therapeutic factors in psychotherapy. *American Journal of Psychotherapy, 25*, 350–361.

Free, N. K., Green, B. L., Grace, M. D., Chermus, L. A., & Whitman, R. M. (1985). Empathy and outcome in brief focal dynamic therapy. *The American Journal of Psychiatry, 142*, 917–921.

Freeman, A., & Freeman, S. (2005). Understanding schemas. In A. Freeman (Ed.), *Encyclopedia of cognitive behavior therapy* (pp. 421–426). New York, NY: Springer. doi:10.1007/0-306-48581-8_117

Freud, S. (1957). Three essays on the theory of sexuality. In J. Strachey (Ed.), *The standard edition of the complete psychological works of Sigmund Freud* (Vol. 7, pp. 123–243). London: Hogarth Press. (Original work published 1905)

Freund, K. (1957). Diagnostika homosexuality u muszi. *Ceskoslovak Medicine, 53*, 382–393.

Freund, K. (1991). Reflections on the development of the phallometric method of assessing sexual preferences. *Annals of Sex Research, 4*, 221–228. doi:10.1007/BF00850054

Friday, R. A. (1989). Contrasts in discussion behaviors of German and American managers. *International Journal of Intercultural Relations, 13*, 429–446. doi:10.1016/0147-1767(89)90022-9

Friendship, C., Beech, A. R., & Browne, K. D. (2002). Reconviction as an outcome measure in research: A methodological note. *The British Journal of Criminology, 42*, 442–444. doi:10.1093/bjc/42.2.442

Fry, P. S. (1975). Affect and resistance to temptation. *Developmental Psychology, 11*, 466–472. doi:10.1037/h0076678

Fuhriman, A., & Burlingame, G. M. (1990). Consistency of matter: A comparative analysis of individual and group process variables. *The Counseling Psychologist, 18*, 6–63. doi:10.1177/0011000090181002

Gallagher, C. A., Wilson, D. B., Hirschfield, P., Coggeshall, M. B., & MacKenzie, D. L. (1999). A quantitative review of the effects of sexual offender treatment on sexual reoffending. *Corrections Management Quarterly, 3*, 19–29.

Gambrill, E. (2002). Assertion training. In M. Hersen & W. Sledge (Eds.), *Encyclopedia of Psychotherapy* (Vol. 1, pp. 117–124). New York, NY: Academic Press.

Gannon, T. A., & Polaschek, D. L. L. (2005). Do child abusers deliberately fake good on cognitive distortion questionnaires? An information processing-based investigation. *Sexual Abuse, 17*, 183–200. doi:10.1177/107906320501700208

Garfield, S. L. (1993). Methodological problems in clinical diagnosis. In P. B. Sutker & H. E. Adams (Eds.), *Comprehensive handbook of psychopathology* (2nd ed., pp. 27–46). New York, NY: Plenum Press.

Garfield, S. L., & Bergin, A. (Eds.). (1986). *Handbook of psychotherapy and behavior change*. New York, NY: Wiley.

Garland, R. J., & Dougher, M. J. (1991). Motivational intervention in the treatment of sex offenders. In W. R. Miller & S. Rollnick (Eds.), *Motivational interviewing: Preparing people to change addictive behavior* (pp. 303–313). New York, NY: Guilford Press.

Garlick, Y., Marshall, W. L., & Thornton, D. (1996). Intimacy deficits and attribution of blame among sexual offenders. *Legal and Criminological Psychology, 1*, 251–258.

Garrett, T., Oliver, C., Wilcox, D. T., & Middleton, D. (2003). Who cares? The views of sexual offenders about the group treatment they receive. *Sexual Abuse, 15*, 323–338. doi:10.1177/107906320301500408

Garrett, T., & Thomas-Peter, B. (2009). Interventions with sex offenders with mental illness. In A. R. Beech, L. A. Craig, & K. D. Browne (Eds.), *Assessment and treatment of sex offenders* (pp. 393–408). Chichester, England: Wiley.

Garrison, J. (1978). Written vs. verbal preparation of patients for group psychotherapy. *Psychotherapy: Theory, Research, & Practice, 15*, 130–134. doi:10.1037/h0085851

Geer, T. M., Becker, J. V., Gray, S. R., & Krauss, D. (2001). Predictors of treatment completion in a correctional sex offender treatment program. *International Journal of Offender Therapy and Comparative Criminology, 45*, 302–313. doi:10.1177/0306624X01453003

Gery, I., Miljkovitch, R., Berthoz, S., & Soussignan, R. (2009). Empathy and recognition of facial expressions of emotion in sex offenders, non-sex offenders and normal controls. *Psychiatry Research, 165*, 252–262. doi:10.1016/j.psychres.2007.11.006

Gibbs, J. C., Potter, G. B., Liau, A. K., Schock, A. M., & Wightkin, S. P. (2001). Peer group therapy. In C. R. Hollin (Ed.), *Handbook of offender assessment and treatment* (pp. 259–268). Chichester, England: Wiley.

Giesen-Bloo, J., van Dyck, R., Spinhoven, P., van Tilburg, W., Dirksen, C., van Asselt, T., . . . Arntz, A. (2006). Outpatient psychotherapy for borderline personality disorder: Randomized trial of schema-focused therapy versus transference-focused psychotherapy. *Archives of General Psychiatry, 63*, 649–658. doi:10.1001/archpsyc.63.6.649

Ginsberg, J. L. D., Mann, R. E., Rotgers, F., & Weekes, J. R. (2002). Motivational interviewing with criminal justice populations. In W. Miller & S. Rollnick (Eds.), *Motivational interviewing: Preparing people to change* (2nd ed., pp. 333–346). New York, NY: Guilford Press.

Giotakis, O. (2005). A combination of viewing reaction time and incidental learning task in child molesters, rapists, and control males and females. *Sexologies, 54*, 13–22.

Glaser, D., & Frosh, S. (1993). *Child sexual abuse* (2nd ed.). Basingstoke, England: Macmillan.

Glaser, W. (2003). Integrating pharmacological treatments. In T. Ward, D. R. Laws, & S. M. Hudson (Eds.), *Sexual deviance: Issues and controversies* (pp. 262–279). Thousand Oaks, CA: Sage.

Goldfried, M. R. (1982). *Converging themes in psychotherapy: Trends in psychodynamic, humanistic, and behavioral practice*. New York, NY: Springer.

Goldfried, M. R., & Wolfe, B. (1996). Psychotherapy practice and research: Repairing a strained alliance. *American Psychologist, 51,* 1007–1016. doi:10.1037/0003-066X.51.10.1007

Gollwitzer, P. M., & Bargh, J. A. (Eds.). (1996). *The psychology of action: Linking cognition and motivation to behavior*. New York, NY: Guilford Press.

Goode, E. (1994, September). Battling deviant behavior. *U.S. News & World Report,* 74–80.

Goodman, A. (1998). *Sexual addiction: An integrated approach*. Madison, CT: International Universities Press.

Green, R. (1995). Psycho-educational modules. In B. K. Schwartz & H. R. Cellini (Eds.), *The sex offender: Corrections, treatment and legal practice* (pp. 13.1–13.10). Kingston, NJ: Civic Research Institute.

Greenberg, D. M., & Bradford, J. M. W. (1997). Treatment of the paraphilic disorders: A review of the role of selective serotonin reuptake inhibitors. *Sexual Abuse, 9,* 349–360.

Greenberg, L. S., & Pavio, S. (1997). *Working with emotions in psychotherapy*. New York, NY: Guilford Press.

Greenberg, L. S., & Pinsof, W. (Eds.). (1986). *Psychotherapeutic process: A research handbook*. New York, NY: Guilford Press.

Greenberg, L. S., Rice, L. N., & Elliott, R. (1993). *Facilitating emotional change: The moment-by-moment process*. New York, NY: Guilford Press.

Greeno, C. G., & Wing, R. R. (1994). Stress-induced eating. *Psychological Bulletin, 115,* 444–464. doi:10.1037/0033-2909.115.3.444

Greenwald, H. (1987). The humor decision. In W. F. Fry & W. A. Salameh (Eds.), *Handbook of humor and psychotherapy: Advances in the clinical use of humor* (pp. 41–54). Sarasota, FL: Professional Resource Exchange.

Gress, C. L. Z. (2005). Viewing time measures and sexual interests: Another piece of the puzzle. *Journal of Sexual Aggression, 11,* 117–125. doi:10.1080/13552600500063666

Gress, C. L. Z., & Laws, D. R. (2009). Measuring sexual deviance: Attention-based measures. In A. R. Beech, L. A. Craig, & K. D. Browne (Eds.), *Assessment and treatment of sex offenders: A handbook* (pp. 109–128). Chichester, England: Wiley.

Gross, J. J. (Ed.). (2007). *Handbook of emotion regulation*. New York, NY: Guilford Press.

Gross, J. J., & Levenson, R. W. (1993). Emotional suppression: Physiology, self-report, and expressive behavior. *Journal of Personality and Social Psychology, 64,* 970–986. doi:10.1037/0022-3514.64.6.970

Gross, J. J., & Levenson, R. W. (1997). Hiding feelings: The acute effects of inhibiting positive and negative emotions. *Journal of Abnormal Psychology, 106*, 95–103. doi:10.1037/0021-843X.106.1.95

Grubin, D. (1997). Inferring predictors of risk: Sex offenders. *International Review of Psychiatry, 9*, 225–232. doi:10.1080/09540269775439

Guinan, J. F., Foulds, M. L., & Wright, J. C. (1973). Do the changes last? A six-month follow-up of a marathon group. *Small Group Research, 4*, 177–180. doi:10.1177/104649647300400205

Guthrie, E. R. (1935). *The psychology of learning.* New York, NY: Harper.

Gutiérrez-Lobos, K., Eher, R., Grünhut, C., Bankier, B., Schmidl-Mohl, B., Frühwald, S., & Semler, B. (2001). Violent sex offenders lack male social support. *International Journal of Offender Therapy and Comparative Criminology, 45*, 70–82. doi:10.1177/0306624X01451005

Haaven, J. L., & Coleman, E. M. (2000). Treatment of the developmentally disabled sex offenders. In D. R. Laws, S. M. Hudson, & T. Ward (Eds.), *Remaking relapse prevention with sex offenders: A sourcebook* (pp. 369–388). Thousand Oaks, CA: Sage.

Haaven, J. L., Little, R., & Petri-Miller, D. (1990). *Treating intellectually disabled sex offenders: Model residential program.* Orwell, VT: Safer Society.

Hahlweg, K., & Klann, N. (1997). The effectiveness of marital counseling in Germany: A contribution to health services research. *Journal of Family Psychology, 11*, 410–421. doi:10.1037/0893-3200.11.4.410-421

Hall, G. C. N. (1995). Sexual offender recidivism revisited: A meta-analysis of recent treatment studies. *Journal of Consulting and Clinical Psychology, 63*, 802–809. doi:10.1037/0022-006X.63.5.802

Hanson, R. K. (1997a). *The development of a brief actuarial risk scale for sexual offense recidivism* (User Report 97-04). Ottawa, Ontario, Canada: Department of the Solicitor General of Canada.

Hanson, R. K. (1997b). Invoking sympathy: Assessment and treatment of empathy deficits among sexual offenders. In B. K. Schwartz & H. R. Cellini (Eds.), *The sex offender: New insights, treatment innovations and legal developments* (Vol. II, pp. 1.1–1.12). Kingston, NJ: Civic Research Institute.

Hanson, R. K. (1998, September). *Working with sex offenders.* Keynote address at the Annual Conference of the National Organization for the Treatment of Abusers, Glasgow, Scotland.

Hanson, R. K. (2003). Empathy deficits of sexual offenders: A conceptual model. *Journal of Sexual Aggression, 9*, 13–23. doi:10.1080/13552600310001379331

Hanson, R. K. (2006a). Does Static-99 predict recidivism among older sexual offenders? *Sexual Abuse, 18*, 343–355. doi:10.1177/107906320601800403

Hanson, R. K. (2006b). Stability and change: Dynamic risk factors for sexual offenders. In W. L. Marshall, Y. M. Fernandez, L. E. Marshall, & G. A. Serran (Eds.), *Sexual offender treatment: Controversial issues* (pp. 17–31). Chichester, England: Wiley.

Hanson, R. K., Bourgon, G., Helmus, L., & Hodgson, S. (2009). The principles of effective correctional treatment also apply to sexual offenders: A meta-analysis. *Criminal Justice and Behavior, 36*, 865–891. doi:10.1177/0093854809338545

Hanson, R. K., & Bussière, M. T. (1998). Predicting relapse: A meta-analysis of sexual offender recidivism studies. *Journal of Consulting and Clinical Psychology, 66*, 348–362. doi:10.1037/0022-006X.66.2.348

Hanson, R. K., Gizzarelli, R., & Scott, H. (1994). The attitudes of incest offenders: Sexual enticement and acceptance of sex with children. *Criminal Justice and Behavior, 21*, 187–202. doi:10.1177/0093854894021002001

Hanson, R. K., Gordon, A., Harris, A. J. R., Marques, J. K., Murphy, W. D., Quinsey, V. L., & Seto, M. C. (2002). First report of the Collaborative Outcome Data Project on the effectiveness of psychological treatment of sex offenders. *Sexual Abuse, 14*, 169–194. doi:10.1177/107906320201400207

Hanson, R. K., & Harris, A. J. R. (2000a). *STABLE-2000.* Unpublished manuscript. Department of the Solicitor General Canada. Available from the authors at Andrew.Harris@psepc-sppcc.gc.ca

Hanson, R. K., & Harris, A. J. R. (2000b). Where should we intervene? Dynamic predictors of sex offender recidivism. *Criminal Justice and Behavior, 27*, 6–35. doi:10.1177/0093854800027001002

Hanson, R. K., & Morton-Bourgon, K. E. (2005). The characteristics of persistent sexual offenders: A meat-analysis of recidivism studies. *Journal of Consulting and Clinical Psychology, 73*, 1154–1163. doi:10.1037/0022-006X.73.6.1154

Hanson, R. K., Morton, K. E., & Harris, A. J. R. (2003). Sexual offender recidivism risk: What we know and what we need to know. *Annals of the New York Academy of Sciences, 989*, 154–166. doi:10.1111/j.1749-6632.2003.tb07303.x

Hanson, R. K., & Scott, H. (1995). Assessing perspective taking among sexual offenders, nonsexual criminals and nonoffenders. *Sexual Abuse, 7*, 259–277.

Hanson, R. K., & Thornton, D. (1999). *Static 99: Improving actuarial risk assessments for sex offenders* (User Report 99-02). Ottawa, Ontario, Canada: Department of the Solicitor General of Canada. Retrieved from www.sgc.gc.ca/publications/corrections/199902_e.pdf

Hanson, R. K., & Thornton, D. (2000). Improving risk assessments for sex offenders: A comparison of three actuarial scales. *Law and Human Behavior, 24*, 119–136. doi:10.1023/A:1005482921333

Hanson, R. K., & Wallace-Capretta, S. (2000). *Predicting recidivism among male batterers.* Ottawa, Ontario, Canada: Department of the Solicitor General of Canada.

Happel, R. M., & Auffrey, J. J. (1995). Sex offender assessment: Interrupting the dance of denial. *The American Journal of Forensic Psychology, 13*, 5–22.

Hare, R. D. (1991). *Manual for the Revised Psychopathy Checklist.* Toronto, Ontario, Canada: Multi-Health Systems.

Hare, R. D., Clarke, D., Grann, M., & Thornton, D. (2000). Psychopathy and the predictive validity of the PCL-R: An international perspective. *Behavioral Sciences*

& the Law, 18, 623–645. doi:10.1002/1099-0798(200010)18:5<623::AID-BSL409>3.0.CO;2-W

Harkins, L., & Beech, A. R. (2007a). Measurement of the effectiveness of sex offender treatment. *Aggression and Violent Behavior, 12*, 36–44. doi:10.1016/j.avb.2006.03.002

Harkins, L., & Beech, A. R. (2007b). A review of the factors that can influence the effectiveness of sexual offender treatment: Risk, need, responsivity, and process issues. *Aggression and Violent Behavior, 12*, 615–627. doi:10.1016/j.avb.2006.10.006

Harris, G. T., Rice, M. E., & Quinsey, V. L. (1993). Violent recidivism of mentally disordered offenders: The development of a statistical prediction instrument. *Criminal Justice and Behavior, 20*, 315–335. doi:10.1177/0093854893020004001

Hart, S., Laws, D. R., & Kropp, P. R. (2003). The promise and peril of sex offender risk assessment. In T. Ward, D. R. Laws, & S. M. Hudson (Eds.), *Sexual deviance: Issues and controversies* (pp. 207–225). Thousand Oaks, CA: Sage.

Hartley, C. C. (1998). How incest offenders overcome internal inhibitions through the use of cognitions and cognitive distortions. *Journal of Interpersonal Violence, 13*, 25–39. doi:10.1177/088626098013001002

Harvey, J. H., Pauwels, B. G., & Zickmund, S. (2005). Relationship connection: The role of minding in the enhancement of closeness. In C. R. Snyder & S. J. Lopez (Eds.), *Handbook of positive psychology* (pp. 423–433). New York, NY: Oxford University Press.

Hazan, C., & Zeifman, D. (1999). Pair bonds as attachments: Evaluating the evidence. In J. Cassidy & P. R. Shaver (Eds.), *Handbook of attachment: Theory, research, and clinical applications* (pp. 336–354). New York, NY: Guilford Press.

Heitler, J. B. (1973). Preparation of lower-class patients for expressive group psychotherapy. *Journal of Consulting and Clinical Psychology, 41*, 251–260. doi:10.1037/h0035173

Hemphill, J. F., & Hart, S. D. (2002). Motivating the unmotivated: Psychopathy, treatment, and change. In M. McMurran (Ed.), *Motivating offenders to change: A guide to enhancing engagement in therapy* (pp. 193–219). Chichester, England: Wiley. doi:10.1002/9780470713471.ch12

Heppner, P. P., & Lee, D. (2005). Problem-solving appraisal and psychological adjustment. In C. R. Snyder & S. J. Lopez (Eds.), *Handbook of positive psychology* (pp. 288–298). New York, NY: Oxford University Press.

Hill, C. E., Carter, J. A., & O'Farrell, M. K. (1983). A case study of the process and outcome of time-limited counselling. *Journal of Counseling Psychology, 30*, 3–18. doi:10.1037/0022-0167.30.1.3

Hirschfeld, M. (1920). *Die homosexualitat des mannes und des weibes*. Berlin, Germany: L. Marcus Verlagsbuchhandlung.

Hoag, M., & Burlingame, G. (1997). Child and adolescent group psychotherapy: A narrative review of effectiveness and the case for meta-analysis. *Journal of Child and Adolescent Group Therapy, 7*, 51–68. doi:10.1007/BF02548949

Hodge, J. E., & Renwick, S. J. (2002). Motivating mentally disorder offenders. In M. McMurran (Ed.), *Motivating offenders to change: A guide to enhancing engagement in therapy* (pp. 221–234). Chichester, England: Wiley. doi:10.1002/9780470713471.ch13

Hodges, T. D., & Clifton, D. O. (2004). Strengths-based development in practice. In P. A. Linley & S. Joseph (Eds.), *Positive psychology in practice* (pp. 256–268). Hoboken, NJ: Wiley.

Hoehn-Saric, D. S., Frank, J., Imber, S., Nash, E., Stone, A., & Battle, C. (1964). Systematic preparation of patients in psychotherapy: I. Effects on therapy behavior and outcome. *Journal of Psychiatric Research, 2*, 267–281. doi:10.1016/0022-3956(64)90013-5

Hoffman, S., Gedanken, S., & Zim, S. (1993). Open group therapy at a university counseling service. *International Journal of Group Psychotherapy, 43*, 485–490.

Hogan, R. (1969). Development of an empathy scale. *Journal of Consulting and Clinical Psychology, 33*, 307–316. doi:10.1037/h0027580

Hogue, T. E. (1994). Goal attainment scaling: A measure of clinical impact and risk assessment with sexual offenders. In N. C. Clark & G. Stephenson (Eds.), *Rights and risks: The application of forensic psychology* (pp. 96–102). Leicester, England: British Psychological Society.

Hogue, T. E. (2009). The Peaks: Assessing sexual offenders in a dangerous and severe personality disorders unit. In A. R. Beech, L. A. Craig, & K. D. Browne (Eds.), *Assessment and treatment of sex offenders: A handbook* (pp. 237–264). Chichester, England: Wiley.

Hojat, M., & Vogel, W. H. (1989). Socioemotional bonding and neurobiochemistry. In M. Hojat & R. Crandall (Eds.), *Loneliness: Theory, research, and applications* (pp. 135–144). Newbury Park, CA: Sage.

Hollin, C. R. (2006). Offending behaviour programmes and contention: Evidence-based practice, manuals, and programme evaluation. In C. R. Hollin & E. J. Palmer (Eds.), *Offending behaviour programmes: Development, application, and controversies* (pp. 33–67). Chichester, England: Wiley. doi:10.1002/9780470713341.ch2

Hollin, C. R. (2009). Treatment manuals: The good, the bad and the useful. *Journal of Sexual Aggression, 15*, 133–137. doi:10.1080/13552600902907304

Hood, R., Shute, S., Feilzer, M., & Wilcox, A. (2002). Sex offenders emerging from long-term imprisonment: A study of their long-term reconviction rates and of parole board members' judgements of their risk. *The British Journal of Criminology, 42*, 371–394. doi:10.1093/bjc/42.2.371

Horvath, A. O. (2000). The therapeutic relationship: From transference to alliance [Special issue: Millennium issue]. *Journal of Counseling Psychology, 56*, 163–173.

Horvath, A. O., & Symonds, B. D. (1991). Relation between working alliance and outcome in psychotherapy: A meta-analysis. *Journal of Counseling Psychology, 38*, 139–149. doi:10.1037/0022-0167.38.2.139

Howells, K. (1979). Some meanings of children for pedophiles. In M. Cook & G. Wilson (Eds.), *Love and attraction: An international conference* (pp. 519–526). Oxford, England: Pergamon Press.

Howitt, D. (1995). *Paedophiles and sexual offences against children*. Chichester, England: Wiley.

Huber, H. P., & Gramer, M. (1991). Influence of age and pre-operative anxiety on preparing children for surgery. *German Journal of Psychology, 15*, 213–221.

Hudson, K. (2005). *Offending identities: Sex offenders' perspectives of their treatment and management*. Portland, OR: Willan.

Hudson, S. M., Marshall, W. L., Wales, D. S., McDonald, E., Bakker, L. W., & McLean, A. (1993). Emotional recognition skills of sex offenders. *Annals of Sex Research, 6*, 199–211. doi:10.1007/BF00849561

Hudson, S. M., & Ward, T. (1997). Intimacy, loneliness, and attachment style in sex offenders. *Journal of Interpersonal Violence, 12*, 323–339. doi:10.1177/088626097012003001

Hudson, S. M., & Ward, T. (2000). Relapse prevention: Assessment and treatment implications. In D. R. Laws, S. M. Hudson, & T. Ward (Eds.), *Remaking relapse prevention with sex offenders: A sourcebook* (pp. 102–122). Thousand Oaks, CA: Sage.

Hudson, S. M., Ward, T., & McCormack, J. C. (1999). Offense pathways in sexual offenders. *Journal of Interpersonal Violence, 14*, 779–798. doi:10.1177/088626099014008001

Hunter, J. A., & Goodwin, D. W. (1992). The clinical utility of satiation therapy with juvenile sex offenders: Variations and efficacy. *Annals of Sex Research, 5*, 71–80. doi:10.1007/BF00849732

Hunter, J. A., & Santos, D. (1990). The use of specialized cognitive-behavioral therapies in the treatment of juvenile sexual offenders. *International Journal of Offender Therapy and Comparative Criminology, 34*, 239–247. doi:10.1177/0306624X9003400307

Huter, J. C., Pfäfflin, F., & Ross, T. (2007). Patient, bezugspflelge und therapeut: Ein empirischer untersuchungsansatz für forensische therapieverläufe [Patient, primary nurse, and therapist: An emperical approach for evaluating forensic treatment]. *Forensische Psychiatrie und Psychotherapie: Werkstattschriften, 14*, 23–35.

Iacono, W. G., & Patrick, C. J. (1999). Polygraph ("lie detector") testing: The state of the art. In A. K. Hess & I. B. Weiner (Eds.), *The handbook of forensic psychology* (2nd ed., pp. 440–473). New York, NY: Wiley.

Jacobson, N. S., & Christensen, A. (1998). *Acceptance and change in couple therapy: A therapist's guide to transforming relationships*. New York, NY: Norton.

James, W. (1902). *The varieties of religious experience: A study in human nature*. New York, NY: Longmans, Green. doi:10.1037/10004-000

Jamieson, S., & Marshall, W. L. (2000). Attachment styles and violence in child molesters. *Journal of Sexual Aggression, 5*, 88–98. doi:10.1080/13552600008413301

Jenkins, A. (1990). *Invitations to responsibility: The therapeutic engagement of men who are violent and abusive*. Adelaide, South Australia: Dulwich Centre Publications.

Johnson, J. A., Cheek, J. M., & Struther, R. (1983). The structure of empathy. *Journal of Personality and Social Psychology, 45*, 1299–1312. doi:10.1037/0022-3514.45.6.1299

Johnson, S., Hunsley, J., Greenberg, L., & Schindler, D. (1999). Emotionally focused couples therapy: Status and challenges. *Clinical Psychology: Science and Practice, 6*, 67–69. doi:10.1093/clipsy/6.1.67

Johnson, S., & Sims, A. (2000). Attachment theory: A map for couples therapy. In T. M. Levy (Ed.), *Handbook of attachment interventions* (pp. 169–191). San Diego, CA: Academic Press.

Johnston, P., Hudson, S. M., & Marshall, W. L. (1992). The effects of masturbatory reconditioning with non-familial child molesters. *Behaviour Research and Therapy, 30*, 559–561. doi:10.1016/0005-7967(92)90043-G

Jolliffe, D., & Farrington, D. P. (2004). Empathy and offending: A systematic review and meta-analysis. *Aggression and Violent Behavior, 9*, 441–476. doi:10.1016/j.avb.2003.03.001

Jones, N., Pelissier, B., & Klein-Saffran, J. (2006). Predicting sex offender treatment entry among individuals convicted of sexual offence crimes. *Sexual Abuse, 18*, 83–98. doi:10.1177/107906320601800106

Jung, C. G. (1933). *Modern man in search of a soul*. New York, NY: Harcourt, Brace & World.

Kafka, M. P. (1994). Sertraline pharmacotherapy for paraphilias and paraphilia-related disorders: An open trial. *Annals of Clinical Psychiatry, 6*, 189–195. doi:10.3109/10401239409149003

Kafka, M. P., & Prentky, R. (1992). Fluoxetine treatment of non-paraphilic sexual addictions and paraphilias in men. *The Journal of Clinical Psychiatry, 53*, 351–358.

Kahn, T. J., & Chambers, H. J. (1991). Assessing reoffense risk with juvenile sex offenders. *Child Welfare, 70*, 333–345.

Kanfer, F. H., & Saslow, G. (1965). Behavioral analysis: An alternative to diagnostic classification. *Archives of General Psychiatry, 12*, 529–538.

Karterud, S. (1988). The influence of task definition, leadership and therapeutic style on inpatient group cultures. *International Journal of Therapeutic Communities, 9*, 231–247.

Kasser, T. (2004). The good life or the goods life? Positive psychology and personal well-being in the culture of consumption. In P. A. Linley & S. Joseph (Eds.), *Positive psychology in practice* (pp. 55–67). Hoboken, NJ: Wiley.

Kasser, T., & Ahuvia, A. C. (2002). Materialistic values and well-being in business students. *European Journal of Social Psychology, 32*, 137–146. doi:10.1002/ejsp.85

Kasser, T., & Ryan, R. M. (1993). A dark side of the American dream: Correlates of financial success as a central life aspiration. *Journal of Personality and Social Psychology, 65*, 410–422. doi:10.1037/0022-3514.65.2.410

Kasser, T., & Ryan, R. M. (1996). Further examining the American dream: Differential correlates of intrinsic and extrinsic goals. *Personality and Social Psychology Bulletin, 22*, 280–287. doi:10.1177/0146167296223006

Kazdin, A. E. (1978). *History of behavior modification: Experimental foundations of contemporary research*. Baltimore, MD: University Park Press.

Kear-Colwell, J., & Pollack, P. (1997). Motivation and confrontation: Which approach to the child sex offender? *Criminal Justice and Behavior, 24*, 20–33. doi:10.1177/0093854897024001002

Keenan, T., & Ward, T. (2000). A theory of mind perspective on cognitive, affective, and intimacy deficits in child sexual offenders. *Sexual Abuse, 12*, 49–60. doi:10.1177/107906320001200106

Keijsers, G. P. J., Schaap, C. P., & Hoogduin, C. A. L. (2000). The impact of interpersonal patient and therapist behaviour on outcome in cognitive-behavior therapy. *Behavior Modification, 24*, 264–297. doi:10.1177/0145445500242006

Kellett, J. M. (2000). Older adult sexuality. In L. T. Szuchman & F. Muscarella (Eds.), *Psychological perspectives on human sexuality* (pp. 355–379). New York, NY: Wiley.

Kemshall, H., & McIvor, G. (Eds.). (2004). *Managing sex offender risk*. London, England: Jessica Kingsley.

Kendall-Tackett, K., Williams, L., & Finkelhor, D. (1993). Impact of sexual abuse on children: A review and synthesis of recent empirical findings. *Psychological Bulletin, 113*, 164–180. doi:10.1037/0033-2909.113.1.164

Kennedy, H. G., & Grubin, D. H. (1992). Patterns of denial in sex offenders. *Psychological Medicine, 22*, 191–196. doi:10.1017/S0033291700032840

Kennedy, W. A., & Foreyt, J. (1968). Control of eating behavior in obese patients by avoidance conditioning. *Psychological Reports, 23*, 571–576.

Kennedy-Moore, E., & Watson, J. C. (1999). *Expressing emotion: Myths, realities, and therapeutic strategies*. New York, NY: Guilford Press.

Keppel, G. (1964). Facilitation in short- and long-term retention of paired associates following distributed practice in learning. *Journal of Verbal Learning and Verbal Behavior, 3*, 91–111. doi:10.1016/S0022-5371(64)80027-X

Kilmann, P. R., & Auerbach, S. M. (1974). Effects of marathon group therapy on trait and state anxiety. *Journal of Consulting and Clinical Psychology, 42*, 607–612. doi:10.1037/h0036726

King, L. A., & Miner, K. N. (2000). Writing about the perceived benefits of traumatic events: Implications for physical health. *Personality and Social Psychology Bulletin, 26*, 220–230. doi:10.1177/0146167200264008

Kingston, D. A., Firestone, P., Moulden, H. A., & Bradford, J. M. (2007). The utility of the diagnosis of pedophilia: A comparison of various classification procedures. *Archives of Sexual Behavior, 36*, 423–436. doi:10.1007/s10508-006-9091-x

Klein, M. H., Mathieu-Coughlan, P., & Kiesler, D. (1986). The experiencing scales. In L. S. Greenberg & W. Pinsoff (Eds.), *The psychotherapeutic process: A research handbook* (pp. 21–71). New York, NY: Guilford Press.

Klerman, G., Weissman, M., Rounsville, B., & Chevron, E. (1984). *Interpersonal therapy of depression*. New York, NY: Basic Books.

Knight, R. A., Prentky, R. A., & Cerce, D. D. (1994). The development, reliability and validity of an inventory for the multidimensional assessment of sex and aggression. *Criminal Justice and Behavior, 21*, 72–94. doi:10.1177/0093854894021001006

Koss, M. P. (1992). The underdetection of rape: Are there differences in the victim's experience? *Psychology of Women Quarterly, 12*, 1–24. doi:10.1111/j.1471-6402.1988.tb00924.x

Kottler, J. A., Sexton, T. L., & Whiston, S. C. (1994). *The heart of healing: Relationship in therapy*. San Francisco, CA: Jossey-Bass.

Krafft-Ebing, R. von (1886). *Psychopathia sexualia*. Stuttgart, Germany: Ferdinand, Enke.

Krug, D., Davis, T. B., & Glover, J. A. (1990). Massed versus distributed repeated reading: A case of forgetting helping recall? *Journal of Educational Psychology, 82*, 366–371. doi:10.1037/0022-0663.82.2.366

Kuyken, W. (2006). Evidence-based case formulation: Is the emperor clothed? In N. Tarrier (Ed.), *Case formulation in cognitive behavior therapy: The treatment of challenging and complex cases* (pp. 12–35). New York, NY: Routledge.

Lalumière, M. L., & Quinsey, V. L. (1994). The discriminability of rapists from non-sex offenders using phallometric measures: A meta-analysis. *Criminal Justice and Behavior, 21*, 150–175. doi:10.1177/0093854894021001010

Lambert, M. J. (1983). Comment on "A case study of the process and outcome of time-limited counseling." *Journal of Counseling Psychology, 30*, 22–25. doi:10.1037/0022-0167.30.1.22

Lambert, M. J. (1989). The individual therapist's contribution to psychotherapy process and outcome. *Clinical Psychology Review, 9*, 469–485. doi:10.1016/0272-7358(89)90004-4

Langevin, R. (1983). *Sexual strands: Understanding and treating sexual anomalies in men*. Hillsdale, NJ: Erlbaum.

Langevin, R., Wright, M. A., & Handy, L. (1988). Empathy, assertiveness, aggressiveness, and defensiveness among sex offenders. *Annals of Sex Research, 1*, 533–547. doi:10.1007/BF00854715

Langström, N., & Grann, M. (2000). Risk for criminal recidivism among young sex offenders. *Journal of Interpersonal Violence, 15*, 855–871. doi:10.1177/088626000015008005

Langton, C. M., Barbaree, H. E., Harkins, L., & Peacock, E. J. (2006). Sexual offenders' response to treatment and its association with recidivism as a function of psychopathy. *Sexual Abuse, 18*, 99–120. doi:10.1177/107906320601800107

Langton, C. M., Barbaree, H. E., Seto, M. C., Harkins, L., & Peacock, E. (2002, October). *How should we interpret behaviour in treatment?* Paper presented at the 21st Annual Research and Treatment Conference of the Association for the Treatment of Sexual Abusers, Montreal, Canada.

Langton, C. M., & Marshall, W. L. (2000). The role of cognitive distortions in relapse prevention programs. In D. R. Laws, S. M. Hudson, & T. Ward (Eds.), *Remaking relapse prevention with sex offenders: A sourcebook* (pp. 167–186). Newbury Park, CA: Sage.

Langton, C. M., & Marshall, W. L. (2001). Cognition in rapists: Theoretical patterns by typological breakdown. *Aggression and Violent Behavior, 6,* 499–518. doi:10.1016/S1359-1789(00)00029-X

Larsen, D. L., Nguyen, T. D., Green, R. S., & Attkisson, C. C. (1983). Enhancing the utilization of outpatient mental health services. *Community Mental Health Journal, 19,* 305–320. doi:10.1007/BF00755411

Larsen, J., Robertson, P., Hillman, D., & Hudson, S. M. (1998). Te Piriti: A bicultlural model for treating child molesters in New Zealand. In W. L. Marshall, Y. M. Fernandez, S. M. Hudson, & T. Ward (Eds.), *Sourcebook of treatment programs for sexual offenders* (pp. 385–398). New York, NY: Plenum Press.

Larsen, R. J., & Prizmic, Z. (2004). Affect regulation. In R. F. Baumeister & K. D. Vohs (Eds.), *Handbook of self-regulation: Research, theory, and application* (pp. 40–61). New York, NY: Guilford Press.

Larson, L. M., Allen, S. J., Imao, R. A. K., & Piersel, W. (1993). Self-perceived effective and ineffective problem solvers' problem-solving styles. *Journal of Counseling and Development, 71,* 528–532.

Lavender, A., & Schmidt, U. (2006). Cognitive-behavioral case formulation in complex eating disorders. In N. Tarrier (Ed.), *Case formulation in cognitive behavior therapy: The treatment of challenging and complex cases* (pp. 238–262). New York, NY: Routledge.

Laws, D. R. (Ed.). (1989). *Relapse prevention with sex offenders.* New York, NY: Guilford Press.

Laws, D. R. (2002). Owning your own data: The management of denial. In M. McMurran (Ed.), *Motivating offenders to change: A guide to enhancing engagement in therapy* (pp. 173–191). Chichester, England: Wiley. doi:10.1002/9780470713471.ch11

Laws, D. R., & Gress, C. L. Z. (2004). Seeing things differently: The viewing time alternative to penile plethysmography. *Legal and Criminological Psychology, 9,* 183–196. doi:10.1348/1355325041719338

Laws, D. R., Hudson, S. M., & Ward, T. (Eds.). (2000). *Remaking relapse prevention with sex offenders.* Thousand Oaks, CA: Sage.

Laws, D. R., & Marshall, W. L. (1990). A conditioning theory of the etiology and maintenance of deviant sexual preference and behavior. In W. L. Marshall, D. R. Laws, & H. E. Barbaree (Eds.), *Handbook of sexual assault: Issues, theories and treatment of the offender* (pp. 209–229). New York, NY: Plenum Press.

Laws, D. R., & Marshall, W. L. (1991). Masturbatory reconditioning: An evaluative review. *Advances in Behaviour Research and Therapy, 13,* 13–25. doi:10.1016/0146-6402(91)90012-Y

Laws, D. R., & Marshall, W. L. (2003). A brief history of behavioral and cognitive behavioral approaches to sexual offenders: Part 1. Early developments. *Sexual Abuse, 15,* 75–92. doi:10.1177/107906320301500201

Laws, D. R., & O'Donohue, W. (Eds.). (1997). *Sexual deviance: Theory, assessment, and treatment.* New York, NY: Guilford Press.

Laws, D. R., & O'Donohue, W. (Eds.). (2008). *Sexual deviance: Theory, assessment, and treatment* (2nd ed.). New York, NY: Guilford Press.

Lawson, J. S., Marshall, W. L., & McGrath, P. (1979). The Social Self-Esteem Inventory. *Educational and Psychological Measurement, 39,* 803–811. doi:10.1177/001316447903900413

Lazarus, R. S., & Folkman, S. (1984). *Stress, appraisal, and coping.* New York, NY: Springer.

Lee, J. K. P., Proeve, M. J., Lancaster, M., & Jackson, H. J. (1996). An evaluation and 1-year follow-up study of a community-based treatment program for sex offenders. *Australian Psychologist, 31,* 147–152. doi:10.1080/00050069608260196

Lees, S. (1996). *Carnal knowledge: Rape on trial.* London, England: Hamish Hamilton.

Lefcourt, H. M. (2005). Humor. In C. R. Snyder & S. J. Lopez (Eds.), *Handbook of positive psychology* (pp. 619–631). New York, NY: Oxford University Press.

Letourneau, E. J. (2002). A comparison of objective measures of sexual arousal and interest: Visual reaction time and penile plethysmography. *Sexual Abuse, 14,* 207–223. doi:10.1177/107906320201400302

Levenson, J. A., & Prescott, D. S. (2007). Considerations in evaluating the effectiveness of sexual offender treatment: Incorporating knowledge into practice. In D. S. Prescott (Ed.), *Knowledge and practice: Challenges in the treatment and supervision of sexual abusers* (pp. 124–142). Oklahoma City, OK: Wood 'N' Barnes.

Licht, H. (1932). *Sexual life in ancient Greece.* London, England: Routledge & Kegan Paul.

Lieberman, M. A., Yalom, I. D., & Miles, M. B. (1973). *Encounter groups: First facts.* New York, NY: Basic Books.

Lietaer, G. (1992). Helping and hindering processes in client-centered/experiential psychotherapy: A content analysis of client and therapist postsession perceptions. In S. G. Toukmanian & D. L. Rennie (Eds.), *Psychotherapy process research: Paradigmatic and narrative approaches* (pp. 134–162). Newbury Park, CA: Sage.

Lindsay, W. R., Steele, L., Smith, A. H. W., Quinn, K., & Allan, R. (2006). A community forensic intellectual disability service: Twelve-year follow-up of referrals, analysis of referral patterns and assessment of harm reduction. *Legal and Criminological Psychology, 11,* 113–130. doi:10.1348/135532505X55669

Linehan, M. (1993). *Skills training manual for treatment borderline personality disorder.* New York, NY: Guilford Press.

Linley, P. A., & Joseph, S. (2004a). Applied positive psychology: A new perspective for professional practice. In P. A. Linley & S. Joseph (Eds.), *Positive psychology in practice* (pp. 3–12). Hoboken, NJ: Wiley.

Linley, P. A., & Joseph, S. (Eds.). (2004b). *Positive psychology in practice*. Hoboken, NJ: Wiley.

Lockwood, C. S., Page, T. E., & Conroy-Hiller, T. (2004). *Comparing the effectiveness of cognitive behaviour therapy using individual or group therapy in the treatment of depression* (JBI Reports, No. 2, pp. 185–206). Sydney, Australia: Blackwell.

Logan, C. (2009). Narcissism. In M. McMurran & R. C. Howard (Eds.), *Personality, personality disorder and violence* (pp. 85–112). Chichester, England: Wiley.

Looman, J. (1999). Mood, conflict, and deviant sexual fantasies. In B. K. Schwartz (Ed.), *The sex offender: Theoretical advances, treating special populations and legal developments* (Vol. III, pp. 3.1–3.11). Kingston, NJ: Civic Research Institute.

Looman, J., Abracen, J., & Nicholaichuk, T. P. (2000). Recidivism among treated sexual offenders and matched controls: Data from the Regional Treatment Centre (Ontario). *Journal of Interpersonal Violence, 15*, 279–290. doi:10.1177/088626000015003004

Looman, J., Abracen, J., Serin, R., & Marquis, P. (2005). Psychopathy, treatment change and recidivism in high risk high need sexual offenders. *Journal of Interpersonal Violence, 20*, 549–568. doi:10.1177/0886260504271583

Lösel, F., & Schmucker, M. (2005). The effectiveness of treatment for sexual offenders: A comprehensive meta-analysis. *Journal of Experimental Criminology, 1*, 117–146. doi:10.1007/s11292-004-6466-7

Loving, J. L. (2002). Treatment planning with the Psychopathy Checklist-Revised (RCL-R). *International Journal of Offender Therapy and Comparative Criminology, 46*, 281–293.

Lovins, B., Lowenkamp, C. T., & Latessa, E. J. (2009). Applying the risk principle to sex offenders: Can treatment make some sex offenders worse? *The Prison Journal, 89*, 344–357. doi:10.1177/0032885509339509

Lowenkamp, C. T., & Latessa, E. (2002). *Evaluation of Ohio's community based correctional facilities and halfway house programs* (Unpublished manuscript). Division of Criminal Justice, University of Cincinnati, OH.

Lowenkamp, C. T., Latessa, E., & Holsinger, A. (2006). The risk principle in action: What have we learned from 13,676 offenders and 97 correctional programs? *Crime and Delinquency, 51*, 1–17.

Luborsky, L. (1994). The benefits to the clinician of psychotherapy research: A clinician-researchers view. In P. F. Talley, H. H. Strupp, & S. F. Butler (Eds.), *Psychotherapy research and practice: Bridging the gap* (pp. 167–180). New York, NY: Basic Books.

Luborsky, L., Crits-Christoph, P., Mintz, J., & Auerbach, A. (1988). *Who will benefit from psychotherapy? Predicting therapeutic outcome*. New York, NY: Basic Books.

Lucas, R., Diener, E., & Larsen, R. (2003). The measurement of positive emotions. In C. R. Snyder & M. Lopez (Eds.), *Handbook of positive psychological assessment* (pp. 201–218). Washington, DC: American Psychological Association. doi:10.1037/10612-013

Lyn, T. S., & Burton, D. L. (2004). Adult attachment and sexual offender status. *American Journal of Orthopsychiatry, 74,* 150–159. doi:10.1037/0002-9432. 74.2.150

Maddux, J. E., Snyder, C. R., & Lopez, S. J. (2004). Toward a positive clinical psychology: Deconstructing the illness ideology and constructing an ideology of human strengths and potential. In P. A. Linley & S. Joseph (Eds.), *Positive psychology in practice* (pp. 320–334). Hoboken, NJ: Wiley.

Mahoney, M. J., & Norcross, J. C. (1993). Relationship styles and therapeutic choices: A commentary. *Psychotherapy: Theory, Research, & Practice, 30,* 423–426. doi:10.1037/0033-3204.30.3.423

Maier, G. J., & Fulton, L. (1998). Inpatient treatment of offenders with mental disorders. In R. M. Wettstein (Ed.), *Treatment of offenders with mental disorders* (pp. 126–167). New York, NY: Guilford Press.

Mailloux, D. L., Abracen, J., Serin, R., Cousineau, C., Malcolm, B., & Looman, J. (2003). Dosage of treatment to sexual offenders: Are we overprescribing? *International Journal of Offender Therapy and Comparative Criminology, 47,* 171–184. doi:10.1177/0306624X03251096

Maletzky, B. M. (1991). *Treating the sex offender.* Newbury Park, CA: Sage.

Maletzky, B. M. (1996). Editorial: Denial of treatment or treatment of denial? *Sexual Abuse, 8,* 1–5. doi:10.1177/107906329600800101

Maletzky, B. M. (1998). Factors associated with success and failure in the behavior and cognitive treatment of sexual offenders. *Annals of Sex Research, 6,* 241–258. doi:10.1007/BF00856862

Mandeville-Norden, R., Beech, A. R., & Hayes, E. (2008). Examining the effectiveness of a UK community-based sexual offender treatment programme for child abusers. *Psychology, Crime & Law, 14,* 493–512. doi:10.1080/106831608 01948907

Mann, R. E. (1996, November). *Measuring the effectiveness of relapse prevention intervention with sex offenders.* Paper presented at the 15th Annual Research and Treatment Conference of the Association for the Treatment of Sexual Abusers, Chicago.

Mann, R. E. (2004). *An investigation of the nature, content and influence of schemas in sexual offending* (Doctoral thesis). University of Leicester, England.

Mann, R. E. (2009). Sex offender treatment: The case for manualization. *Journal of Sexual Aggression, 15,* 121–131. doi:10.1080/13552600902907288

Mann, R. E., & Beech, A. R. (2003). Cognitive distortions, schemas, and implicit theories. In T. Ward, D. R. Laws, & S. M. Hudson (Eds.), *Sexual deviance: Issues and controversies* (pp. 135–153). Thousand Oaks, CA: Sage.

Mann, R. E., Ginsburg, J. I. D., & Weekes, J. R. (2002). Motivational interviewing with offenders. In M. McMurran (Ed.), *Motivating offenders to change* (pp. 87–102). Chichester, England: Wiley. doi:10.1002/9780470713471.ch6

Mann, R. E., & Hollin, C. R. (2001, November). *Schemas: A model for understanding cognition in sexual offending.* Paper presented at the 20th Annual Research and

Treatment Conference of the Association for the Treatment of Sexual Abusers, San Antonio, TX.

Mann, R. E., & Rollnick, S. (1996). Motivational interviewing with a sex offender who believed he was innocent. *Behavioural and Cognitive Psychotherapy, 24,* 127–134. doi:10.1017/S1352465800017392

Mann, R. E., & Shingler, J. (2006). Schema-driven cognition in sexual offenders: Theory, assessment and treatment. In W. L. Marshall, Y. M. Fernandez, L. E. Marshall, & G. A. Serran (Eds.), *Sexual offender treatment: Controversial issues* (pp. 173–185). Chichester, England: Wiley.

Mann, R. E., & Thornton, D. (1998). The evolution of a multisite sexual offender treatment program. In W. L. Marshall, Y. M. Fernandez, S. M. Hudson, & T. Ward (Eds.), *Sourcebook of treatment programs for sexual offenders* (pp. 47–57). New York, NY: Plenum Press.

Mann, R. E., & Webster, S. D. (2002, October). *Understanding resistance and denial.* Paper presented at the 21st Annual Research and Treatment Conference of the Association for the Treatment of Sexual Abusers, Montreal, Canada.

Mann, R. E., Webster, S. D., Schofield, C., & Marshall, W. L. (2004). Approach versus avoidance goals in relapse prevention with sexual offenders. *Sexual Abuse, 16,* 65–75.

Mann, R. E., Webster, S. D., Wakeling, H. C., & Marshall, W. L. (2007). The measurement and influence of child sexual abuse supportive beliefs. *Psychology, Crime & Law, 13,* 443–458. doi:10.1080/10683160601061141

Mark, P. (1992). Training staff to work with sex offenders. *Probation Journal, 39,* 1–13.

Marlatt, G. A. (1982). Relapse prevention: A self-control program for the treatment of addictive behaviors. In R. B. Stuart (Ed.), *Adherence, compliance and generalization in behavioral medicine* (pp. 329–378). New York, NY: Brunner/Mazel.

Marlatt, G. A., & Gordon, J. R. (1985). *Relapse prevention: Maintenance strategies in the treatment of addictive behaviors.* New York, NY: Guilford Press.

Marques, J. K. (1982, March). *Relapse prevention: A self-control model for the treatment of sex offenders.* Paper presented at the 7th Annual Forensic Mental Health Conference, Asilomar, CA.

Marques, J. K., Day, D. M., Nelson, C., & West, M. A. (1994). Effects of cognitive-behavioral treatment on sex offender recidivism: Preliminary results of a longitudinal study. *Criminal Justice and Behavior, 21,* 28–54. doi:10.1177/0093854894021001004

Marques, J. K., Weideranders, M., Day, D. M., Nelson, C., & van Ommeren, A. (2005). Effects of a relapse prevention program on sexual recidivism: Final results from California's Sex Offender Treatment and Evaluation Project (SOTEP). *Sexual Abuse, 17,* 79–107. doi:10.1177/107906320501700108

Marquis, J. N. (1970). Orgasmic reconditioning: Changing sexual object choice through controlling masturbation fantasies. *Journal of Behavior Therapy and Experimental Psychiatry, 1,* 263–271. doi:10.1016/0005-7916(70)90050-9

Marsa, F., O'Reilly, G., Carr, A., Murphy, P., O'Sullivan, M., Cotter, A., & Hevey, D. (2004). Attachment styles and psychological profiles of child sex offenders in Ireland. *Journal of Interpersonal Violence, 19,* 228–251. doi:10.1177/0886260503260328

Marshall, L. E., Bailey, W., Mailett, G., & Marshall, W. L. (2009). *Changes in shame and guilt as a result of sexual offender treatment.* Manuscript submitted for publication.

Marshall, L. E., & Marshall, W. L. (2001). Excessive sexual desire disorder among sexual offenders: The development of a research project. *Sexual Addiction & Compulsivity: The Journal of Treatment and Prevention, 8,* 301–307. doi:10.1080/107201601753459982

Marshall, L. E., & Marshall, W. L. (2006). Sexual addiction in incarcerated sexual offenders. *Sexual Addiction & Compulsivity: The Journal of Treatment and Prevention, 13,* 377–390. doi:10.1080/10720160601011281

Marshall, L. E., & Marshall, W. L. (2007). Preparatory programs for sexual offender treatment. In D. Prescott (Ed.), *Applying knowledge to practice: The treatment and supervision of sexual abusers* (pp. 108–123). Oklahoma City, OK: Wood 'N' Barnes.

Marshall, L. E., & Marshall, W. L. (2008, August). *Treatment program for sexual offenders in categorical denial.* Paper presented at the 10th Conference of the International Association for the Treatment of Sexual Offenders Capetown, South Africa.

Marshall, L. E., & Marshall, W. L. (in press). The role of attachments in sexual offenders: An examination of pre-occupied attachment style offending behavior. In B. K. Schwartz (Ed.), *Handbook of sexual offender treatment.* Kingston, NJ: Civic Research.

Marshall, L. E., Marshall, W. L., Fernandez, Y. M., Malcolm, P. B., & Moulden, H. M. (2008). The Rockwood Preparatory Program for sexual offenders: Description and preliminary appraisal. *Sexual Abuse, 20,* 25–42. doi:10.1177/1079063208314818

Marshall, L. E., Marshall, W. L., Moulden, H. M., & Serran, G. A. (2008). The prevalence of sexual addiction in incarcerated sexual offenders and matched community nonoffenders. *Sexual Addiction & Compulsivity: The Journal of Treatment and Prevention, 15,* 271–283. doi:10.1080/10720160802516328

Marshall, L. E., & O'Brien, M. D. (2009). Assessment of sexual addiction. In A. R. Beech, L. A. Craig, & K. D. Browne (Eds.), *Assessment and treatment of sex offenders: A handbook* (pp. 163–177). Chichester, England: Wiley.

Marshall, L. E., O'Brien, M. D., & Marshall, W. L. (2010). *Sexual prudish attitudes among sexual offenders.* Manuscript in preparation.

Marshall, L. E., Serran, G. A., & Marshall, W. L. (2008, October). *Group climate in an open-ended versus a closed sexual offender treatment program.* Paper presented at the 27th Annual Research and Treatment Conference of the Association for the Treatment of Sexual Abusers, Atlanta, GA.

Marshall, W. L. (1971). A combined treatment method for certain sexual deviations. *Behaviour Research and Therapy, 9,* 293–294. doi:10.1016/0005-7967(71)90016-7

Marshall, W. L. (1975). Reducing masturbatory guilt. *Journal of Behavior Therapy and Experimental Psychiatry, 6,* 260–261. doi:10.1016/0005-7916(75)90116-0

Marshall, W. L. (1979). Satiation therapy: A procedure for reducing deviant sexual arousal. *Journal of Applied Behavior Analysis, 12,* 377–389. doi:10.1901/jaba. 1979.12-377

Marshall, W. L. (1989). Invited essay: Intimacy, loneliness and sexual offenders. *Behaviour Research and Therapy, 27,* 491–504. doi:10.1016/0005-7967(89)90083-1

Marshall, W. L. (1992). The social value of treatment for sexual offenders. *The Canadian Journal of Human Sexuality, 1,* 109–114.

Marshall, W. L. (1993a). The role of attachment, intimacy, and loneliness in the etiology and maintenance of sexual offending. *Sexual and Marital Therapy, 8,* 109–121.

Marshall, W. L. (1993b). The treatment of sex offenders: What does the outcome data tell us? A reply to Quinsey et al. *Journal of Interpersonal Violence, 8,* 524–530. doi:10.1177/088626093008004007

Marshall, W. L. (1994). Treatment effects on denial and minimization in incarcerated sex offenders. *Behaviour Research and Therapy, 32,* 559–564. doi:10.1016/0005-7967(94)90145-7

Marshall, W. L. (1996). The sexual offender: Monster, victim, or everyman? *Sexual Abuse, 8,* 317–335.

Marshall, W. L. (1997). The relationship between self-esteem and deviant sexual arousal in nonfamilial child molesters. *Behavior Modification, 21,* 86–96. doi: 10.1177/01454455970211005

Marshall, W. L. (2002). Historical foundations and current conceptualizations of empathy. In Y. M. Fernandez (Ed.), *In their shoes: Examining the issue of empathy and its place in the treatment of offenders* (pp. 1–15). Oklahoma City, OK: Wood 'N' Barnes.

Marshall, W. L. (2005). Therapist style in sexual offender treatment: Influence on indices of change. *Sexual Abuse, 17,* 109–116. doi:10.1177/107906320501700202

Marshall, W. L. (2006a). Ammonia aversion with an exhibitionist: A case study. *Clinical Case Studies, 5,* 15–24. doi:10.1177/1534650103259755

Marshall, W. L. (2006b). Olfactory aversion and directed masturbation in the modification of deviant preferences: A case study of a child molester. *Clinical Case Studies, 5,* 3–14. doi:10.1177/1534650103259754

Marshall, W. L. (2007a). Covert association: A case illustration. *Clinical Case Studies, 6,* 218–231. doi:10.1177/1534650105280329

Marshall, W. L. (2007b). Diagnostic issues, multiple paraphilias, and comorbid disorders in sexual offenders: Their incidence and treatment. *Aggression and Violent Behavior, 12,* 16–35. doi:10.1016/j.avb.2006.03.001

Marshall, W. L. (2008). Czy pedofilia jest uleczalna? Wyniki badan pólnocno-amerykanskich [Are pedophiles treatable? Evidence from North American studies]. *Seksuologia Polska, 6,* 1–6.

Marshall, W. L. (2009). Manualization: A blessing or a curse? *Journal of Sexual Aggression, 15,* 109–120. doi:10.1080/13552600902907320

Marshall, W. L., & Anderson, D. (2000). Do relapse prevention components enhance treatment effectiveness? In D. R. Laws, S. M. Hudson, & T. Ward (Eds.), *Remaking relapse prevention with sex offenders: A sourcebook* (pp. 39–55). Newbury Park, CA: Sage.

Marshall, W. L., Anderson, D., & Champagne, F. (1997). Self-esteem and its relationship to sexual offending. *Psychology, Crime & Law, 3,* 161–186. doi:10.1080/10683169708410811

Marshall, W. L., Anderson, D., & Fernandez, Y. M. (1999). *Cognitive behavioural treatment of sexual offenders.* Chichester, England: Wiley.

Marshall, W. L., & Barbaree, H. E. (1988). The long-term evaluation of a behavioral treatment program for child molesters. *Behaviour Research and Therapy, 26,* 499–511. doi:10.1016/0005-7967(88)90146-5

Marshall, W. L., & Barbaree, H. E. (1990). Outcome of comprehensive cognitive behavioral treatment programs. In W. L. Marshall, D. R. Laws, & H. E. Barbaree (Eds.), *Handbook of sexual assault: Issues, theories and treatment of the offender* (pp. 363–385). New York, NY: Plenum Press.

Marshall, W. L., Barbaree, H. E., & Butt, J. (1988). Sexual offenders against male children: Sexual preferences. *Behaviour Research and Therapy, 26,* 383–391. doi:10.1016/0005-7967(88)90071-X

Marshall, W. L., & Barrett, S. (1990). *Criminal neglect: Why sex offenders go free.* Toronto, Ontario, Canada: Doubleday.

Marshall, W. L., Booth, B., Bradford, J. M. W., & Marshall, L. E. (2009, April). *Management of mentally disordered sexual offenders.* Workshop presented at the World Congress of Psychiatry, Florence, Italy.

Marshall, W. L., Bryce, P., Hudson, S. M., Ward, T., & Moth, B. (1996). The enhancement of intimacy and reduction of loneliness among child molesters. *Legal and Criminological Psychology, 1,* 95–102.

Marshall, W. L., Champagne, F., Brown, C., & Miller, S. (1998). Empathy, intimacy, loneliness, and self-esteem in nonfamilial child molesters. *Journal of Child Sexual Abuse, 6,* 87–98. doi:10.1300/J070v06n03_06

Marshall, W. L., Champagne, F., Sturgeon, C., & Bryce, P. (1997). Increasing the self-esteem of child molesters. *Sexual Abuse, 9,* 321–333.

Marshall, W. L., & Christie, M. M. (1982). The enhancement of social self-esteem. *Canadian Counsellor, 16,* 82–89.

Marshall, W. L., Christie, M. M., Lanthier, R. D., & Cruchley, J. (1982). The nature of the reinforcer in the enhancement of social self-esteem. *Canadian Counsellor, 16,* 90–96.

Marshall, W. L., Cripps, E., Anderson, D., & Cortoni, F. A. (1999). Self-esteem and coping strategies in child molesters. *Journal of Interpersonal Violence, 14*, 955–962. doi:10.1177/088626099014009003

Marshall, W. L., Earls, C. M., Segal, Z. V., & Darke, J. (1983). A behavioral program for the assessment and treatment of sexual aggressors. In K. Craig & R. McMahon (Eds.), *Advances in clinical behavior therapy* (pp. 148–174). New York, NY: Brunner/Mazel.

Marshall, W. L., Eccles, A., & Barbaree, H. E. (1991). Treatment of exhibitionists: A focus on sexual deviance versus cognitive and relationship features. *Behaviour Research and Therapy, 29*, 129–135. doi:10.1016/0005-7967(91)90041-Z

Marshall, W. L., & Fernandez, Y. M. (2003). *Phallometric testing with sexual offenders: Theory, research, and practice*. Brandon, VT: Safer Society Press.

Marshall, W. L., Fernandez, Y. M., Hudson, S. M., & Ward, T. (Eds.). (1998). *Sourcebook of treatment programs for sexual offenders*. New York, NY: Plenum Press.

Marshall, W. L., & Hambley, L. S. (1996). Intimacy and loneliness, and their relationship to rape myth acceptance and hostility toward women among rapists. *Journal of Interpersonal Violence, 11*, 586–592. doi:10.1177/088626096011004009

Marshall, W. L., Hamilton, K., & Fernandez, Y. M. (2001). Empathy deficits and cognitive distortions in child molesters. *Sexual Abuse, 13*, 123–130. doi:10.1177/107906320101300205

Marshall, W. L., Hudson, S. M., Jones, R., & Fernandez, Y. M. (1995). Empathy in sex offenders. *Clinical Psychology Review, 15*, 99–113. doi:10.1016/0272-7358(95)00002-7

Marshall, W. L., Keltner, A., & Griffiths, E. (1974). *An apparatus for the delivery of foul odours: Clinical applications* (Unpublished manuscript). Queen's University, Kingston, Ontario, Canada.

Marshall, W. L., & Kennedy, P. (2003). Sexual sadism in sexual offenders: An elusive diagnosis. *Aggression and Violent Behavior, 8*, 1–22. doi:10.1016/S1359-1789(01)00052-0

Marshall, W. L., & Laws, D. R. (2003). A brief history of behavioral and cognitive behavioral approaches to sexual offender treatment: Part 2. The modern era. *Sexual Abuse, 15*, 93–120. doi:10.1177/107906320301500202

Marshall, W. L., & Lippens, K. (1977). The clinical value of boredom: A procedure for reducing inappropriate sexual interests. *Journal of Nervous and Mental Disease, 165*, 283–287. doi:10.1097/00005053-197710000-00009

Marshall, W. L., & Marshall, L. E. (2000). The origins of sexual offending. *Trauma, Violence & Abuse, 1*, 250–263. doi:10.1177/1524838000001003003

Marshall, W. L., & Marshall, L. E. (2007). The utility of the Random Controlled Trial for evaluating sexual offender treatment: The gold standard or an inappropriate strategy? *Sexual Abuse, 19*, 175–191. doi:10.1177/107906320701900207

Marshall, W. L., & Marshall, L. E. (2008). Good clinical practice and the evaluation of treatment: A response to Seto et al. *Sexual Abuse, 20*, 256–260. doi:10.1177/1079063208323839

Marshall, W. L., & Marshall, L. E. (2010a). *Are the cognitive distortions of child molesters in need of treatment?* Manuscript submitted for publication.

Marshall, W. L., & Marshall, L. E. (2010b). Attachment and intimacy in sexual offenders: An update. *Sexual and Marital Therapy, 25,* 86–90.

Marshall, W. L., Marshall, L. E., Sachdev, S., & Kruger, R. L. (2003). Distorted attitudes and perceptions, and their relationship with self-esteem and coping in child molesters. *Sexual Abuse, 15,* 171–181. doi:10.1177/107906320301500302

Marshall, W. L., Marshall, L. E., & Serran, G. A. (2009). Empathy and offending behavior. In M. McMurran & R. C. Howard (Eds.), *Personality, personality disorder and violence* (pp. 229–244). Chichester, England: Wiley.

Marshall, W. L., Marshall, L. E., Serran, G. A., & Fernandez, Y. M. (2006). *Treating sexual offenders: An integrated approach.* New York, NY: Routledge.

Marshall, W. L., Marshall, L. E., Serran, G. A., & O'Brien, M. D. (2008). Sexual offender treatment: A positive approach. *The Psychiatric Clinics of North America, 31,* 681–696. doi:10.1016/j.psc.2008.06.001

Marshall, W. L., Marshall, L. E., Serran, G. A., & O'Brien, M. D. (2009). Self-esteem, shame, cognitive distortions and empathy in sexual offenders: Their integration and treatment implications. *Psychology, Crime & Law, 15,* 217–234. doi:10.1080/10683160802190947

Marshall, W. L., Marshall, L. E., & Ware, J. (2009). Cognitive distortions in sexual offenders: Should they all be treatment targets? *Sexual Abuse in Australia and New Zealand: An Interdisciplinary Journal, 2,* 70–78.

Marshall, W. L., & Mazzucco, A. (1995). Self-esteem and parental attachments in child molesters. *Sexual Abuse, 7,* 279–285.

Marshall, W. L., & McGuire, J. (2003). Effect sizes in treatment of sexual offenders. *International Journal of Offender Therapy and Comparative Criminology, 46,* 653–663.

Marshall, W. L., & Moulden, H. (2001). Hostility toward women and victim empathy in rapists. *Sexual Abuse, 13,* 249–255. doi:10.1177/107906320101300403

Marshall, W. L., O'Brien, M. D., & Marshall, L. E. (2009). Modifying sexual preferences. In A. R. Beech, L. A. Craig, & K. D. Browne (Eds.), *Assessment and treatment of sex offenders: A handbook* (pp. 311–327). Chichester, England: Wiley.

Marshall, W. L., O'Sullivan, C., & Fernandez, Y. M. (1996). The enhancement of victim empathy among incarcerated child molesters. *Legal and Criminological Psychology, 1,* 95–102.

Marshall, W. L., & Pithers, W. D. (1994). A reconsideration of treatment outcome with sex offenders. *Criminal Justice and Behavior, 21,* 10–27. doi:10.1177/0093854894021001003

Marshall, W. L., & Serran, G. A. (2000). Current issues in the assessment and treatment of sexual offenders. *Clinical Psychology & Psychotherapy, 7,* 85–96. doi:10.1002/(SICI)1099-0879(200005)7:2<85::AID-CPP234>3.0.CO;2-F

Marshall, W. L., Serran, G. A., Fernandez, Y. M., Mulloy, R., Mann, R. E., & Thornton, D. (2003). Therapist characteristics in the treatment of sexual offenders:

Tentative data on their relationship with indices of behaviour change. *Journal of Sexual Aggression, 9,* 25–30. doi:10.1080/355260031000137940

Marshall, W. L., Serran, G. A., Moulden, H., Mulloy, R., Fernandez, Y. M., Mann, R. E., & Thornton, D. (2002). Therapist features in sexual offender treatment: Their reliable identification and influence on behaviour change. *Clinical Psychology & Psychotherapy, 9,* 395–405. doi:10.1002/cpp.335

Marshall, W. L., Thornton, D., Marshall, L. E., Fernandez, Y. M., & Mann, R. E. (2001). Treatment of sex offenders who are in categorical denial: A pilot project. *Sexual Abuse, 13,* 205–215. doi:10.1177/107906320101300305

Marshall, W. L., Ward, T., Mann, R. E., Moulden, H., Fernandez, Y. M., Serran, G. A., & Marshall, L. E. (2005). Working positively with sexual offenders: Maximizing the effectiveness of treatment. *Journal of Interpersonal Violence, 20,* 1096–1114. doi:10.1177/0886260505278514

Marshall, W. L., & Williams, S. (1975). A behavioral approach to the modification of rape. *Quarterly Bulletin of the British Association for Behavioural Psychotherapy, 4,* 78.

Marshall, W. L., & Yates, P. M. (2005). Comment on Mailloux et al.'s (2003) study "Dosage of treatment to sexual offenders: Are we overprescribing?" *International Journal of Offender Therapy and Comparative Criminology, 49,* 221–224. doi:10.1177/0306624X04268351

Martin, D. J., Garske, J. P., & Davis, M. K. (2000). Relation of the therapeutic alliance with outcome and other variables: A meta-analytic review. *Journal of Consulting and Clinical Psychology, 68,* 438–450. doi:10.1037/0022-006X.68.3.438

Martin, G., & Pear, J. (1992). *Behavior modification: What is it and how to do it.* Englewood Cliffs, NJ: Prentice Hall.

Maruna, S. (2001). *Making good: How ex-convicts reform and rebuild their lives.* Washington, DC: American Psychological Association. doi:10.1037/10430-000

Maruna, S. (2004). Desistance and explanatory style: A new direction in the psychology of reform. *Journal of Contemporary Criminal Justice, 20,* 184–200. doi:10.1177/1043986204263778

Maruna, S., & Mann, R. E. (2006). A fundamental attribution error? Rethinking cognitive distortions. *Legal and Criminological Psychology, 11,* 155–177. doi:10.1348/135532506X114608

Maslow, A. H. (1968). *Toward a psychology of being* (2nd ed.). New York, NY: Van Nostrand Reinhold.

Masters, W., & Johnson, B. (1966). *Human sexual response.* Boston: Little, Brown.

Mathews, A. M., Johnston, D. W., Lancashire, M., Munby, M., Shaw, P. M., & Gelder, M. G. (1976). Imaginal flooding and exposure to real phobic situations: Treatment outcome with agoraphobic patients. *The British Journal of Psychiatry, 129,* 361–371. doi:10.1192/bjp.129.4.361

Mayall, A., & Gold, S. R. (1995). Definitional issues and mediating variables in the sexual revictimization of women sexually abused as children. *Journal of Interpersonal Violence, 10,* 26–42. doi:10.1177/088626095010001002

Mayer, A. P. (2008). Expanding opportunities for high academic achievement: An international baccalaureate diploma program in an urban high school. *Journal of Advanced Academics, 19*, 202–235.

Mayerson, N. G. (1984). Preparing clients for group therapy: A critical review and theoretical formulation. *Clinical Psychology Review, 4*, 191–213. doi:10.1016/0272-7358(84)90028-X

McCarthy, B., & McCarthy, E. (2002). *Sexual awareness: Couple sexuality for the twenty-first century*. New York, NY: Carroll & Graf.

McCarthy, B., & McCarthy, E. (2003). *Rekindling desire: A step-by-step program to help low-sex and no-sex marriages*. New York, NY: Brummer-Routledge.

McClure, B. A., & Hodge, R. W. (1987). Measuring countertransference and attitude in therapeutic relationships. *Psychotherapy: Theory, Research, & Practice, 24*, 325–335. doi:10.1037/h0085723

McConnaughy, E. M., Prochaska, J. O., & Velicer, W. F. (1983). Stages of change in psychotherapy: Measurement and sample profiles. *Psychotherapy: Theory, Research, & Practice, 20*, 368–375. doi:10.1037/h0090198

McCord, W., & McCord, J. (1964). *The psychopath: An essay on the criminal mind*, Princeton, NJ: van Nostrand.

McGlinn, S., & Jackson, E. W. (1989). Predicting the medical school progress of minority students who participated in a preparatory program. *Academic Medicine, 64*, 164–166. doi:10.1097/00001888-198903000-00012

McGrath, R. J., Cumming, G. F., & Burchard, B. L. (2003). *Current practices and trends in sexual abuser management: Safer Society 2002 nationwide survey*. Brandon, VT: Safer Society Press.

McGrath, R. J., Cumming, G., Livingston, J. A., & Hoke, S. E. (2003). Outcome of a treatment program for adult sex offenders: From prison to community. *Journal of Interpersonal Violence, 18*, 3–17. doi:10.1177/0886260502238537

McGuff, R., Gitlin, D., & Enderlin, D. (1996). Clients' and therapists' confidence and attendance at planned individual therapy sessions. *Psychological Reports, 79*, 537–538.

McGuire, R. J., Carlisle, J. M., & Young, B. G. (1965). Sexual deviation as conditioned behaviour: A hypothesis. *Behaviour Research and Therapy, 3*, 185–190.

McIntyre, A. (1984). *After virtue: A study in moral theory*. Notre Dame, IN: University of Notre Dame Press.

McKibben, A., Proulx, J., & Lusignan, R. (1994). Relationship between conflict, affect and deviant sexual behavior in rapists and pedophiles. *Behaviour Research and Therapy, 32*, 571–575. doi:10.1016/0005-7967(94)90147-3

McLeod, J. (1990). The client's experience of counselling and psychotherapy: A review of the research literature. In D. Mearns & W. Dryden (Eds.), *Experiences of counselling in action* (pp. 66–79). London: Sage.

McMurran, M. (2001). Offenders with drink and drug problems. In C. R. Hollin (Ed.), *Handbook of offender assessment and treatment* (pp. 481–493). Chichester, England: Wiley.

McPherson, M., Chein, D., Van Maren, N., & Swenson, D. (1994). Sex offender treatment programs. Saint Paul, MN: Program Evaluation Division, Office of the Legislative Auditor State of Minnesota.

McRoberts, C., Burlingame, G. M., & Hoag, M. J. (1998). Comparative efficacy of individual and group psychotherapy: A meta-analytic perspective. *Group Dynamics, 2,* 101–117. doi:10.1037/1089-2699.2.2.101

Mehrabian, A., & Epstein, N. (1972). A measure of emotional empathy. *Journal of Personality, 40,* 525–543. doi:10.1111/j.1467-6494.1972.tb00078.x

Melamed, Y., & Szor, H. (1999). The therapist and the patient: Coping with non-compliance. *Comprehensive Psychiatry, 40,* 391–395. doi:10.1016/S0010-440X(99)90146-3

Mennonite Central Committee of Ontario. (1996). *The green manual.* Toronto, Ontario, Canada: Author.

Middleton, D. (2009). Internet sex offenders. In A. R. Beech, L. A. Craig, & K. D. Browne (Eds.), *Assessment and treatment of sex offenders: A handbook* (pp. 199–215). Chichester, England: Wiley.

Miller, P. A., & Eisenberg, M. (1988). The relation of empathy to aggressive and externalizing/antisocial behavior. *Psychological Bulletin, 103,* 324–344. doi:10.1037/0033-2909.103.3.324

Miller, R. S., & Lefcourt, H. M. (1982). The assessment of social intimacy. *Journal of Personality Assessment, 46,* 514–518. doi:10.1207/s15327752jpa4605_12

Miller, S. D., Duncan, B. L., & Hubble, M. A. (1997). *Escape from Babel: Toward a unifying language for psychotherapy practice.* New York, NY: Norton.

Miller, W. R., Benefield, R. G., & Tonigan, J. S. (1993). Enhancing motivation for change in problem drinking: A controlled comparison to two therapist styles. *Journal of Consulting and Clinical Psychology, 61,* 455–461. doi:10.1037/0022-006X.61.3.455

Miller, W. R., & Rollnick, S. (Eds.). (1991). *Motivational interviewing: Preparing people to change their addictive behavior.* New York, NY: Guilford Press.

Miller, W. R., & Rollnick, S. (Eds.). (2002). *Motivational Interviewing: Preparing people for change* (2nd ed.). New York, NY: Guilford Press.

Miller, W. R., & Sovereign, R. G. (1989). The check-up: A model for early intervention in addictive behaviors. In T. Loberg, W. R. Miller, P. E. Nathan, & G. A. Marlatt (Eds.), *Addictive behaviors: Prevention and early intervention* (pp. 219–231). Amsterdam: Swets & Zeitlinger.

Miller, W. R., Taylor, C. A., & West, J. C. (1980). Focused versus broad-spectrum behavior therapy for problem drinkers. *Journal of Consulting and Clinical Psychology, 48,* 590–601. doi:10.1037/0022-006X.48.5.590

Millon, T., Antoni, M., Millon, C., Meagher, S., & Grossman, S. (2001). *Millon Behavioral Medicine Diagnostic.* Minnetonka, MN: NCS Assessments.

Mills, J. F., & Kroner, D. G. (1999). *Measures of Criminal Attitudes and Associates: User guide.* Available from Jeremy F. Mills, Bath Institution, 5775 Bath Road, PO Box 1500, Bath, Ontario, K0H 1G0, Canada.

Miner, M. H., Day, D. M., & Nafpaktitis, M. K. (1989). Assessment of coping skills: Development of a Situational Competency Test. In D. R. Laws (Ed.), *Relapse prevention with sex offenders* (pp. 127–136). New York, NY: Guilford Press.

Miner, M. H., & Dwyer, S. M. (1995). Analysis of dropouts from outpatient sex offender treatment. *Journal of Psychology & Human Sexuality, 7,* 77–93. doi:10.1300/J056v07n03_06

Mintz, E. E. (1967). Time-extended marathon groups. *Psychotherapy: Theory, Research, & Practice, 4,* 65–70. doi:10.1037/h0087939

Mintz, J., Luborsky, L., & Auerbach, A. H. (1971). Dimensions of psychotherapy: A factor-analytic study of ratings of psychotherapy sessions. *Journal of Consulting and Clinical Psychology, 36,* 106–120. doi:10.1037/h0030481

Moll, A. (1893). *Les perversions de l'instinct génital. Etude sur l'inversion sexuelle basée sur des documents officials* [Perversions of the genital instinct]. Paris, France: G. Carré.

Moll, A. (1911). Die behandlung sexueller perversioner mit versonderer beruchsichtigung der assoziationstherapie [The treatment of sexual perversions with particular consideration of association therapy]. *Zeitschrift Psychotherapie, 3,* 1–10.

Moore, D. L., Bergman, B. A., & Knox, P. L. (1999). Predictors of sex offender treatment completion. *Journal of Child Sexual Abuse, 7,* 73–88. doi:10.1300/J070v07n03_05

Moos, R. H. (1986). *Group Environment Scale manual* (2nd ed.). Palo Alto, CA: Consulting Psychologists' Press.

Morgan, R. D., Luborsky, L., Crits-Christoph, P., Curtis, H., & Solomon, J. (1982). Predicting outcomes of psychotherapy by the Penn Helping Alliance Rating Method. *Archives of General Psychiatry, 39,* 397–402.

Morgan, R. D., Winterowd, C. L., & Ferrell, S. W. (1999). A national survey of group psychotherapy services in correctional facilities. *Professional Psychology, Research and Practice, 30,* 600–606. doi:10.1037/0735-7028.30.6.600

Morganstern, K. (1974). Cigarette smoking as a noxious and self-managed aversion therapy for compulsive eating. *Behavior Therapy, 5,* 255–260. doi:10.1016/S0005-7894(74)80141-3

Moulden, H. M., Firestone, P., Kingston, D. A., & Bradford, J. M. W. (2009). *Recidivism in pedophiles: An investigation using different methods of defining pedophilia.* Manuscript submitted for publication.

Moulden, H. M., & Marshall, W. L. (2005). Hope in the treatment of sexual offenders: The potential application of hope theory. *Psychology, Crime & Law, 11,* 329–342. doi:10.1080/10683160512331316361

Murphy, C. M., & Baxter, V. A. (1997). Motivating batterers to change in the treatment context. *Journal of Interpersonal Violence, 12,* 607–619. doi:10.1177/088626097012004009

Murphy, G., & Sinclair, N. (2009). Treatment for men with intellectual disabilities and sexually abusive behaviour. In A. R. Beech, L. A. Craig, & K. D. Browne

(Eds.), *Assessment and treatment of sex offenders: A handbook* (pp. 369–392). Chichester, England: Wiley.

Murphy, J. J., & Berry, D. J. (1995, October). *Treating sex offenders who deny their guilt: A six month adapted version of the denier's pilot study.* Paper presented at the 14th Annual Research and Treatment Conference of the Association for the Treatment of Sexual Abusers, New Orleans, LA.

Murphy, W. D. (1990). Assessment and modification of cognitive distortions in sex offenders. In W. L. Marshall, D. R. Laws, & H. E. Barbaree (Eds.), *Handbook of sexual assault: Issues, theories, and treatment of the offender* (pp. 331–342). New York, NY: Plenum Press.

Murphy, W. D., & Barbaree, H. E. (1994). *Assessments of sex offenders by measures of erectile response: Psychometric properties and decision making.* Brandon, VT: The Safer Society Press.

Murphy, W. D., & Carich, M. S. (2001). Cognitive distortions and restructuring in sexual abuser treatment. In M. S. Carich & S. E. Mussack (Eds.), *Handbook for sexual abuser assessment and treatment* (pp. 65–75). Brandon, VT: Safer Society Press.

Mussack, S. E., & Carich, M. S. (2001). Sexual abuser evaluation. In M. S. Carich & S. E. Mussack (Eds.), *Handbook for sexual abuser assessment and treatment* (pp. 11–29). Brandon, VT: Safer Society Press.

Myers, R. (2000). *Identifying schemas in child and adult sex offenders and violent offenders* (Unpublished MSc thesis). University of Leicester, England.

Myhill, A., & Allen, J. (2002). *Rape and sexual assault of women: The extent of the problem* (Home Office Study, 237). London, England: Home Office Publications Unit.

National Research Council. (2003). *The polygraph and lie detection.* Washington, DC: National Academies Press.

Nezu, A. M., & Nezu, C. M. (1989). Clinical predictions, judgment and decision making: An overview. In A. M. Nezu & C. M. Nezu (Eds.), *Clinical decision making in behavior therapy: A problem solving perspective* (pp. 9–34). Champaign, IL: Research Press.

Nezu, A. M., Nezu, C. M., & Blissett, S. E. (1988). Sense of humor as a moderator of the relation between stressful events and psychological distress: A prospective analysis. *Journal of Personality and Social Psychology, 54,* 520–525. doi:10.1037/0022-3514.54.3.520

Nicholaichuk, T., Gordon, A., Gu, D., & Wong, S. (2000). Outcome of an institutional sexual offender treatment program: A comparison between treated and matched untreated offenders. *Sexual Abuse, 12,* 139–153. doi:10.1177/107906320001200205

Nichols, H. R., & Molinder, I. (1984). *Multiphasic Sex Inventory.* Tacoma, WA: Authors.

Nichols, M., & Taylor, T. (1975). Impact of therapist interventions on early sessions of group therapy. *Journal of Clinical Psychology, 31,* 726–729. doi:10.1002/1097-4679(197510)31:4<726::AID-JCLP2270310438>3.0.CO;2-S

Nietzel, M. T., Russell, R. L., Hemmings, K. A., & Gretter, M. L. (1987). The clinical significance of psychotherapy for unipolar depression: A meta-analytic approach to social comparison. *Journal of Consulting and Clinical Psychology, 55*, 156–161. doi:10.1037/0022-006X.55.2.156

Norcross, J. C. (2002). Empirically supported therapy relationships. In J. C. Norcross (Ed.), *Psychotherapy relationships that work: Therapist contributions and responsiveness to patient needs* (pp. 3–10). New York, NY: Oxford University Press.

Norman, C. (1892). Sexual perversion. In H. Tuke (Ed.), *Dictionary of psycho-logical medicine* (pp. 220–321). London, England: Churchill.

Norris, C. (1993). *An approach to treating incarcerated sex offenders who are resistant to treatment involvement.* Paper presented at the 12th Annual Research and Treatment Conference of the Association for the Treatment of Sexual Abusers, Boston.

Nunes, K. L., & Cortoni, F. (2007). Dropout from sex-offender treatment and dimensions of risk of sexual recidivism. *Criminal Justice and Behavior, 35*, 24–33. doi:10.1177/0093854807309037

O'Brien, M. D. (2004). *Healthy sexual functioning programme: Training manual.* London, England: Offending Behaviour Programmes Unit, Her Majesty's Prison Service.

O'Brien, M. D., Marshall, L. E., & Marshall, W. L. (2009). The Rockwood Preparatory Program for Sexual Offenders: The goals and methods employed to achieve them. In D. Prescott (Ed.), *Building motivation for change in sexual offenders* (pp. 118–138). Brandon, VT: Safer Society Press.

O'Donohue, W., & Letourneau, E. (1993). A brief group treatment for the modification of denial in child sexual abusers: Outcome and follow-up. *Child Abuse & Neglect, 17*, 299–304. doi:10.1016/0145-2134(93)90049-B

O'Guinn, T. C., & Faber, R. J. (1989). Compulsive buying: A phenomenological exploration. *The Journal of Consumer Research, 16*, 147–157. doi:10.1086/209204

Olver, M. E., & Wong, S. C. P. (2009). Therapeutic responses of psychopathic sexual offenders: Treatment attrition, therapeutic change, and long-term recidivism. *Journal of Consulting and Clinical Psychology, 77*, 328–336. doi:10.1037/a0015001

Orlinsky, D. E., Grawe, K., & Parks, B. K. (1994). Process and outcome in psychotherapy—noch einmal. In A. E. Garfield & S. L. Garfield (Eds.), *Handbook of psychotherapy and behaviour change* (4th ed., pp. 270–376). New York, NY: Wiley.

Orlinsky, D. E., & Howard, K. I. (1986). Process and outcome in psychotherapy. In S. L. Garfield & A. E. Bergin (Eds.), *Handbook of psychotherapy and behaviour change* (3rd ed., pp. 311–384). New York, NY: Wiley.

Padesky, C. A. (1994). Schema change processes in cognitive therapy. *Clinical Psychology & Psychotherapy, 1*, 267–278. doi:10.1002/cpp.5640010502

Paolucci, E., Genuis, M., & Violato, C. (2001). A meta-analysis of the published research on the effects of child sexual abuse. *Journal of Psychology: Interdisciplinary & Applied, 135*, 17–36. doi:10.1080/00223980109603677

Parkinson, B., Totterdell, P., Briner, R. B., & Reynolds, S. (1996). *Changing moods: The psychology of mood and mood regulation*. London, England: Longman.

Patterson, G. R., & Forgatch, M. S. (1985). Therapist behavior as a determinant for client noncompliance: A paradox for the behavior modifier. *Journal of Consulting and Clinical Psychology, 53*, 846–851. doi:10.1037/0022-006X.53.6.846

Paulhaus, E. L. (1991). Measurement and control of response bias. In J. P. Robinson, P. R. Shaver, & L. S. Wrightman (Eds.), *Measures of personality and social psychological attitudes* (pp. 17–59). New York, NY: Academic Press.

Peck, C. P. (1986). Risk-taking behavior and compulsive gambling. *American Psychologist, 41*, 461–465. doi:10.1037/0003-066X.41.4.461

Pence, E., & Paymar, M. (1993). *Education groups for men who batter: The Duluth model*. New York, NY: Springer.

Pennebaker, J. W. (1997). Writing about emotional experiences as a therapeutic process. *Psychological Science, 8*, 162–166. doi:10.1111/j.1467-9280.1997.tb00403.x

Persons, J. B. (1989). *Cognitive therapy in practice: A case formulation approach*. New York, NY: Norton.

Persons, J. B. (2008). *The case formulation approach to cognitive-behavior therapy*. New York, NY: Guilford Press.

Persons, J. B., & Silberschaltz, G. (1998). Are the results of randomized controlled trials useful to psychotherapists? *Journal of Consulting and Clinical Psychology, 66*, 126–135. doi:10.1037/0022-006X.66.1.126

Peters, S. D., Wyatt, G. E., & Finkelhor, D. (1986). Prevalence. In D. Finkelhor (Ed.), *A sourcebook in child sexual abuse* (pp. 15–59). Beverly Hills, CA: Sage.

Pfäfflin, F., Böhmer, M., Cornehl, S., & Mergenthaler, F. (2005). What happens in therapy with sexual offenders? A model of process research. *Sexual Abuse, 17*, 141–151. doi:10.1177/107906320501700205

Piper, W. E., Ogrodniczuk, J. S., Joyce, A. S., McCallum, M., Rosie, J. S., O'Kelly, J. G., & Steinberg, P. I. (1999). Prediction of dropping out in time-limited interpretive individual psychotherapy. *Psychotherapy: Theory, Research, & Practice, 36*, 114–122. doi:10.1037/h0087787

Pithers, W. D. (1990). Relapse prevention with sexual aggressors: A method for maintaining therapeutic change and enhancing external supervision. In W. L. Marshall, D. R. Laws, & H. E. Barbaree (Eds.), *The handbook of sexual assault: Issues, theories and treatment of the offender* (pp. 363–385). New York, NY: Plenum.

Pithers, W. D. (1994). Process evaluation of a group therapy component designed to enhance sex offenders' empathy for sexual abuse survivors. *Behaviour Research and Therapy, 32*, 565–570. doi:10.1016/0005-7967(94)90146-5

Pithers, W. D. (1997). Maintaining treatment integrity with sexual abusers. *Criminal Justice and Behavior, 24*, 34–51. doi:10.1177/0093854897024001003

Pithers, W. D., Marques, J. K., Gibat, C. C., & Marlatt, G. A. (1983). Relapse prevention with sexual aggressors: A self-control model of treatment and maintenance of change. In J. G. Greer & I. R. Stuart (Eds.), *The sexual aggressor: Current perspectives on treatment* (pp. 214–239). New York, NY: Van Nostrand Reinhold.

Prendergast, W. E. (1991). *Treating sex offenders in correctional institutions and outpatient clinics: A guide to clinical practice*. New York, NY: Haworth Press.

Prentky, R. A., & Burgess, A. W. (1990). Rehabilitation of child molesters: A cost-benefit analysis. *American Journal of Orthopsychiatry, 60*, 108–117. doi:10.1037/h0079197

Prentky, R. A., & Edmunds, S. B. (1997). *Assessing sexual abuse: A resource guide for practitioners*. Brandon, VT: Safer Society Press.

Preston, D. (2001). Addressing treatment resistance in correction. In L. L. Motiuk & R. C. Serin (Eds.), *Compendium 2000 on effective correctional programming* (pp. 47–55). Ottawa, Ontario, Canada: Ministry of Supply and Services Canada.

Prochaska, J. O., & DiClemente, C. C. (1982). Transtheoretical therapy: Toward a more integrative model of change. *Psychotherapy: Theory, Research, & Practice, 19*, 276–288. doi:10.1037/h0088437

Prochaska, J. O., & DiClemente, C. C. (1994). *The transtheoretical approach: Crossing traditional boundaries of therapy*. Malabar, FL: Krieger.

Proeve, M., & Howells, K. (2006). Shame and guilt in child molesters. In W. L. Marshall, Y. M. Fernandez, L. E. Marshall, & G. A. Serran (Eds.), *Sexual offender treatment: Controversial issues* (pp. 125–139). Chichester, England: Wiley.

Proulx, J., Brien, T., Ciampi, A., Allaire, J. F., McDonald, M., & Chouinard, A. (2004, October). *Treatment attrition in sexual offenders*. Paper presented at the 23rd Annual Research and Treatment Conference of the Association for the Treatment of Sexual Abusers, Albuquerque, NM.

Proulx, J., McKibben, A., & Lusignan, R. (1996). Relationship between affective components and sexual behaviors in sexual aggressors. *Sexual Abuse, 8*, 279–289.

Quaker Peace and Social Justice. (2005). *Circles of support and accountability in the Thames Valley: The first three years, April 2002 to March 2005*. London, England: Author.

Quinsey, V. L. (1986). Men who have sex with children. In D. N. Weisstub (Ed.), *Law and mental health: International perspectives* (Vol. 2, pp. 140–172). New York, NY: Pergamon Press.

Quinsey, V. L., Chaplin, T. C., & Carrigan, W. F. (1980). Biofeedback and signalled punishment in the modification of inappropriate sexual age preferences. *Behavior Therapy, 11*, 567–576. doi:10.1016/S0005-7894(80)80072-4

Quinsey, V. L., Harris, G. T., Rice, M. E., & Lalumière, M. L. (1993). Assessing treatment efficacy in outcome studies of sex offenders. *Journal of Interpersonal Violence, 8*, 512–523. doi:10.1177/088626093008004006

Quinsey, V. L., & Lalumière, M. L. (2001). *Assessment of sexual offenders against children* (2nd ed.). Newbury Park, CA: Sage.

Quinsey, V. L., Rice, M. E., & Harris, G. T. (1995). Actuarial prediction of sexual recidivism. *Journal of Interpersonal Violence, 10*, 85–105. doi:10.1177/088626095010001006

Rabavilas, A. D., Boulougouris, I. C., & Perissaki, C. (1979). Therapist qualities related to outcome with exposure in vivo in neurotic patients. *Journal of Behavior Therapy and Experimental Psychiatry, 10*, 293–294. doi:10.1016/0005-7916(79)90005-3

Rafanelli, C., Park, S. K., Ruini, C., Ottolini, F., Cazzaro, M., & Fava, G. A. (2000). Rating well-being and distress. *Stress Medicine, 16*, 55–61. doi:10.1002/(SICI)1099-1700(200001)16:1<55::AID-SMI832>3.0.CO;2-M

Rasmussen, D. B. (1999). Human flourishing and the appeal to human nature. In E. F. Paul, F. D. Miller, & J. Paul (Eds.), *Human flourishing* (pp. 1–43). New York, NY: Cambridge University Press.

Rathus, S. A. (1973). A 30-item schedule for assessing assertive behavior. *Behavior Therapy, 4*, 398–406. doi:10.1016/S0005-7894(73)80120-0

Reder, L. M. (1982). Plausibility judgment versus fact retrieval: Alternative strategies for sentence verification. *Psychological Review, 89*, 250–280. doi:10.1037/0033-295X.89.3.250

Renjilian, D. A., Perri, M. G., Nezu, A. M., McKelvey, W. F., Shermer, R. L., & Anton, S. D. (2001). Individual vs. group therapy for obesity: Effects of matching participants to their treatment preference. *Journal of Consulting and Clinical Psychology, 69*, 717–721. doi:10.1037/0022-006X.69.4.717

Resick, P. (1993). The psychological impact of rape. *Journal of Interpersonal Violence, 8*, 223–255. doi:10.1177/088626093008002005

Rhodes, W., & Brown, W. (1991). *Why some children succeed despite the odds.* New York, NY: Praeger.

Rice, M. E., & Harris, G. T. (2003). The size and sign of treatment effects in sex offender therapy. *Annals of the New York Academy of Sciences, 989*, 428–440. doi:10.1111/j.1749-6632.2003.tb07323.x

Rice, M. E., Harris, G. T., & Cormier, C. A. (1992). An evaluation of a maximum security therapeutic community for psychopaths and other mentally disordered offenders. *Law and Human Behavior, 16*, 399–412. doi:10.1007/BF02352266

Rice, M. E., Quinsey, V. L., & Harris, G. T. (1991). Sexual recidivism among child molesters released from a maximum security psychiatric institution. *Journal of Consulting and Clinical Psychology, 59*, 381–386. doi:10.1037/0022-006X.59.3.381

Ringler, M. (1977). The effect of democratic versus authoritarian therapist behaviour on success, success-expectation and self-attribution in desensitization of examination anxiety. *Zeitschrift für Klinische Psychologie, 6*, 40–58.

Robinson, D., & Porporino, F. J. (2001). Programming cognitive skills: The reasoning and rehabilitation programme. In C. R. Hollin (Ed.), *Handbook of offender assessment and treatment* (pp. 179–193). Chichester, England: Wiley.

Roemer, L., & Borkovec, T. (1994). Effects of expressing thoughts about emotional material. *Journal of Abnormal Psychology, 103*, 467–474. doi:10.1037/0021-843X.103.3.467

Roger, D., & Masters, R. (1997). The development and evaluation of an emotional control training program for sexual offenders. *Legal and Criminological Psychology, 2*, 51–64.

Rogers, C. R. (1957). The necessary and sufficient conditions of therapeutic personality change. *Journal of Consulting Psychology, 21*, 95–103. doi:10.1037/h0045357

Rosenberg, M. (1965). *Society and the adolescent self-image*. Princeton, NJ: Princeton, University Press.

Ross, D. F., Read, J. D., & Toglia, M. P. (Eds.). (1994). *Adult eyewitness testimony: Current trends and developments*. Cambridge, England: Cambridge University Press.

Ross, R. R., & Fabiano, E. (1985). *Time to think: A cognitive model of delinquency prevention and offender rehabilitation*. Johnson City, TN: Institute of Social Sciences and Arts.

Rothschild, A. J. (2000). Sexual side effects of antidepressants. *The Journal of Clinical Psychiatry, 61*, 28–36.

Ruini, C., & Fava, G. A. (2002, August). *Well-being therapy of generalized anxiety disorder*. Paper presented at the 2nd Positive Psychology Summer Institute, Philadelphia.

Ruini, C., & Fava, G. A. (2004). Clinical applications of well-being therapy. In P. A. Linley & S. Joseph (Eds.), *Positive psychology in practice* (pp. 371–387). Hoboken, NJ: Wiley.

Russell, D., Peplau, L. A., & Cutrona, C. E. (1980). The Revised UCLA Loneliness Scale. *Journal of Personality and Social Psychology, 39*, 472–480. doi:10.1037/0022-3514.39.3.472

Russell, D. E. H. (1984). *Sexual exploitation: Rape, child sexual abuse and workplace harassment*. Thousand Oaks, CA: Sage.

Rutherford, K. (1994). Humor in psychotherapy. *Individual Psychology: Journal of Adlerian Theory, Research, and Practice, 50*, 207–222.

Ryan, G., & Miyoshi, T. (1990). Summary of a pilot follow-up study of adolescent sexual perpetrators after treatment. *Interchange, 1*, 6–8.

Ryan, R. M., & Deci, W. L. (2000). Self-determination theory and the facilitation of intrinsic motivation, social development, and well being. *American Psychologist, 55*, 68–78. doi:10.1037/0003-066X.55.1.68

Ryan, V. L., & Gizynski, M. N. (1971). Behavior therapy in retrospect: Patients' feelings and their behavior therapies. *Journal of Consulting and Clinical Psychology, 37*, 1–9. doi:10.1037/h0031293

Ryff, C. D., & Singer, B. H. (1996). Psychological well-being: Meaning, measurement, and implications for psychotherapy research. *Psychotherapy and Psychosomatics, 65*, 14–23. doi:10.1159/000289026

Safran, J. D., & Segal, Z. V. (1990). *Interpersonal process in cognitive therapy*. New York, NY: Basic Books.

Saleeby, D. (Ed.). (2002). *The strength perspective in social work practice*. White Plains, NY: Longman.

Saleh, F. M. (2009). Pharmacological treatment of paraphilic sex offenders. In F. M. Saleh, A. J. Grudzinskas, J. M. Bradford, & D. J. Brodsky (Eds.), *Sex offenders:*

Identification, risk assessment, treatment, and legal issues (pp. 189–207). New York, NY: Oxford University Press.

Salekin, R. T. (2002). Psychopathy and therapeutic pessimism: Clinical lore or clinical reality? *Clinical Psychology Review, 22*, 79–112. doi:10.1016/S0272-7358(01)00083-6

Salkovskis, P. M. (Ed.). (1996). *Frontiers of cognitive therapy*. New York, NY: Guilford Press.

Salter, A. C. (1988). *Treating child sex offenders and victims? Assessment and treatment of child sex offenders: A practical guide*. Beverly Hills, CA: Sage.

Samstag, L. W., Batchelder, S. T., Muran, J. C., Safran, J. D., & Winston, A. (1998). Early identification of treatment failures in short-term psychotherapy: An assessment of therapeutic alliance and interpersonal behavior. *The Journal of Psychotherapy Practice and Research, 7*, 126–143.

Saul, J. R. (1992). *Voltaire's bastards: The dictatorship of reason in the West*. New York, NY: Penguin Books.

Saunders, M. (1999). Clients' assessments of the affective environment of the psychotherapy session: Relationship to session quality and treatment effectiveness. *Journal of Clinical Psychology, 55*, 597–605. doi:10.1002/(SICI)1097-4679(199905)55:5<597::AID-JCLP7>3.0.CO;2-M

Sawyer, S. (2002). Group therapy with adult sex offenders. In B. K. Schwartz & H. Cellini (Eds.), *The sex offender: Current treatment modalities and systems issues* (Vol. 4, pp. 14.1–14.15). Kingston, NJ: Civic Research Institute.

Sayette, M. A. (1993). An appraisal-disruption model of alcohol's effectiveness on stress responses in social drinkers. *Psychological Bulletin, 114*, 459–476. doi:10.1037/0033-2909.114.3.459

Schaap, C., Bennun, I., Schindler, L., & Hoogduin, K. (1993). *The therapeutic relationship in behavioural psychotherapy*. Chichester, England: Wiley.

Schindler, L., Revenstorf, D., Hahlweg, K., & Brenglemann, J. C. (1983). Therapeuten-verthalten in der Verhaltenstherapie: Entwicklumg eines instruements zur Beurteilung dunch den Klienten [Therapist behavior in behavioral therapy: Development of an instrument for evaluation by the client]. *Partnerberaturing, 20*, 149–157.

Schlank, A. M., & Shaw, T. (1996). Treating sexual offenders who deny their guilt: A pilot study. *Sexual Abuse, 8*, 17–23.

Schlank, A. M., & Shaw, T. (1997). Treating sex offenders who deny—a review. In B. K. Schwartz & H. R. Cellini (Eds.), *The sex offender: New insights, treatment innovations and legal developments* (pp. 6.1–6.7). Kingston, NJ: Civic Research Institute.

Schlenker, B. R., Pontari, B. A., & Christopher, A. N. (2001). Excuses and character: Personal and social implications of excuses. *Personality and Social Psychology Review, 5*, 15–32. doi:10.1207/S15327957PSPR0501_2

Schmauk, F. J. (1970). Punishment, arousal, and avoidance learning in sociopaths. *Journal of Abnormal Psychology, 76*, 325–335. doi:10.1037/h0030398

Schmuck, P., & Sheldon, K. M. (Eds.). (2001). *Life goals and well-being.* Toronto, Ontario, Canada: Hogrefe & Huber.

Schneider, S. L., & Wright, R. C. (2004). Understanding denial in sexual offenders: A review of cognitive and motivational processes to avoid responsibility. *Trauma, Violence & Abuse, 5*, 3–20. doi:10.1177/1524838003259320

Schwartz, B. K. (1995). Group therapy. In B. K. Schwartz & H. Cellini (Eds.), *The sex offender: Corrections, treatment and legal practice* (Vol. 1, pp. 14.1–14.15). Kingston, NJ: Civic Research Institute.

Seager, J. A., Jellicoe, D., & Dhaliwal, G. K. (2004). Refusers, dropouts, and completers: Measuring sex offender treatment efficacy. *International Journal of Offender Therapy and Comparative Criminology, 48*, 600–612. doi:10.1177/0306624X04263885

Sefarbi, R. (1990). Admitters and deniers among adolescent sex offenders and their families: A preliminary study. *American Journal of Orthopsychiatry, 60*, 460–465. doi:10.1037/h0079180

Seidman, B. T., Marshall, W. L., Hudson, S. M., & Robertson, P. J. (1994). An examination of intimacy and loneliness in sex offenders. *Journal of Interpersonal Violence, 9*, 518–534. doi:10.1177/088626094009004006

Seligman, L. (1990). *Selecting effective treatments: A comprehensive systematic guide to treating adult mental disorders.* San Francisco, CA: Jossey-Bass.

Seligman, M. E. P. (1991). *Learned optimism.* New York, NY: Knopf.

Seligman, M. E. P. (2002). *Authentic happiness: Using the new positive psychology to realize your potential for lasting fulfillment.* New York, NY: Free Press.

Seligman, M. E. P. (2003). *Authentic happiness* (2nd ed.). London, England: Nicholas Brealey.

Seligman, M. E. P., & Csikszentmihalyi, M. (2000). Positive psychology: An introduction. *American Psychologist, 55*, 5–14. doi:10.1037/0003-066X.55.1.5

Seligman, M. E. P., & Levant, R. F. (1998). Managed care policies rely on inadequate science. *Professional Psychology, Research and Practice, 29*, 211–212. doi:10.1037/0735-7028.29.3.211

Seligman, M. E. P., & Peterson, C. (2003). Positive clinical psychology. In L. G. Aspinwall & U. M. Staudinger (Eds.), *A psychology of human strengths: Fundamental questions and future directions for a positive psychology* (pp. 305–317). Washington, DC: American Psychological Association. doi:10.1037/10566-021

Selzer, M. L. (1971). The Michigan Alcoholism Screening Test (MAST): The quest for a new diagnostic instrument. *The American Journal of Psychiatry, 127*, 1653–1658.

Serber, M. (1970). Shame aversion therapy. *Journal of Behavior Therapy and Experimental Psychiatry, 1*, 213–215. doi:10.1016/0005-7916(70)90005-4

Serin, R. C., & Kennedy, S. (1997). *Treatment readiness responsivity: Contributing to effective correctional programming* (Research Report R-54). Ottawa, Ontario, Canada: Correctional Service of Canada.

Serran, G. A. (2002). The measure of empathy. In Y. M. Fernandez (Ed.), *In their shoes: Examining the issue of empathy and its place in the treatment of offender* (pp. 16–35). Oklahoma City, OK: Wood 'N' Barnes.

Serran, G. A., Fernandez, Y. M., Marshall, W. L., & Mann, R. E. (2003). Process issues in treatment: Application to sexual offender programs. *Professional Psychology, Research and Practice, 34*, 368–374. doi:10.1037/0735-7028.34.4.368

Serran, G. A., Firestone, P., Marshall, W. L., & Moulden, H. (2007). Changes in coping following treatment for child molesters. *Journal of Interpersonal Violence, 22*, 1199–1210. doi:10.1177/0886260507303733

Serran, G. A., Looman, J., & Dickie, I. (2004, October). *The role of schemas in sexual offending.* Paper presented at the 23rd Annual Research and Treatment Conference of the Association for the Treatment of Sexual Abusers. Albuquerque, NM.

Serran, G. A., & Marshall, W. L. (2010). Therapeutic process in the treatment of sexual offenders: A review article. *British Journal of Forensic Practice, 12*, 4–16. doi:10.5042/bjfp.2010.0421

Serran, G. A., Marshall, L. E., & Marshall, W. L. (2007). Attachment, intimacy and loneliness in sexual offenders: Treatment strategies for enhancing functioning. *International Journal of Psychology Research, 1*, 47–57.

Seto, M. C. (2005, November). *The evolution of sex offender treatment: Taking the next step.* Paper presented at the 24th Annual Research and Treatment Conference of the Association for the Treatment of Sexual Abusers, Salt Lake City, UT.

Seto, M. C. (2008). *Pedophilia and sexual offending against children: Theory, assessment, and intervention.* Washington, DC: American Psychological Association. doi:10.1037/11639-000

Seto, M. C., & Barbaree, H. E. (1999). Psychopathy, treatment behavior and sex offender recidivism. *Journal of Interpersonal Violence, 14*, 1235–1248. doi:10.1177/088626099014012001

Seto, M. C., Harris, G. T., Rice, M. E., & Barbaree, H. E. (2004). The screening scale for pedophilic interests predicts recidivism among adult sex offenders with child victims. *Archives of Sexual Behavior, 33*, 455–466. doi:10.1023/B:ASEB.0000037426.55935.9c

Seto, M. C., & Lalumière, M. L. (2001). A brief screening scale to identify pedophilic interests among child molesters. *Sexual Abuse, 13*, 15–25. doi:10.1177/107906320101300103

Seto, M. C., Marques, J. K., Harris, G. T., Chaffin, M., Lalumière, M. L., Miner, M. H., . . . Quinsey, V. L. (2008). Good science and progress in sex offender treatment are intertwined: A response to Marshall & Marshall (2009). *Sexual Abuse, 20*, 247–255. doi:10.1177/1079063208317733

Shadish, W. R., & Baldwin, S. A. (2005). Effects of behavioral marital therapy: A meta-analysis of randomized controlled trials. *Journal of Consulting and Clinical Psychology, 73*, 6–14. doi:10.1037/0022-006X.73.1.6

Shaw, T. A., Herkov, J. M., & Greer, R. A. (1995). Examination of treatment completion and predicted outcome among incarcerated sex offenders. *The Bulletin of the American Academy of Psychiatry and the Law, 23*, 35–41.

Shaw, T. A., & Schlank, A. J. (1992, October). *Treating sexual offenders who deny their guilt.* Paper presented at the 11th Annual Research and Treatment Conference of the Association for the Treatment of Sexual Abusers, Portland, OR.

Shaw, T. A., & Schlank, A. J. (1993, November). *Update: Treating sexual offenders who deny their guilt.* Paper presented at the 12th Annual Research and Treatment Conference of the Association for the Treatment of Sexual Abusers, Boston.

Sheldon, K. M., & King, L. (2001). Why positive psychology is necessary. *American Psychologist, 56*, 216–217. doi:10.1037/0003-066X.56.3.216

Sheldon, K. M., & Lyubomirsky, S. (2004). Achieving sustainable new happiness: Prospects, practices, and prescriptions. In P. A. Linley & S. Joseph (Eds.), *Positive psychology in practice* (pp. 127–145). Hoboken, NJ: Wiley.

Sherer, M., Madduz, J. E., Mercandante, B., Prentice-Dunn, S., Jacobs, B., & Rogers, R. (1982). The Self-Efficacy Scale: Construction and validation. *Psychological Reports, 51*, 663–671.

Shingler, J., & Mann, R. E. (2006). Collaboration in clinical work with sexual offenders: Treatment and risk assessment. In W. L. Marshall, Y. M. Fernandez, L. E. Marshall, & G. A. Serran (Eds.), *Sexual offender treatment: Controversial issues* (pp. 225–239). Chichester, England: Wiley.

Simon, G. M. (2006). The heart of the matter: A proposal for placing the self of the therapist at the center of family therapy research and training. *Family Process, 45*, 331–344. doi:10.1111/j.1545-5300.2006.00174.x

Simons, D., Tyler, C., & Lins, R. (2005, November). *Influence of therapist characteristics on treatment progress.* Paper presented at the 24th Annual Research and Treatment conference of the Association for the Treatment of Sexual Abusers, Salt Lake City, UT.

Simourd, D. J. (1997). The Criminal Sentiments Scale—Modified and Pride in Delinquency Scale: Psychometric properties and construct validity of two measures of criminal attitudes. *Criminal Justice and Behavior, 24*, 52–70. doi:10.1177/0093854897024001004

Simourd, D. J., & Malcolm, P. B. (1998). Reliability and validity of the level of service inventory-revised among federally incarcerated sex offenders. *Journal of Interpersonal Violence, 13*, 261–274. doi:10.1177/088626098013002006

Sinclair, L. (2009, October). *Rebooting: Incorporating healthy sexuality programming in sex offender treatment.* Paper presented at the 28th Research and Treatment Conference of the Association for the Treatment of Sexual Abusers, Dallas, TX.

Skinner, B. F. (1957). *Verbal behavior*. New York, NY: Appleton. doi:10.1037/11256-000

Skinner, H. A. (1982). The drug abuse screening test. *Addictive Behaviors, 7,* 363–371. doi:10.1016/0306-4603(82)90005-3

Smallbone, S. W., & Dadds, M. R. (1998). Childhood attachment and adult attachment in incarcerated adult male sex offenders. *Journal of Interpersonal Violence, 13,* 555–573. doi:10.1177/088626098013005001

Smallbone, S., Marshall, W. L., & Wortley, R. (2008). *Preventing child sexual abuse: Evidence, policy and practice*. Portland, OR: Willan.

Smith, W. R., & Monastersky, C. (1986). Assessing juvenile sexual offenders' risk for reoffending. *Criminal Justice and Behavior, 13,* 115–140. doi:10.1177/0093854886013002001

Snyder, C. R. (1994). *The psychology of hope: You can get there from here*. New York, NY: Free Press.

Snyder, C. R. (2000). The past and possible futures of hope. *Journal of Social and Clinical Psychology, 19,* 11–28.

Snyder, C. R., Harris, C., Anderson, J. R., Holleran, S. A., Irving, L. M., Sigmon, S. T., . . . Harney, P. (1991). The will and the ways: Development and validation of an individual difference measure of hope. *Journal of Personality and Social Psychology, 60,* 570–585. doi:10.1037/0022-3514.60.4.570

Snyder, C. R., & Lopez, S. J. (Eds.). (2005). *Handbook of positive psychology*. New York, NY: Oxford University Press.

Snyder, C. R., Rand, K. L., & Sigmon, D. R. (2005). Hope theory: A member of the positive psychology family. In C. R. Snyder & S. J. Lopez (Eds.), *Handbook of positive psychology* (pp. 257–276). New York, NY: Oxford University Press.

Snyder, C. R., Sympson, S. C., Ybasco, F. C., Borders, T. F., Babyak, M. A., & Higgins, R. L. (1996). Development and validation of the State Hope Scale. *Journal of Personality and Social Psychology, 70,* 321–335. doi:10.1037/0022-3514.70.2.321

Sparks, J., Bailey, W., Marshall, W. L., & Marshall, L. E. (2003, October). *Shame and guilt in sex offenders*. Paper presented at the 22nd Annual Research and Treatment Conference of the Association for the Treatment of Sexual Abusers, St. Louis, MO.

Spiegler, M. D., & Guevremont, D. C. (1998). *Contemporary behavior therapy* (3rd ed.). Pacific Grove, CA: Brooks/Cole.

Spielberger, C. D. (1988). *State-Trait Anger Expression Inventory (STAXI) professional manual*. Odessa, FL: Psychological Assessment Resources.

Spielberger, C. D., Gorsuch, R. L., & Lushene, R. E. (1970). *Manual for the State-Trait Anxiety Inventory*. Palo Alto, CA: Consulting Psychologists Press.

Sporer, S. L., Malpass, R. S., & Koehnken, G. (Eds.). (1996). *Psychological issues in eyewitness identification*. Hillside, NJ: Erlbaum.

Stalans, L. J. (2004). Adult sex offenders on community supervision: A review of recent assessment strategies and treatment. *Criminal Justice and Behavior, 31,* 564–608. doi:10.1177/0093854804267093

Stanton, A. L., Danoff-Burg, S., Cameron, C. L., & Ellis, A. P. (1994). Coping through emotional approach: Problems of conceptualization and confounding. *Journal of Personality and Social Psychology, 66,* 350–362. doi:10.1037/0022-3514.66.2.350

Stanton, A. L., Kirk, S. B., Cameron, C. L., & Danoff-Burg, S. (2000). Coping through emotional approach: Scale construction and validation. *Journal of Personality and Social Psychology, 78,* 1150–1169. doi:10.1037/0022-3514.78.6.1150

Stanton, A. L., Parsa, A., & Austenfeld, J. L. (2005). The adaptive potential of coping through emotional approach. In C. R. Snyder & S. J. Lopez (Eds.), *Handbook of positive psychology* (pp. 148–158). New York, NY: Oxford University Press.

Starzyk, K. B., & Marshall, W. L. (2003). Childhood family and personological risk factors for sexual offending. *Aggression and Violent Behavior, 8,* 93–105. doi:10.1016/S1359-1789(01)00053-2

Stewart, L., Hill, J., & Cripps, J. (2001). Treatment of family violence in correctional settings. In L. Motiuk & R. Serin (Eds.), *Compendium 2000 on effective correctional programming* (pp. 87–97). Ottawa, Ontario, Canada: Correctional Service of Canada.

Stewart, L., & Montplaisir, G. (1999). *Reasons for drop-outs among participants in the Cognitive Skills and Anger and Other Emotions Management programs.* Available from L. Stewart, Correctional Service of Canada, Parole Office, Toronto, Ontario, Canada.

Stinson, J. D., Sales, B. D., & Becker, J. V. (2008). *Sex offending: Causal theories to inform research, prevention, and treatment.* Washington, DC: American Psychological Association. doi:10.1037/11708-000

Stirpe, T. S., Wilson, R. J., & Long, C. (2001). Goal attainment scaling with sexual offenders: A measure of clinical impact at post-treatment and at community follow-up. *Sexual Abuse, 13,* 65–77. doi:10.1177/107906320101300201

Strupp, H. H. (1980). Success and failure in time-limited psychotherapy: A systematic comparison of two cases. *Archives of General Psychiatry, 37,* 595–603.

Strupp, H. H., & Bloxom, A. L. (1973). Preparing lower class patients for group psychotherapy: Development and evaluation of a role-induction film. *Journal of Consulting and Clinical Psychology, 41,* 373–384. doi:10.1037/h0035380

Strupp, H. H., & Hadley, S. W. (1979). Specific vs. nonspecific factors in psychotherapy. *Archives of General Psychiatry, 36,* 1125–1136.

Stukenberg, K. W. (2001). Object relations and transference in group treatment of incest offenders. *Bulletin of the Menninger Clinic, 65,* 489–502. doi:10.1521/bumc.65.4.489.19839

Suchy, Y., Whittaker, W. J., Strassberg, D. S., & Eastvold, A. (2009). Facial and prosodic affect recognition among pedophilic and nonpedophilic criminal child molesters. *Sexual Abuse, 21,* 93–110. doi:10.1177/1079063208326930

Swanston, H. Y., Tebbutt, J. S., O'Toole, P., & Oates, R. K. (1997). Sexually abused children 5 years after presentation: A case-control study. *Pediatrics, 100,* 600–608. doi:10.1542/peds.100.4.600

Taft, C. T., & Murphy, C. M. (2007). The working alliance in intervention for partner violence perpetrators: Recent research and theory. *Journal of Family Violence, 22,* 11–18. doi:10.1007/s10896-006-9053-z

Tangney, J. P., & Dearing, R. L. (2002). *Shame and guilt.* New York, NY: Guilford Press.

Tarrier, N. (2006). An introduction to case formulation and its challenges. In N. Tarrier (Ed.), *Case formulation in cognitive behavior therapy: The treatment of challenging and complex cases* (pp. 1–11). New York, NY: Routledge.

Tarrier, N., & Calam, R. (2002). New developments in cognitive-behavioral case formulation. Epidemiological, systemic and social context: An integrative approach. *Cognitive and Behavioral Psychotherapy, 30,* 311–328.

Taylor, G. R. (1954). *Sex in history.* New York, NY: Ballantine.

Taylor, M., & Quayle, E. (2006). The Internet and abuse images of children: Search, precriminal situations and opportunity. In R. Wortley & S. Smallbone (Eds.), *Situational prevention of child sexual abuse* (pp. 169–195). New York, NY: Criminal Justice Press/Willan.

Taylor, S. (2006). *Clinician's guide to PTSD: A cognitive-behavioral approach.* New York, NY: Guilford Press.

Tennen, H., & Affleck, G. (2005). Benefit-finding and benefit-reminding. In C. R. Snyder & S. J. Lopez (Eds.), *Handbook of positive psychology* (pp. 584–597). New York, NY: Oxford University Press.

Thakker, J., Collie, R. M., Gannon, T. A., & Ward, T. (2008). Rape: Assessment and treatment. In D. R. Laws & W. T. O'Donohue (Eds.), *Sexual deviance: Theory, assessment, and treatment* (2nd ed., pp. 356–383). New York, NY: Guilford Press.

Thompson, R. A. (1994). Emotion regulation: A theme in search of definition. *Monographs of the Society for Research in Child Development, 59,* 25–52. doi:10.2307/1166137

Thornton, D. (2002). Constructing and testing a framework for dynamic risk assessment. *Sexual Abuse, 14,* 139–153. doi:10.1177/107906320201400205

Thornton, D., & Beech, A. R. (2002, October). *Integrating statistical and psychological factors through the structured risk assessment model.* Paper presented at the 21st Annual Research and Treatment Conference of the Association of the Treatment of Sexual Abusers, Montreal, Canada.

Thornton, D., Beech, A., & Marshall, W. L. (2004). Pretreatment self-esteem and posttreatment sexual recidivism. *International Journal of Offender Therapy and Comparative Criminology, 48,* 587–599. doi:10.1177/0306624X04265286

Thornton, D., Mann, R. E., Webster, S. D., Blud, L., Travers, R., Friendship, C., & Erikson, M. (2003). Distinguishing and combining risks for sexual and violent recidivism. *Annals of the New York Academy of Sciences, 989*, 225–235. doi:10.1111/j.1749-6632.2003.tb07308.x

Thornton, D., Mann, R. E., & Williams, F. M. S. (2000). *Therapeutic style in sex offender treatment*. Unpublished manuscript, Offending Behaviour Programming Unit, HM Prison Service, London.

Thornton, D., & Shingler, J. (2001, November). *Impact of schema level work on sexual offenders' cognitive distortions*. Paper presented at the 20th Annual Research and Treatment Conference of the Association for the Treatment of Sexual Abusers, San Antonio, TX.

Thunedborg, K., Black, C. H., & Bech, P. (1995). Beyond the Hamilton depression scores in long-term treatment of manic-melancholic patients: Prediction of recurrence of depression by quality of life measurements. *Psychotherapy and Psychosomatics, 64*, 131–140. doi:10.1159/000289002

Tingle, D., Barnard, G. W., Robbins, L., Newman, G., & Hutchinson, D. (1986). Childhood and adolescent characteristics of pedophiles and rapists. *International Journal of Law and Psychiatry, 9*, 103–116. doi:10.1016/0160-2527(86)90020-8

Tobin, D. L., Holroyd, K. A., Reynolds, R. V., & Wigal, J. K. (1989). The hierarchical factor structure of the Coping Strategies Inventory. *Cognitive Therapy and Research, 13*, 343–361. doi:10.1007/BF01173478

Tromp, S., Koss, M. P., Figueredo, A. J., & Tharan, M. (1995). Are rape memories different? A comparison of rape, other unpleasant, and pleasant memories among employed women. *Journal of Traumatic Stress, 8*, 607–627. doi:10.1002/jts.2490080406

Tyron, G. S., & Kane, A. S. (1990). The helping alliance and premature termination. *Counselling Psychology Quarterly, 3*, 233–238. doi:10.1080/09515079008254254

Tyron, G. S., & Kane, A. S. (1993). Relationship of working alliance to mutual and unilateral termination. *Journal of Counseling Psychology, 40*, 33–36. doi:10.1037/0022-0167.40.1.33

Tyron, G. S., & Winograd, G. (2001). Goal consensus and collaboration. *Psychotherapy: Theory, Research, & Practice, 38*, 385–389. doi:10.1037/0033-3204.38.4.385

Ullmann, L. P., & Krasner, L. (Eds.). (1965). *Case studies in behavior modification*. New York, NY: Holt, Rinehart & Winston.

Underwood, B. J. (1961). Ten years of massed practice and distributed practice. *Psychological Review, 68*, 229–247. doi:10.1037/h0047516

U.S. Bureau of Justice Statistics (2000, August). U.S. Department of Justice. Office of Justice Programs. NCJ 183014.

U.S. Department of Health and Human Services, Administration on Children, Youth and Families (2006). *Child Maltreatment 2004*. Washington, DC: U.S. Government Printing Office.

Vaillant, G. E. (2004). Positive aging. In P. A. Linley & S. Joseph (Eds.), *Positive psychology in practice* (pp. 561–578). Hoboken, NJ: Wiley.

van Dijk, J. J. M., & Mayhew, P. (1992). *Criminal victimization in the Industrialized World: Key findings of the 1989 and 1992 International Crime Surveys*. The Hague, Netherlands: Ministry of Justice, Department of Crime Prevention.

Von Schrenck-Notzing, A. (1956). *The use of hypnosis in psychopathia sexualis with special reference to contrary sexual instinct* (C. G. Chaddock, Trans.). New York, NY: The Institute of Research in Hypnosis Publication Society and the Julien Press. (Original work published 1895)

Ward, T. (1999). A self-regulation model of the relapse process in sexual offenders. In B. K. Schwartz (Ed.), *The sex offender: Theoretical advances, treating special populations and legal developments* (Vol. III, pp. 6.1–6.8). Kingston, NJ: Civic Research Institute.

Ward, T. (2002). Good lives and the rehabilitation of offenders: Promises and problems. *Aggression and Violent Behavior, 7*, 513–528. doi:10.1016/S1359-1789 (01)00076-3

Ward, T., & Brown, M. (2003). The risk-need model of offender rehabilitation: A critical analysis. In T. Ward, D. R. Laws, & S. M. Hudson (Eds.), *Sexual deviance: Issues and controversies* (pp. 338–353). Thousand Oaks, CA: Sage.

Ward, T., Collie, R. M., & Bourke, P. (2009). Models of offender rehabilitation: The good lives model and the risk-need-responsivity model. In A. R. Beech, L. A. Craig, & K. D. Browne (Eds.), *Assessment and treatment of sex offenders* (pp. 293–310). Chichester, England: Wiley.

Ward, T., & Gannon, T. A. (2006). Rehabilitation, etiology, and self-regulation: The good lives model of sexual offender treatment. *Aggression and Violent Behavior, 11*, 77–94. doi:10.1016/j.avb.2005.06.001

Ward, T., & Haig, B. D. (1997). Abductive method and clinical assessment. *Australian Psychologist, 32*, 93–100. doi:10.1080/00050069708257360

Ward, T., & Hudson, S. M. (1996). Relapse prevention: A critical analysis. *Sexual Abuse, 8*, 177–200.

Ward, T., & Hudson, S. M. (2000). A self-regulation model of relapse prevention. In D. R. Laws, S. M. Hudson, & T. Ward (Eds.), *Remaking relapse prevention with sex offenders: A sourcebook* (pp. 79–101). Thousand Oaks, CA: Sage.

Ward, T., Hudson, S. M., & Marshall, W. L. (1994). The abstinence violation effect in child molesters. *Behaviour Research and Therapy, 32*, 431–437. doi:10.1016/ 0005-7967(94)90006-X

Ward, T., Hudson, S. M., & Marshall, W. L. (1996). Attachment style in sex offenders: A preliminary study. *Journal of Sex Research, 33*, 17–26. doi:10.1080/ 00224499609551811

Ward, T., Hudson, S. M., Marshall, W. L., & Siegert, R. (1995). Attachment style and intimacy deficits in sex offenders: A theoretical framework. *Sexual Abuse, 7*, 317–335.

Ward, T., Hudson, S. M., & McCormack, J. (1997). Attachment style, intimacy deficits, and sexual offending. In B. K. Schwartz (Ed.), *The sex offender: New insights, treatment innovations, and legal developments* (Vol. II, pp. 2.1–2.14). Kingston, NJ: Civic Research Institute.

Ward, T., Hudson, S. M., & Siegert, R. J. (1995). A critical comment on Pithers' relapse prevention model. *Sexual Abuse, 7,* 167–175.

Ward, T., & Keenan, T. (1999). Child molesters' implicit theories. *Journal of Interpersonal Violence, 14,* 821–838. doi:10.1177/088626099014008003

Ward, T., Keown, K., & Gannon, T. A. (2007). Cognitive distortions as belief, value, and action judgments. In T. A. Gannon, T. Ward, A. R. Beech, & D. D. Fisher (Eds.), *Aggressive offenders' cognition: Theory, research, and practice* (pp. 53–70). Chichester, England: Wiley. doi:10.1002/9780470746295.ch3

Ward, T., & Mann, R. E. (2004). Good lives and the rehabilitation of offenders: A positive approach to sex offender treatment. In P. A. Linley & S. Joseph (Eds.), *Positive psychology in practice* (pp. 598–616). Hoboken, NJ: Wiley.

Ward, T., Mann, R. E., & Gannon, T. A. (2007). The good lives model of rehabilitation: Clinical implications. *Aggression and Violent Behavior, 12,* 208–228. doi:10.1016/j.avb.2006.07.001

Ward, T., & Marshall, W. L. (2004). Good lives, aetiology and the rehabilitation of sex offenders: A bridging theory. *Journal of Sexual Aggression, 10,* 153–169. doi:10.1080/13552600412331290102

Ward, T., & Maruna, S. (2007). *Rehabilitation: Beyond the risk paradigm.* New York, NY: Routledge.

Ward, T., Nathan, P., Drake, C. R., Lee, J. K. P., & Pathé, M. (2000). The role of formulation based treatments for sexual offenders. *Behaviour Change, 17,* 251–264. doi:10.1375/bech.17.4.251

Ward, T., Polaschek, D. L. L., & Beech, A. R. (2006). *Theories of sexual offending.* Chichester, England: Wiley.

Ward, T., & Stewart, C. (2003a). Good lives and the rehabilitation of sexual offenders. In T. Ward, D. R. Laws, & S. M. Hudson (Eds.), *Sexual deviance: Issues and controversies* (pp. 21–44). Thousand Oaks, CA: Sage.

Ward, T., & Stewart, C. A. (2003b). The treatment of sex offenders; Risk management and good lives. *Professional Psychology, Research and Practice, 34,* 353–360. doi:10.1037/0735-7028.34.4.353

Ward, T., Vertue, F. M., & Haig, B. D. (1999). Abductive reasoning and clinical assessment in practice. *Behaviour Change, 16,* 49–63. doi:10.1375/bech.16.1.49

Ward, T., Vess, J., Collie, R. M., & Gannon, T. A. (2006). Risk management or goods promotion: The relationship between approach and avoidance goals in treatment for sex offenders. *Aggression and Violent Behavior, 11,* 378–393. doi:10.1016/j.avb.2006.01.001

Ware, J., & Bright, D. A. (2008). Evolution of a treatment programme for sex offenders: Changes to the NSW Custody-Based Intensive Treatment (CUBIT). *Psychiatry, Psychology and Law, 15,* 340–349. doi:10.1080/13218710802014543

Ware, J., Mann, R. E., & Wakeling, H. C. (2009). What is the best modality for treating sexual offenders? *Sexual Abuse in Australia and New Zealand, 2*, 2–13.

Ware, J., & Marshall, W. L. (2008). Treatment engagement with a sexual offender who denies committing the offense. *Clinical Case Studies, 7*, 592–603. doi:10.1177/1534650108319913

Warren, A. R., Woodall, C. E., Hunt, J. S., & Perry, N. W. (1996). "It sounds good in theory but": Do investigative interviewers follow guidelines based on memory research? *Child Maltreatment, 1*, 231–245. doi:10.1177/1077559596001003006

Watson, D., & Friend, R. (1969). Measurement of social-evaluative anxiety. *Journal of Consulting and Clinical Psychology, 33*, 448–457. doi:10.1037/h0027806

Webster, S. D., & Beech, A. R. (2000). The nature of sexual offenders' affective empathy: A grounded theory analysis. *Sexual Abuse, 12*, 249–261. doi:10.1177/107906320001200402

Webster, S. D., Bowers, L. E., Mann, R. E., & Marshall, W. L. (2005). Developing empathy in sex offenders: The value of offence re-enactments. *Sexual Abuse, 17*, 63–77. doi:10.1177/107906320501700107

Webster, S. D., Mann, R. E., Carter, A. J., Long, J., Milner, R. J., O'Brien, M. D., . . . Ray, N. L. (2006). Inter-rater reliability of dynamic risk assessment with sexual offenders. *Psychology, Crime & Law, 12*, 439–452. doi:10.1080/10683160500036889

Wells, A. (2006). Cognitive therapy case formulation in anxiety disorders. In N. Tarrier (Ed.), *Case formulation in cognitive behavior therapy: The treatment of challenging and complex cases* (pp. 52–80). New York, NY: Routledge.

Wertheim, E. H., & Schwartz, J. C. (1983). Depression, guilt, and self-management of pleasant and unpleasant events. *Journal of Personality and Social Psychology, 45*, 884–889. doi:10.1037/0022-3514.45.4.884

Westerlund, E. (1992). *Women's sexuality after childhood incest.* New York, NY: Norton.

Whalen, C. (1969). Effects of a model and instructions on group verbal behaviors. *Journal of Consulting and Clinical Psychology, 33*, 509–521. doi:10.1037/h0028282

Whittaker, M. K., Brown, J., Beckett, R., & Gerhold, C. (2006). Sexual knowledge and empathy: A comparison of adolescent child molesters and non-offending adolescents. *Journal of Sexual Aggression, 12*, 143–154. doi:10.1080/13552600600823621

Widom, C. S., & Ames, M. A. (1994). Criminal consequences of childhood sexual victimization. *Child Abuse & Neglect, 18*, 303–318. doi:10.1016/0145-2134(94)90033-7

Williams, D. J. (2004). Sexual offenders' perceptions of correctional therapy: What can we learn? *Sexual Addiction & Compulsivity, 11*, 145–162. doi:10.1080/10720160490882633

Willis, G. (2008). The quality of community reintegration planning for child molesters: Effects on sexual recidivism. *ATSA Forum, 20*, 218–240.

Wilson, G. T. (1996). Manual-based treatments: The clinical application of research findings. *Behaviour Research and Therapy, 34*, 295–314. doi:10.1016/0005-7967(95)00084-4

Wilson, R. J. (2007). Circles of Support and Accountability: Empowering communities. In D. S. Prescott (Ed.), *Knowledge & practice: Challenges in the treatment and supervision of sexual abusers* (pp. 280–309). Oklahoma City, OK: Wood 'N' Barnes.

Wilson, R. J., Cortoni, F., & McWhinnie, A. J. (2009). Circles of Support & Accountability: A Canadian national replication of outcome findings. *Sexual Abuse, 21*, 412–430. doi:10.1177/1079063209347724

Winn, M. E. (1996). The strategic and systemic management of denial in the cognitive/behavioral treatment of sexual offenders. *Sexual Abuse, 8*, 25–36.

Wiseman, H. (1992). Conceptually-based interpersonal process recall (IPR) of change events: What clients tell us about our micro theory of change. In S. G. Toukmanian & D. L. Rennie (Eds.), *Psychotherapy process research: Paradigms and narrative approaches* (pp. 51–76). Newbury Park, CA: Sage.

Wolpe, J. (1969). *The practice of behavior therapy*. New York, NY: Pergamon Press.

Wong, S. (2000). Psychopathic offenders. In S. Hodgins & R. Muller-Isbemer (Eds.), *Violence, crime, and mentally disordered offenders* (pp. 87–112). Chichester, England: Wiley.

Wright, L. W., Jr., & Adams, H. E. (1994). Assessment of sexual preference using a choice reaction time task. *Journal of Psychopathology and Behavioral Assessment, 16*, 221–231. doi:10.1007/BF02229209

Wyre, R. (1989). Working with the paedophile. In M. Farrell (Ed.), *Understanding the paedophile* (pp. 17–23). London: ISTD/The Portman Clinic.

Yates, P. M. (2007). Taking the leap: Abandoning relapse prevention and applying the self-regulation model to the treatment of sexual offenders. In D. Prescott (Ed.), *Applying knowledge to practice: The treatment and supervision of sexual abusers* (pp. 143–174). Oklahoma City, OK: Wood 'N' Barnes.

Yates, P. M., & Ward, T. (2008). Good lives, self-regulation, and risk management: An integrated model of sexual offender assessment and treatment. *Sexual Abuse in Australia and New Zealand: An Interdisciplinary Journal, 1*, 3–20.

Yates, P. M., & Ward, T. (2009). Yes, relapse prevention should be abandoned: A reply to Carich, Dobkowski, and Delehanty (2008). *ATSA Forum, 21*, 9–21.

Yates, T. M., & Masten, A. S. (2004). Fostering the future: Resilience theory and the practice of positive psychology. In P. A. Linley & S. Joseph (Eds.), *Positive psychology in practice* (pp. 521–539). Hoboken, NJ: Wiley.

Young, J. E. (1999). *Cognitive therapy for personality disorders: A schema-focused approach*. Sarasota, FL: Professional Resource Press.

Young, J. E., & Brown, G. (2001). *Young Schema Questionnaire: Special edition*. New York, NY: Schema Therapy Institute.

Young, J. E., Klosko, J. S., & Weishaar, M. E. (2003). *Schema therapy: A practitioner's guide*. New York, NY: Guilford Press.

Zwick, R., & Attkisson, C. C. (1985). Effectiveness of a client pre-therapy orientation program. *Journal of Counseling Psychology, 32*, 514<

INDEX

ABOUT THE AUTHORS

William L. Marshall, OC, FRSC, PhD, is the director of Rockwood Psychological Services, which provides assessment and treatment for sexual offenders in Canadian federal prisons and for juvenile offenders in the community. He is also director of groups and evaluations at a center for mentally disordered offenders. Dr. Marshall has over 370 publications, including 19 books, and has been on (or still is on) the editorial boards of 16 journals. He was elected a Fellow of the Royal Society of Canada in 2000 and was appointed an Officer of the Order of Canada in 2006.

Liam E. Marshall, PhD, has been conducting research on and treating sexual offenders for more than 14 years. He has delivered trainings for correctional services and those who work with sexual and violent offenders in 14 countries, and has designed anger management and domestic violence programs for mentally disordered offenders. Dr. Marshall has also contributed to the development of the preparatory, regular, maintenance, deniers, and low-functioning sexual offender treatment programs, and occasionally acts as a therapist for these programs. He has numerous publications, including a coedited and two coauthored books, and is on the editorial board of the journals *Sexual*

Aggression and *Sexual Addiction and Compulsivity*. Currently, he is the research director for Rockwood Psychological Services, and evaluation chairman and codirector of treatment programs at a secure treatment unit for incarcerated mentally disordered offenders.

Geris A. Serran, PhD, graduated with a doctoral degree in clinical psychology from the University of Ottawa in 2003. A registered psychologist, Dr. Serran is currently employed at Rockwood Psychological Services as the clinical director of the sexual offender treatment programs at Bath Institution (a medium security federal penitentiary), and she also conducts assessments interventions with juvenile sexual offenders. Her research interests include therapeutic processes, coping strategies, maladaptive schemas, and treatment of sexual offenders. She has authored several book chapters and journal articles, coedited and coauthored books, and presented at international conferences. Dr. Geris is also on the editorial board for the journal *Sexual Aggression*.

Matt D. O'Brien, MA, MSc, graduated with a master's degree in applied criminological psychology from the University of London in 1997. Dr. O'Brien worked in the delivery and design of offending behavior programs, primarily with sexual offenders, in Her Majesty's Prison Service for 10 years. He has authored a number of book chapters and journal articles, presented at international conferences, and trained and consulted with staff in a number of different jurisdictions. He is currently employed at Rockwood Psychological Services as a therapist for the preparatory, deniers', and maintenance programs for sexual offenders in Canadian federal correctional settings as well as with juvenile sexual offenders in community settings.